The Oxford 50th Anniversary
Book of the

# UNITED
# NATIONS

UNITED NATIONS
聯合國
ОБЪЕДИНЕННЫЕ НАЦИИ
WE THE PEOPLES OF THE UNITED NATIONS DETERMINED TO SAVE SUCCEEDING GENERATIONS FROM THE SCOURGE OF WAR
15c
NACIONES UNIDAS
NATIONS UNIES

The Oxford 50th Anniversary
Book of the

# UNITED
# NATIONS

CHARLES PATTERSON

Oxford University Press
New York • Oxford

Oxford University Press

Oxford  New York
Athens  Auckland  Bangkok  Bombay
Calcutta  Cape Town  Dar es Salaam  Delhi
Florence  Hong Kong  Istanbul  Karachi
Kuala Lumpur  Madras  Madrid  Melbourne
Mexico City  Nairobi  Paris  Singapore
Taipei  Tokyo  Toronto

and associated companies in

Berlin  Ibadan

Design: Valerie Sauers
Picture research: Amla Sanghvi

Library of Congress Cataloging-in-Publication Data
Patterson, Charles.
The Oxford 50th anniversary book of the United Nations / Charles Patterson
    p.  cm.
    Includes bibliographical references and index.
    ISBN  0-19-508280-X (library ed.)
    1. United Nations—Juvenile literature.  [1. United Nations.]
    I. Title.
REF JX1977.Z8P3   1995
    341.23'09—dc20                        94-35280
                                          CIP

9 8 7 6 5 4 3 2 1

Printed in the United States of America
on acid-free paper

*On the cover:* (left) Soviet sculptor Evgeny Vuchetich created this statue, *Let Us Beat Our
Swords into Ploughshares,* which now sits in the garden of UN headquarters in New York
City; (top) children from countries around the world gather for a UNICEF-sponsored
event in New York City; (middle) Cambodians returning from refugee camps in Thailand aboard a UN train in June 1992; (bottom) the Security Council meets to discuss
the situation in South Africa in July 1992.

*Frontispiece:* This UN stamp takes its message from the opening lines of the UN Charter.

# CONTENTS

CHAPTER 1

# The Road to Peace: Origins of the UN

*The damage and destruction wrought by World War I inspired world leaders to create the League of Nations as a way to guard against another war.*

As World War II—the most destructive war in history—neared its end in 1945, many people hoped and prayed that the world could find a way to avoid such wars in the future. In February 1945, the Big Three—British prime minister Winston Churchill, President Franklin D. Roosevelt of the United States, and Joseph Stalin, leader of the Soviet Union—held their final wartime meeting in the Soviet city of Yalta to discuss the shape of the postwar world. The three leaders agreed to divide Germany and its capital city, Berlin, into British, French, American, and Soviet zones of occupation and decided that the Soviet Union would enter the war against Japan in exchange for territory in East Asia.

The Allied leaders also united on the need for a world body whose role would be to try to prevent future great wars like World War II. This organization—which Churchill, Roosevelt, and Stalin said was essential "to prevent aggression and to remove political, economic, and social causes of war through close and continuing collaboration of all peace-loving peoples"—was to be called the United Nations.

*In February 1945, as World War II drew to a close, the Big Three—Churchill, Roosevelt, and Stalin—met in the Soviet seaport of Yalta to make plans for postwar Europe. Those plans included the creation of the United Nations.*

*One of the first international organizations was the International Telegraphic Union, created in 1865. This map, from that year, shows telegraph lines circling the globe. Dotted lines indicate parts of the system not yet completed.*

To organize this international body, the Big Three, along with the governments of China and France, called for a meeting of the world's nations in San Francisco. However, the roots of this search for world peace go back much further than World War II. The quest for international peace and security has had a long and difficult history.

### First Steps

From earliest times, clans and tribes have chosen cooperation over conflict. In ancient Greece, city-states formed alliances and leagues for mutual defense and assistance. Later, toward the end of the Middle Ages in Europe, many feudal states (those tied together by the authority of kings, dukes, and other powerful nobles) joined together to form larger political units such as the nation-states of France and England.

In the modern era of European history, economic rivalries, commercial expansion, and the race to acquire overseas colonies created a need for international rules to help nations recognize each other's colonial claims, settle boundary disputes, and join forces to curb piracy on the seas. Along with the growth of national rivalries and conflicts came the need for peaceful cooperation.

After the fall of the French emperor Napoleon in the early 19th century, England, Austria, Prussia, Russia, and later France created what was called the Concert of Europe to keep the peace and pursue goals by diplomacy rather than force. The main accomplishments of the Concert of Europe were the establishment of rules to make warfare less brutal, a system that encouraged talks for the resolution of conflicts, and the world's first proposals for disarmament (reduction of weapons).

### First International Institutions

Following the invention of the steamship, railroad, telegraph, and telephone, people could move and communicate with greater speed from city to city and nation to nation. This technological jump also caused trade and commerce to expand. Old patterns of isolation and fear of foreigners began to erode. Farsighted people, especially in Europe, which had suffered horribly from centuries of increasingly violent warfare, began to see the need for a cooperative approach among nations to solve common problems.

The first organizations in modern Europe created for international cooperation were river commissions. In 1804, France and Germany formed the Central Rhine Commission to oversee river traffic, operate lighthouses and other navigation facilities, and settle violations of commission rules. The next river commission was the European Danube Commission, which was established to regulate international traffic on the Danube River. Both these river commissions still function in much the same way they did when they were first created.

Later in the 19th century, European nations organized other groups to aid cooperation—the International Telegraphic Union (1865), the Universal Postal Union (1874), and other international agencies dealing with agriculture, health, railroads, weights and measures, patents and copyrights, and tariffs. Governments joined and cooperated with these agencies because it was good for their national economies and made life easier for their citizens. The rapid growth of these international agencies, several of which later became agencies of the United Nations, shows how quickly time and distance were shrinking as new scientific and technological advances helped people communicate across national borders and even oceans.

One important result of this growing commercial and technological cooperation was the hope that nations might now be able to cooperate to avoid war and maintain peace. In the early 19th century, men and women who believed that peace could be achieved by reducing armaments and developing nonmilitary ways to settle conflicts established peace societies in Great Britain, France, Switzerland, and the United States. Settling disputes among nations by arbitration—submitting the issue to a third country or the head of a neutral government—became an internationally accepted means for resolving disagreements. After the American Civil War, for example, the United States demanded payment from Great Britain for the damage done by Confederate warships built in British shipyards. The two countries agreed to settle the dispute by arbitration, and $15.5 million was awarded to the United States.

In the late 19th and early 20th centuries, the potential for a major conflict in Europe increased when England, France, Italy, Germany, Austria, and Russia formed alliances with each other to protect themselves in the event of war. However, this system of military alliances only increased uneasiness among the great European powers.

Czar Nicholas II of Russia, who realized that his country was having trouble keeping up with Western nations in the production of advanced weapons, called for two peace conferences in hopes of curbing the arms race and reducing international tensions. In 1899, at his invitation, representatives from 26 nations (mostly European) attended the First Hague Peace Conference in the Netherlands. Although the conference failed to cut the number of weapons held by European nations, it did reach agreements about the treatment of war prisoners, the rights of the Red Cross in wartime, and the outlawing of the use of poison

*Czar Nicholas II of Russia (left), and King George V of England at the First Hague Peace Conference in 1899*

*In 1899 representatives from 26 nations gathered in the Netherlands for the First Hague Peace Conference.*

gas and other new methods of warfare considered inhumane.

The conference also established a Permanent Court of Arbitration in The Hague in a "peace palace" built by the American industrialist Andrew Carnegie. Each member nation nominated four people to the court. From their number a panel could then be chosen to decide any case voluntarily submitted to it by a nation or group of nations.

In 1907, at the suggestion of President Theodore Roosevelt of the United States, the czar called the Second Hague Conference. Delegates from 44 nations, including most of the countries of Latin America, attended. This conference continued the work begun in 1899, but it failed to break new ground. Although the two Hague conferences were not able to control the arms race or greatly reduce tensions among national governments, they strengthened the idea that independent nations could resolve their differences peacefully and kept alive the possibility of an organiza-

tion to keep the peace and promote international cooperation.

## The League of Nations

On June 28, 1914, Archduke Francis Ferdinand, nephew and heir to the aging Austrian emperor Francis Joseph, paid a formal visit to Sarajevo, the capital of Bosnia. As he rode with his wife, Sophie, in an open car, a 19-year-old student member of the Black Hand, a secret Serbian terrorist society, shot and killed the couple. The assassination of the heir to the throne of Austria-Hungary created an international crisis. Austria-Hungary, supported by Germany, blamed Serbia, an ally of Russia, for the murder. Failure to resolve the crisis plunged Europe into war.

World War I (1914–18) involved almost all the European nations and their overseas colonies, as well as Japan and eventually the United States. As nations on both sides of the conflict poured their resources into the struggle, the war dragged on at great human cost. In April 1917, the United States joined the war and sent troops to France, where they helped withstand a German offensive in the spring of 1918. In November the war ended when Germany signed a treaty of surrender.

It took this disastrous war to persuade world leaders to establish the League of Nations. Though the roots of the league lay in the international conferences and agreements of the 19th and early 20th centuries, it was the urgent need to prevent another war like World War I that led to the creation of the world's first international organization for the promotion of peace and international security.

President Woodrow Wilson of the United States, who had said the purpose of the war was to "make the world safe for democracy," submitted his peace plan, called the Fourteen Points, to Congress on January 8, 1918. It was designed to prevent future international crises like the one that had led to war in 1914. Because Wilson believed

that secret diplomacy had contributed to the war, the first of his Fourteen Points called for "open covenants [treaties] of peace openly arrived at." Other points called for freedom of the seas, free trade, reduction of armaments, and the peaceful adjustment of colonial claims among European nations over territories they controlled or wanted to control in Africa and Asia. Wilson also demanded the realignment of borders and territorial settlements in Europe according to "clearly recognizable lines of nationality," that is, borders drawn so that they included a majority of any ethnic group that would make up the population of the new country. His final point—the 14th—proposed the creation of "a general association of nations" to guarantee political independence and secure borders for great and small powers alike. Wilson

*The first page of the speech President Woodrow Wilson delivered to Congress in which he outlined his Fourteen Points for building a lasting peace in Europe.*

*An American soldier stands atop the ruins of a bombed-out church on the outskirts of Verdun, the site of some of the fiercest fighting in World War I.*

*President Woodrow Wilson rides with French premier Georges Clemenceau to the signing of the Treaty of Versailles.*

firmly believed that such a league of nations could prevent future wars by settling disputes peacefully.

President Wilson's support was crucial to the creation of the League of Nations. While other Allied leaders sought to translate their victory into national advantage, Wilson remained true to his dream of a just peace. His vision, which appealed to millions of Europeans who had been through the pain of the war, convinced the leaders to go along with his idea. At the Paris Peace Conference in 1919, they accepted Wilson's demand that the League of Nations be included as part of the peace treaty of the conference—the Treaty of Versailles.

Nevertheless, the original members of the League of Nations consisted of the victorious Allies and some neutral states—but not the United States. It is one of the great ironies of history that the league, which embodied Wilson's hope for maintaining peace in the postwar world, was launched and operated without U.S. support. When Wil-

son returned home after the Paris Peace Conference, he discovered that many Americans and members of Congress preferred isolationism to involvement in international affairs. The Republican-controlled Senate refused to ratify the Treaty of Versailles because many senators objected to U.S. involvement in the League of Nations.

Although ensuring international peace and security was the main purpose of the league, it dealt with other matters that required international cooperation as well. The league covenant created three permanent organs within the league—the Assembly, the Council, and the Secretariat—and two semi-independent bodies outside the framework of the covenant—the Permanent Court of International Justice and the International Labour Organization. These were the political, economic, social, and judicial structures upon which the league's successor—the United Nations—would later be modeled.

All member states of the League of Nations were represented in the Assembly, while the Council consisted of the great powers who were its permanent members and other members elected on a rotating basis. The Assembly and Council both served as models for two main bodies of the later United Nations—the General Assembly and Security Council. The Assembly of the league discussed pressing international problems, but it was left to the Council to deal with conflicts that threatened the peace. The Secretariat was responsible for keeping records, planning meetings, and managing the day-to-day business of the league.

Each of the league's member states undertook to "respect and preserve . . . against external aggression the territorial integrity and existing political independence of all Members of the League"—that is, all nations pledged to help any country threatened or invaded by another. Members also agreed that all disputes should be judged and settled by the Council and that war should be seen as a last resort, not to be begun until at least three months after the Council proposed a settlement between the conflicting sides.

If any nation resorted to war or the threat of war in violation of the league covenant, members could discipline that nation by applying diplomatic and economic penalties. If the violation was regarded as an act of war against the community of nations, members were authorized to organize a military attack against the aggressor. Members of the league also agreed to work together to control armaments and to cooperate in solving other common problems.

The Permanent Court of International Justice was established to resolve international legal disputes. The International Labour Organization, whose constitution was part of the Treaty of Versailles, was organized to study labor conditions around the world and make recommendations about how to improve the lives of working people in different parts of the world.

After World War I, as European nations sought to rebuild their economies, in-

*The League of Nations meeting in Geneva on September 5, 1921—without a representative from the United States. The U.S. Senate, wanting to pursue an isolationist foreign policy, refused to ratify the Treaty of Versailles, which called for U.S. participation in the League of Nations.*

*A column of German soldiers roars through the wreckage of a Polish town at the start of World War II in September 1939.*

flation, unemployment, and a worldwide depression contributed to the rise of totalitarian states (nations in which a single political party gained total control over the lives of citizens) in Italy, Germany, and Japan. In the 1930s, when these fascist dictatorships embarked on an aggressive foreign policy, the League of Nations possessed neither the will nor the means to stop them. (Fascism derived its name from the *fascio,* or bundle of sticks, a symbol of ancient Roman power that was adopted by Benito Mussolini, the first of these dictators.)

Italy and Germany met little resistance when they threatened the peace of Europe between 1936 and 1939. World War II began in September 1939 when Germany in-

vaded Poland, and Great Britain and France in turn declared war on Germany. After the Germans conquered most of Western Europe, they invaded the Soviet Union in June 1941. In December a Japanese attack on Pearl Harbor brought the United States into the war on the side of the Allies. The addition of Russian and U.S. forces to the Allied war effort helped turn the tide of battle. World War II ended in the summer of 1945 with the unconditional surrender of Germany and Japan.

Although the League of Nations failed to prevent war, it did do some useful work while it lasted. It supervised the nations that were allowed temporary rule (called mandates) over former German colonies and former parts of the Ottoman Empire. The league also provided aid to refugees and helped resolve a number of border disputes. However, because the league was not able to force strong nations to act against their own interests, it could not curb the aggression that led to a second, even more destructive world war. In 1946 the league dissolved itself and turned its assets, property, and some of its functions over to the newly created United Nations.

Although the League of Nations died, its vision of international cooperation lived on. In fact, all three bodies of the League of Nations—the Assembly, Council, and Secretariat—and both its associated organizations were to become part of the United Nations. The Permanent Court of International Justice went on to become the International Court of Justice, and the International Labour Organization became the first of the specialized UN agencies.

## Allied Wartime Meetings

World War II gave a new boost to the idea of an international organization committed to the promotion of peace and cooperation, just as World War I had done a generation earlier. At the beginning of the war, when the Allies were losing, there was little time or thought given to postwar peace plans.

However, on June 12, 1941, in London, representatives of Britain, Australia, Canada, New Zealand, South Africa, and the governments-in-exile of Belgium, Czechoslovakia, Greece, Luxembourg, the Netherlands, Norway, Poland, Yugoslavia, and free France signed an agreement known as the Inter-Allied Declaration. The Declaration stated that "the only true basis of enduring peace is the willing cooperation of free peoples in a world in which, relieved of the menace of aggression, all may enjoy economic and social security."

Two months later—on August 14, 1941—President Franklin Roosevelt of the United States and Prime Minister Winston

In August 1941, as U.S. involvement in World War II seemed more and more inevitable, President Franklin Delano Roosevelt (center), met with British Prime Minister Winston Churchill (left), aboard the HMS Prince of Wales. They issued a joint declaration— the Atlantic Charter—outlining their postwar goals.

Churchill of Britain, meeting on a battleship in the North Atlantic Ocean, issued a joint declaration known as the Atlantic Charter. In it the two governments called for a safer world, promised "to aid and encourage all other . . . measures which will lighten for peace-loving peoples the crushing burden of armaments," and suggested the future "establishment of a wider and permanent system of general security." The Atlantic Charter, signed by the heads of the world's two leading democracies, was a declaration of postwar goals that included the establishment of what Churchill called "an effective international organization" with security and economic responsibilities.

On January 1, 1942, 26 Allied nations (including the United States, which was now in the war) signed a document called the Declaration of the United Nations. This declaration marked the official appearance of the term *United Nations,* which had been first used by Roosevelt. In the declaration, the Allied nations committed themselves to the "common struggle against savage and brutal forces seeking to subjugate the world" (at that time Germany, Italy, and Japan) and to the goals of the Atlantic Charter. During the course of the war, representatives of 21 more nations added their signatures to the Declaration of the United Nations.

After the Allies launched their offensives in 1942, more thought was given to the shape of the postwar world. The calls for a future international organization suggested in early Allied documents were strengthened in the Moscow Declaration on General Security, which Great Britain, China, the Soviet Union, and the United States signed on October 30, 1943.

The four Allied governments pledged to continue their wartime cooperation "for the organization and maintenance of peace and security" and affirmed "the necessity of establishing at the earliest practicable date a general international organization, based on the principle of the sovereign equality of all peace-loving States, and open to membership by all such States, large and small, for the maintenance of international peace and security."

In the late summer and fall of 1944, representatives of the four major Allied powers met in Washington, D.C., at a mansion called Dumbarton Oaks, to discuss the framework of the new international organization and to draw up a blueprint for its creation. A spirit of unity and cooperation created by the Allies pressing their offensives on all fronts helped the conference reach agreement on many issues. At the conclusion of the conference, the four governments published the Dumbarton Oaks Proposals, which outlined the goals, structure, and operation of an international organization.

The proposals made clear that the main purpose of the new organization was to maintain international peace and security. The Dumbarton Oaks plan provided for a General Assembly with membership for all nations and a Security Council with limited

membership, but with the great powers—Britain, France, China, the Soviet Union, and the United States—serving as its permanent representatives. The Security Council was to have primary responsibility for maintaining peace and security, with decisions in this important area reached only by agreement of all five permanent members. The Dumbarton Oaks Proposals also called for a Secretariat, an Economic and Social Council, and an international court.

Disagreements about the shape of the organization were resolved at Yalta. At Dumbarton Oaks the Soviets had sought the admission of all 15 Soviet republics as members of the new organization, but at Yalta they settled for the admission of two—the Ukraine and Byelorussia—in addition to the Soviet Union itself. At Yalta the Big Three also reached agreement on the question of territories governed under mandates from the League of Nations. They agreed that the new world body would have a trusteeship system administered by a Trusteeship Council that would oversee the governing of these territories as well as the colonies of enemy states and other territories voluntar-

*By the fall of 1944 Allied victory in World War II seemed assured. Representatives of the four major Allied powers met at Dumbarton Oaks, an estate in Washington, D.C., to work out the details of the creation and organization of the United Nations.*

President Harry S. Truman addresses the delegates from 50 nations who gathered for the San Francisco Conference.

ily placed under the system at the conclusion of World War II.

When the Big Three decided at Yalta to convene a conference in San Francisco to write a charter to bring the international organization proposed at Dumbarton Oaks into existence, they did so against the advice of some of their own diplomats. These advisers cautioned against proceeding with the creation of the new world organization until the plan underwent further revisions and improvements and until there was more public support. President Roosevelt disagreed. On his return from Yalta he told Congress, "This time we shall not make the mistake of waiting until the end of the war to set up the machinery of peace."

## The Birth of the United Nations

Countries around the world studied the Dumbarton Oaks Proposals. Representa-

tives of 20 Latin American countries met in Mexico City early in 1945 to discuss the proposals, and the nations of the British Commonwealth held similar meetings in London that April.

On April 25, the San Francisco Conference—officially called the United Nations Conference on International Organization—opened, attended by representatives from 46 nations. Delegations from Argentina, Denmark, Byelorussia, and the Ukraine were later admitted and participated in the drafting of the charter.

Although conference rules provided for free discussion, voting equality, and decisions made by a two-thirds vote of those present and voting, the five major powers, especially the United States, played the leading role. Nevertheless, with Latin American and Arab countries acting as blocs to advance their interests more effectively, the smaller nations did exercise

## RALPH BUNCHE:
## CITIZEN OF THE WORLD

The American statesman Ralph Bunche (1904–71) was one of the architects of the United Nations. In 1944 he was a member of the U.S. State Department group responsible for the research and analysis needed to plan the new organization. He also helped draft the UN charter at the Dumbarton Oaks Conference, advised the U.S. delegation at the San Francisco Conference, and served on the Preparatory Commission of the United Nations.

Grandson of a slave and son of a barber, Bunche was born in Detroit and grew up in poverty. After he was orphaned at age 12, he was raised by his grandmother, who moved him and his sister to Los Angeles. Bunche attended the University of California at Los Angeles with the help of an athletic scholarship and a job as a janitor. In 1927 he graduated at the top of his class with a degree in international relations.

Bunche continued his studies at Harvard and in 1932–33 traveled to Africa to complete research for his doctoral dissertation, *French Administration in Togoland and Dahomey.* He received his Ph.D. from Harvard in 1934, becoming the first African American to receive a doctorate in political science. While completing his graduate studies, Bunche taught at Howard University, where he became a professor. He also did postdoctoral work at Northwestern University, the London School of Economics, and the University of Cape Town in South Africa.

During World War II, Bunche worked for the U.S. government, first in the Office of Strategic Services as an expert on colonial affairs, then in the State Department as a specialist on Africa. In 1944, as a member of the U.S. delegation to the Dumbarton Oaks Conference, he helped draft the trusteeship section of the UN Charter, which the delegates at the San Francisco Conference accepted the following year. He also attended the San Francisco Conference as an adviser to the U.S. delegation.

Bunche then became, in his words, an "international servant." In January 1946 he was a member of the U.S. delegation to the First General Assembly of the United Nations. Later in the year, he left the State Department to join the United Nations at the request of Trygve Lie, the UN's first secretary-general.

At the United Nations, Bunche became deeply involved in shaping the new organization. In 1947 he became director of the UN Department of Trusteeship and Information from Non-Self-Governing Territories. As a strong voice for decolonization, he helped many former colonies win their independence in the 1950s and 1960s.

The world learned about Bunche's diplomatic skills during and after the Arab-Israeli War of 1948. As the secretary-general's special representative, he accompanied UN-appointed mediator Count Folke Bernadotte of Sweden to the

Middle East. After Bernadotte's assassination, the Security Council put Bunche in charge of the negotiations.

Because Arabs refused to sit down at the same table with Israelis, Bunche organized committees that met in small rooms and took up one issue at a time. Bunche persevered with energy and patience. He cajoled the negotiators, threatened them, even joked with them, and in the end he successfully created an atmosphere of trust and compromise. His determination and hard work paid off in 1949 when Israel, Egypt, Lebanon, Jordan, and Syria hammered out four separate armistice agreements. For his remarkable achievement, Ralph Bunche was awarded the Nobel Peace Prize in 1950.

Bunche, who called the UN "the greatest peace effort in human history," spent the rest of his life working to make it more effective. During the 1956 Suez crisis, he directed the United Nations Emergency Force in Egypt. In 1960 Secretary-General Dag Hammarskjöld sent him to the Congo. As conditions there deteriorated, Bunche found himself in charge of the military and civilian UN operation that had to run the country.

In 1964 Bunche helped establish the UN peacekeeping force in Cyprus, and in 1965 he monitored the India-Pakistan cease-fire. He also helped resolve conflicts in Lebanon and Bahrain.

True to his ideals, Bunche followed the civil rights struggle in his own country and lent support to it whenever he could. In 1965 he walked with Dr. Martin Luther King, Jr., and Rabbi Abraham Heschel of the Jewish Theological Seminary at the head of the historic march from Selma to Montgomery, Alabama.

At the UN, Bunche served as undersecretary for special political affairs and as undersecretary-general until he retired in 1971. His biographer, Brian Urquhart, concluded that Ralph Bunche was an "extraordinary American who, by character, education and historical circumstance, became a citizen of the world."

*The Arab-Israeli War of 1948 provided a showcase for the diplomatic skills of Ralph Bunche. Here, in his role as UN Mediator for Palestine, he confers with Gen. A. Lundström, the UN's chief military observer for Palestine.*

*After months of intense negotiations, the UN Charter was officially adopted on June 25, 1945. A member of the Guatemalan delegation signs the charter at the official signing ceremony the next day.*

considerable influence on the conference.

Although the smaller countries were not able to keep the Security Council's permanent members from having veto power over council actions, they did succeed in putting some limits on the permanent members by preventing them from being able to veto what the council discusses. The smaller nations also succeeded in getting the UN to assume more responsibility for economic, social, and colonial issues. For example, the Economic and Social Council (ECOSOC), a minor component of the organization under the Dumbarton Oaks Proposals, was raised to the status of a principal organ, with its authority increased and its functions enlarged and defined. ECOSOC coordinates all the economic, social, cultural, educational, and health work of the UN.

After two months of negotiations, the UN Charter was ready for adoption. On June 25, 1945, the conference, meeting in full session at the San Francisco Opera House, adopted the charter unanimously. On the same day, the conference delegates also established a preparatory commission made up of representatives from all the member states. The commission met in London in November to organize the first meetings of the new organization's major organs.

The next day, at the signing ceremony in the auditorium of the Veterans' Memorial Hall, delegates representing 50 nations signed the charter (see Appendix 2 for the complete text of the charter). Although Poland did not participate in the San Francisco Conference because the United States and Britain refused to recognize its Soviet-sponsored government, it was later permitted to sign the charter and thus be recognized as one of the 51 original member states of the United Nations.

After the signing ceremony, the nations that had participated in creating the charter submitted the agreement to their respective governments for ratification. Although the process varied from country to country, ratification generally involved approval by the national legislature. In democratic countries like the United States, where treaties were closely studied and hotly debated, passage was by no means a sure thing.

Although the great majority of treaties submitted to the U.S. Senate over the years had been passed, it had rejected some of the most important ones, like the covenant of the League of Nations and the statute of the first World Court. Other treaties remained buried in the Senate Foreign Relations Committee, where they died without ever reaching the Senate floor for a vote.

*The UN Security Council officially began its work in January 1946 with a meeting in London.*

However, this time the Senate rose to the occasion. The same Senate that had rejected the covenant of the League of Nations 26 years earlier now approved the United Nations Charter by a vote of 89 to 2. On August 8, 1945, President Harry Truman signed the bill that gave U.S. approval to the United Nations Charter.

On October 24, 1945—the date now celebrated as United Nations Day—the UN officially came into existence when the Soviet Union deposited its ratification and the U.S. secretary of state signed a document called the Protocol of Deposit of Ratification, affirming that a majority of the 51 original signers, including all five great powers, had deposited their ratifications. By December 27, 1945, all 51 signers of the UN Charter had ratified it.

In early 1946 the United Nations began its work in London, where the first General Assembly held its opening meeting on January 10. The Security Council met for the first time a week later. In December 1946 the General Assembly accepted a $8.5 million gift from John D. Rockefeller, Jr., to buy land along the East River in New York City to build a permanent UN headquarters. The principal buildings of the New York headquarters—the Secretariat, the General Assembly, and the Conference Building—were finished in 1952. The Dag Hammarskjöld Memorial Library was dedicated in 1961.

CHAPTER 2

# The New Organization

The United Nations Charter is the document that serves as the UN constitution. The charter can be amended, but amendment requires the approval of two-thirds of the General Assembly and ratification by two-thirds of all UN member states, including all five permanent members of the Security Council.

In the history of the UN, the charter has been amended only three times. In each case the purpose of the amendment was to increase the size of either the Security Council or the Economic and Social Council in response to the growing membership of the UN. Since it was founded in 1945, the United Nations has more than tripled in size (from 51 to 184 members).

kind, and to reaffirm faith in fundamental human rights, in the dignity and worth of the human person, in the equal rights of men and women and of nations large and small, and to establish conditions under which justice and respect for the obligations arising from treaties and other sources of international law can be maintained, and to promote social progress and better standards of life . . . HAVE RESOLVED TO COMBINE OUR EFFORTS TO ACCOMPLISH THESE AIMS.

Accordingly, our respective Governments, through representatives assembled in the city of San Francisco, . . . do hereby establish an international organization to be known as the United Nations.

## Preamble

The preamble to the UN Charter expressed the hopes of many people from the countries who were to join the United Nations:

WE THE PEOPLES OF THE UNITED NATIONS, DETERMINED to save succeeding generations from the scourge of war, which twice in our lifetime has brought untold sorrow to man-

## Purposes and Principles

As set forth in the charter, the purposes of the United Nations are to maintain international peace and security; to develop friendly relations among nations based on respect for equality and self-determination; to cooperate in solving economic, social, cultural, and humanitarian problems; and to promote respect for human rights and basic freedoms.

CHARTER OF THE UNITED NATIONS
AND
STATUTE OF THE
INTERNATIONAL COURT OF JUSTICE

SAN FRANCISCO · 1945

*The UN Charter. Versions of the charter exist in Chinese, English, French, Russian, and Spanish— the original five official languages of the UN.*

Article 2 of the charter sets forth these basic principles of the UN, which member states accept when they ratify the charter. These principles recognize the sovereign equality of members (equal representation of all countries) and demand good faith fulfillment of charter obligations, peaceful settlement of international disputes, refusal to use force or the threat of force, support for UN enforcement action, and pressure on nonmember states to act in accordance with UN principles to maintain international peace and security.

The same article declares that nothing in the charter should be interpreted to "authorize the United Nations to intervene in matters that are essentially within the domestic jurisdiction of any state." However, in recent years the scope of what is an international, as opposed to a national or domestic, issue has been expanding to include such concerns as human rights, environmental pollution, and the creation of democratic

institutions. All of these areas were once considered outside the scope of the UN.

## The General Assembly

The General Assembly, which is the first of the six principal parts of the UN described by the charter, is the focus of all UN activities. It is the only body in which all member states are represented equally. Each UN member state belongs to the General Assembly and has one vote, no matter how large or small the country may be. Large states may have as many as 10 delegates, but they are allowed only one vote. That means that tiny UN members such as Cape Verde, Fiji, the Maldives, the Marshall Islands, Monaco, Saint Kitts–Nevis, and the Seychelles have the same vote as China, which has more than a billion people.

Unlike the Assembly of the League of Nations, which required a unanimous vote for most of its actions, the UN General Assembly requires a simple majority, except on "important questions" that require a two-thirds majority. Resolutions that need a two-thirds majority to pass include recommendations about international peace and security; the election of nonpermanent members of the Security Council, members of the Economic and Social Council, and members of the Trusteeship Council; the admission of new members to the United Nations; the suspension of the rights and privileges of membership; the expulsion of members; and questions relating to the operation of the trusteeship system and the UN budget.

The General Assembly meets once a year in a regular session that usually begins on the third Tuesday in September and ends in mid-December. Each session opens with a three-week period of general debate, during which most delegations express their views on a wide range of global issues. Heads

of state—U.S. presidents, Russian presidents, and other government leaders from all over the world—often participate in this opening phase of the session.

One of the most raucous General Assembly sessions occurred in 1960, when Soviet premier Nikita Khrushchev visited New York for a couple of weeks in late September and early October. It was during an especially bitter time in the cold war, when the UN was little more than a battleground between East and West. During sessions, each side used the assembly rostrum to attack the other. Delegates interrupted each other's speeches, and sometimes entire delegations stormed out of the hall because they did not like what was being said or who was saying it.

The assembly sessions Khrushchev attended were wild. To show disapproval of speeches he did not like, the bald, squat,

*The 46th session of the General Assembly, held in 1991.*

*In 1960, Soviet premier Nikita Khrushchev amazed the other delegates with his shoe-pounding, desk-banging reaction to speeches he objected to.*

feisty head of the Soviet Union pounded his desk with his fists, shouted insults at speakers, and stood up and shook his finger menacingly at delegates. During the October 13 debate on colonialism, when one Western delegate accused the Soviet Union of subjugating Eastern Europe, Khrushchev got so angry he took off his shoe, shook it at the speaker, then pounded it loudly on his desk. He left his shoe on his desk, and later, when he heard another speech he did not like, he pounded the desk again.

The Khrushchev-led heckling of Western delegates by the Soviet bloc (nations allied with the Soviet Union) caused the assembly meeting to become so disorderly that assembly president Frederick Boland of Ireland broke his gavel when he banged it down to end the meeting. "Because of the scene you have just witnessed," he said, "I think the assembly had better adjourn." He was so flustered that he omitted to say when the assembly would hold its next meeting.

Another memorable appearance at the UN took place on October 4, 1965, when Pope Paul VI flew to New York to address a special session of the General Assembly. Secretary-General U Thant went to Kennedy International Airport to welcome the pope

on behalf of the United Nations. In the hall of the General Assembly, after an introduction by assembly president Amintore Fanfani of Italy, Pope Paul delivered a moving plea for peace, which radio and television stations carried to millions of people around the world.

On November 13, 1974, the Palestinian leader Yasir Arafat became the first representative of a nongovernmental organization—the Palestine Liberation Organization (PLO)—to address a full session of the General Assembly. Invited to the UN to speak during the debate on the "question of Palestine," the flamboyant Arafat raised diplomatic eyebrows when he appeared at the rostrum with a pistol strapped to his waist. In his speech he called on the UN to help the Palestinian people achieve self-determination. "The chairman of the PLO has come bearing an olive branch and a freedom-fighter's gun," he said. "He asks that the assembly not let the olive branch fall."

Special emergency sessions of the assembly take place after the regular assembly session closes when important international issues come up that demand immediate attention. If a veto in the Security Council blocks action on a peace and security issue, an emergency special session of the assembly can be called within 24 hours at the request of nine members of the Security Council or a majority of UN member states. Special emergency sessions have been called to deal with such crises as the invasion of Hungary (1956), the civil war in Lebanon (1958), the struggle

*Yasir Arafat, the chairman of the Palestine Liberation Organization, addressed the General Assembly on November 13, 1974, with a pistol strapped to his waist.*

*Under the watchful eye of UN Secretary-General Trygve Lie (top), officials tally the votes to see who will be elected president of the General Assembly in 1948.*

for the independence of the Congo (1960), the Arab-Israeli War (1967), the war in Afghanistan (1980), and the independence of Namibia (1981).

The first task of every new assembly is to elect a president, 21 vice presidents, and chairpersons for the assembly's six standing committees. To ensure representative geographical balance, the presidency of the assembly rotates each year among Africa, Asia, Eastern Europe, Latin America, and Western Europe and other states. Five vice presidents come from the five permanent members of the Security Council; the remaining 16 are from different parts of the world.

Because of the large number of issues the General Assembly addresses, most questions are assigned to the assembly's six standing committees, where they are discussed and recommendations are prepared for a vote by the full assembly. The votes usually take place toward the end of the regular session after the main committees have completed their recommendations—called draft resolutions—for the assembly.

The six standing committees of the General Assembly (the First through the Sixth Committees) deal with disarmament and international security; world economy and finance; social, humanitarian, and cultural issues; special political issues and decolonization (that is, the giving up of colonies, mostly by European nations); administration and budget; and legal matters.

Although the regular session of the General Assembly lasts only three months, its work continues during the rest of the year through its committees. In addition to its six standing committees, the General Assembly has established special committees to deal with such issues as disarmament, human rights, science and technology, and outer space. The assembly also created such bodies as the World Food Council and the United Nations Children's Fund and calls international conferences to address important world problems.

The assembly operates somewhat like a legislature when it adopts resolutions, declarations, and conventions. Assembly resolutions that govern matters within the UN itself (for instance, about rules, funds, property, and staff) have the force of law. The assembly functions most like an international lawmaking body when it drafts multilateral treaties, that is, treaties among more than two different nations. Multilateral treaties such as the Law of the Sea and the Genocide Convention become legally binding on the participating nations when they are ap-

*After the horror of the Holocaust, the Draft Convention on the Crime of Geno-cide was one of the first multilateral treaties approved by the UN.*

From time to time, the General Assembly holds international conferences to deal with important world problems. At this conference, held in the 1970s, the topic was the status of women in society. This was the first meeting of the General Assembly with predominantly female delegates.

proved by the congresses or parliaments of the required number of states.

The General Assembly supervises all UN programs and activities, since it controls all the finances of the UN. The assembly considers and approves the United Nations budget and decides how much money each member state will contribute to running the UN. The Security Council, the Economic and Social Council, and the Trusteeship Council submit annual and special reports on their operations to the General Assembly.

The assembly has ultimate responsibility for the Economic and Social Council and the Trusteeship Council. By making regular decisions about the organization, personnel, work, and budget of the secretary-general and his staff, the assembly also supervises the Secretariat.

The charter not only empowers the General Assembly to make recommendations to the Security Council and call peace-threatening situations to its attention, but it also assigns the assembly an important role in the maintenance of international peace and security. Although the primary UN responsibility in this area belongs to the Secu-

rity Council, Article 11 of the charter states that the General Assembly "may consider the general principles of cooperation in the maintenance of international peace and security . . . and may make recommendations with regard to such principles to the Members or to the Security Council or both."

Since 1947 the General Assembly has adopted a series of resolutions and declarations designed to advance international peace and cooperation. These have called for the prohibition of force by one member state against another, the peaceful settlement of all international disputes, the elimination of the threat of nuclear war, international control over nuclear energy, the elimination of weapons of mass destruction, and the reduction of resources set aside for the production of weapons of war.

## The Security Council

Article 24 of the UN Charter states that the Security Council bears "primary responsibility for the maintenance of international peace and security." The council may act on a complaint by a UN member or nonmem-

*The 15 members of the Security Council meet to discuss the crisis created by the Soviet downing of a Korean airliner in 1983.*

ber, on notification by the secretary-general or General Assembly, or by its own decision.

In general, the Security Council considers two kinds of situations—disputes between nations and more serious threats to the peace. In the case of disputes, the Security Council limits itself to making recommendations to the parties involved. However, in the case of more serious threats the council may vote that UN members cut off economic or diplomatic relations or may even vote for military action against the aggressor nation. Although the charter forbids the United Nations from interfering in a country's internal affairs, this limitation was not intended to prevent the use of diplomatic or economic pressure or military force to protect the peace. During an interna-

tional crisis—such as the Soviet occupation of Czechoslovakia (1968) or war in the Middle East (1956, 1967, 1973)—the council will meet in emergency session to discuss the situation and take steps to solve or defuse the crisis.

The Security Council shares other responsibilities related to international peace and security with the General Assembly, such as the election of a secretary-general, the admission of new members, the election of judges to the International Court of Justice, revoking and restoring the rights and privileges of member states, and the expulsion of UN members. Various UN observer and peacekeeping missions report directly to the Security Council. Under the charter, the council also had the responsibility of supervising trust territories that were considered "strategic," that is, important because of their geographic significance during the cold war between the two superpowers—the United States and the Soviet Union. Actually, the only strategic trust territory established by the UN was the Pacific Islands Trust Territory of the United States.

The Security Council has 15 members. The charter designated five countries—Great Britain, France, China (until 1971 the Republic of China—that is, Taiwan—but since then the People's Republic of China), the Soviet Union (now Russia), and the United States—as permanent members. The remaining 10 members are chosen by the General Assembly for two-year terms, with 5 new nonpermanent members elected each year. Retiring members are not eligible for reelection immediately. Although all members of the UN, except the five permanent members, are eligible for election to the council, the charter says that the General Assembly should consider the candidate's contribution "to the maintenance of international peace and security and to the other purposes of the organization" as well as "to [equal] geographic distribution."

In the early years of the UN the Western powers had a majority on the Security Council, but in the late 1950s states from Africa, Asia, and Eastern Europe began requesting more representation for their areas. After a charter amendment that enlarged the council from 11 to 15 increased the number of elected members from 6 to 10, the General Assembly passed a resolution that designated the proportion of the council's 10 nonpermanent members. Five of the 10 nonpermanent members now must come from Africa and Asia, 2 from Latin America, 1 from Eastern Europe, and 2 from Western Europe and other states. Since the same amendment increased the majority needed for a council decision from 7 to 9, the Western powers no

longer have the automatic voting majority they used to have.

Each country on the council appoints a delegate and an alternate. The council delegate is usually head of his or her country's UN delegation, which in the case of large nations can have up to 10 members. That person—called the country's ambassador to the United Nations—may or may not be a career diplomat.

Some U.S. Presidents have given the UN job to a politician from their own party whom they defeated in the Presidential primaries (President Dwight Eisenhower appointed Henry Cabot Lodge and President John Kennedy appointed Adlai Stevenson). Other Americans appointed to serve on the U.S. delegation to the UN had also gained prominence in their fields before their appointments. For example, Andrew Young, who served as U.S. ambassador to the UN from 1977 to 1979, was a colleague of Dr. Martin Luther King, Jr., in the civil rights movement, while Shirley Temple Black, who served as a UN delegate in 1969 and 1970, first came to public attention as a child movie star in Hollywood.

The current U.S. ambassador to the UN and the second woman to hold the

*The Security Council has five permanent members. The remaining 10 members are elected by the General Assembly for two-year terms. Newly elected delegates from Cuba, Norway, and Egypt, gather in front of the entrance to the Security Council in 1949.*

# IN THE DARK

Sometimes when governments fail to inform their UN ambassadors about government actions and operations, the ambassador is left to defend his country's mistakes and say things that are not true. That is what happened to Adlai Stevenson in 1961.

Stevenson, a former Democratic Presidential candidate who lost the race against Dwight Eisenhower in 1952 and 1956, was a man of great intelligence and experience. In 1945, as a special assistant to the U.S. Secretary of State, he attended the San Francisco Conference that founded the United Nations. He was also a member of the U.S. mission to the UN General Assembly in 1946 and 1947. In 1949 he was elected Governor of Illinois. Because he was so widely respected at home and abroad, President John Kennedy chose him for the UN post.

On the morning of Monday, April 17, 1961, a small army of about 1,500 armed Cuban exiles who lived in the United States and who opposed Fidel Castro's dictatorship went ashore at the Bay of Pigs (Bahia de Cochinos) on the southwestern coast of Cuba. Short of ammunition and supplies, the Cuban exiles had to fight it out with Castro's army without American support, since President Kennedy refused to send in U.S. troops to rescue them. The heavily outnumbered invaders were wiped out in a couple of days.

Despite intense pressure from the U.S. military and the Central Intelligence Agency (CIA), which had organized the operation, the President refused to risk war by attacking Cuba. Such an action would have intensified cold war tensions and branded Kennedy as a ruthless aggressor. At the UN, the Cuban foreign minister charged that the invasion was "by a force of mercenaries organized, financed, and armed by the government of the United States." He said—correctly—that the CIA was behind it.

Stevenson, who received his information and instructions from the White House and State Department, denied the charge for several days. Later in the week he gave a speech at the UN in which he said, "The United States has committed no aggression against Cuba and no offense has been launched from Florida or any other part of the United States." He assured the world there was no U.S. military involvement in the attack on Cuba.

The true nature of the operation, however, was quickly becoming known through press reports, so that by the time Stevenson left the UN after his speech and returned to the embassy suite in the Waldorf Tower he looked "ghastly," as one of his aides, Jane Dick, put it. She was on her way to a diplomatic reception when she spotted him in the lobby. She said something to him, but he walked past her "as if in a trance, his face drawn, pale, tense." She had never seen him look like that before. She knew something must be terribly wrong, so she turned around and took the next elevator up to the suite.

When Stevenson opened the door, he looked very upset. She listened to his anguished words as she watched him pace back and forth in the suite. He had

*Adlai Stevenson (left) meets with President John F. Kennedy in the White House.*

told lies to the UN, he told her. He did not know they were lies, but he told them just the same and what he said to his UN colleagues was now exposed as false. By denying U.S. involvement he had lost all respect at the UN. His credibility was destroyed, his effectiveness ruined. There was only one thing left for him to do—resign.

But he could not do that. Resigning would only betray the country and the President. If he quit, that would only make matters worse. What could he do? Nothing, he decided.

At first, Stevenson blamed President Kennedy for making such a blunder and then using Stevenson's honor to lend plausibility to the government's lies. However, Stevenson soon learned that the young President had not been in charge of the events that led to the Bay of Pigs invasion even though he assumed public responsibility for the fiasco. Kennedy told one of his aides, "All my life I've known better than to depend on the experts. How could I have been so stupid?"

Kennedy was deeply sorry about the incident and the way Stevenson had been treated. The President let him know he would never again let Stevenson be kept in the dark about any development relevant to his work at the UN. "The integrity and credibility of Adlai Stevenson constitute one of our greatest national assets," Kennedy told an aide. "I don't want anything done which might jeopardize that."

*Madeleine Albright, U.S. ambassador to the UN, calls the Security Council to order. The presidency of the Security Council rotates monthly among the members.*

post—Madeleine Albright—has a background in international relations. Born in Prague and educated at Wellesley College and Columbia University (where she earned her Ph.D. in Russian studies), Albright served on President Jimmy Carter's National Security Council staff from 1978 to 1980. At the time of her UN appointment by President Bill Clinton, she was professor of international affairs at Georgetown University's School of Foreign Policy.

The presidency of the Security Council rotates each month among its members, with representatives serving in alphabetical order according to their last names in English. When debate on a question has been completed, a vote is taken. Each member of the Security Council has one vote. For what are called "substantive matters," that is, matters of great importance that involve using military force or diplomatic or economic pressure, the charter calls for decisions to be made "by an affirmative [yes] vote of nine members including the concurring [yes] votes of the permanent members." This means that any one of the five

permanent members can veto a Security Council decision on a substantive matter by voting against it.

All five permanent members have exercised the right of veto at one time or another, but the Soviet Union cast more vetoes than anybody else. During the early years of the cold war especially, conflict between the Soviet Union and the other four members blocked the work of the council on many important issues. In the first 10 years of the UN the veto was cast 78 times, 75 of them by the Soviet Union.

During the cold war, the threat of a veto kept the Security Council from taking action against the superpowers and their allies or passing resolutions critical of their behavior (for example, the U.S. mining of Nicaraguan waters in the 1980s and the Soviet downing of a Korean airliner in 1983). Nonetheless, bringing issues to the council helped cool tempers and opened the way for diplomatic compromises.

At the San Francisco Conference there had been a good deal of opposition, especially by smaller nations, to the idea of permanent members of the Security Council having veto power. They worried that the veto would paralyze the work of the UN and give too much power to the Big Five. The veto idea was accepted and became part of the UN Charter largely because of the belief that the resolution of major crises required the unity of the great powers.

Serious consideration is now being given to possible changes in the composition of the Security Council in order to give major donor nations (those who pay a large percent of the UN budget) and major developing nations a stronger voice on the council. Recommendations include expanding the membership of the council to give Japan and Germany permanent, but not veto-bearing, seats and to give Africa, Asia, and Latin America an additional rotating seat so that large countries such as India, Nigeria, and Brazil can sit on the council with greater regularity.

## The Economic and Social Council

The UN Charter established the Economic and Social Council (ECOSOC) as the United Nation's principal arm to coordinate economic and social work throughout the world. Although UN peacekeeping operations are better known because they receive more media coverage, economic and social projects account for more than 80 percent of the work of the United Nations. ECOSOC's purpose is to consider a wide range of international economic and social questions and to report its conclusions and policy recommendations to the General Assembly and other UN bodies.

The Economic and Social Council originally had 18 nations as members, but its size has since been expanded to 54. The General Assembly elects ECOSOC members for staggered three-year terms by a two-

thirds vote. Each year it adds 18 members to replace the 18 members whose three-year terms have expired. Retiring members are eligible for reelection.

Each year ECOSOC elects a president from one of the member states represented on the council. Sessions, which last about a month, are held twice a year—first in New York in the spring, then in Geneva in the summer. Decisions are made by a simple majority of those present and voting. Much of the work of ECOSOC is carried out by the commissions and committees it creates. These meet at regular intervals throughout the year and report to the council.

One of the Economic and Social Council's most important contributions is its studies of economic and social problems throughout the world. Its reports, which are distributed to governments and private groups, help launch discussions on how to solve problems in rich and poor nations alike. Through its large network of agencies, programs, committees, commissions, and study groups, ECOSOC acts as an international research group and information center.

The Economic and Social Council's studies are especially helpful in the developing world, where accurate and complete in-

*The Economic and Social Council meeting in Geneva in June of 1994.*

*A worker from Save the Children feeds hungry children in Zimbabwe. The Economic and Social Council works closely with such nongovernmental organizations.*

formation is necessary for planning and putting into place development projects. For example, the United Nations Development Programme, whose work the Economic and Social Council supervises, is presently contributing nearly $3 million to data collecting in the African countries of Burkina Faso, Congo, Gambia, and Zambia in order to measure the economic contributions of women more accurately. Better and more complete statistics will help to persuade governments in those countries to allow women to have greater access to job training, loans, and new technologies.

The Economic and Social Council also supervises the activities of an array of other agencies that report through it to the General Assembly. These include the United Nations Children's Fund (UNICEF), the Human Rights Commission, the Office of the UN High Commissioner for Refugees, the UN Population Fund, the World Food Program, the UN Institute for Training and Research, the UN Environment Programme, the UN Center for Human Settle-

ments (Habitat), and the UN Development Programme, which has an annual budget of well over $1 billion. Today, more than 40 UN agencies, commissions, committees, funds, and other bodies report to the General Assembly through ECOSOC. This makes ECOSOC an umbrella organization covering virtually all the thousands of humanitarian programs the UN conducts around the world.

The Economic and Social Council also works with hundreds of nongovernmental organizations (NGOs), such as CARE, Save the Children, and the International Red Cross. The council recognizes that these organizations possess special experience and technical expertise and should have the opportunity to express their views. NGOs are allowed to send observers and submit reports to meetings of ECOSOC and its subsidiary bodies. They are also allowed to consult with the Secretariat.

NGOs play an important part in the work of the UN. They were very influential at the 1993 Human Rights Conference in

Vienna, for example. Before the conference opened, close to 1,000 human rights NGOs gathered in the city to hold their own forum—"All Human Rights for All."

More than 2,000 participants in the forum divided into five working groups to discuss issues scheduled to come before the conference. Many recommendations made by the fifth working group—"Beyond Vienna: Building the Human Rights Movement"—were incorporated into the Vienna Declaration and Programme of Action that came out of the conference two weeks later.

The NGO proposals included a human rights education campaign, more UN financial support for human rights work, the establishment of an Office of the UN High Commissioner for Human Rights, and a permanent human rights court.

NGOs were also conspicuous at the Earth Summit in Rio de Janeiro in 1992. They took part in meetings in 23 countries leading up to the conference, and at the conference itself about 250 NGOs were given official "observer" status. Some NGOs were official members of national

delegations, but many hundreds more gathered in Rio and held sessions concurrent with those of the conference.

Although not officially part of the United Nations, NGOs are involved in almost all aspects of its work. They help the UN by cooperating, recommending, complaining, urging, supporting, and giving advice.

In addition to coordinating economic and social policy, the Economic and Social Council acts like a legislature, since the UN Charter allows it to make recommendations to the General Assembly, UN member states, and specialized UN agencies. The recommendations may take the form of declarations that the General Assembly approves, such as the Universal Declaration of Human Rights (1948). Or the recommendations may take the form of conventions that require the approval of the assembly and the subsequent approval (ratification) of a specified number of member states. An example is the Convention on the Political Rights of Women, which the General Assembly adopted in 1952.

*At the UN-sponsored Earth Summit, held in Rio de Janeiro in 1992, an unprecedented number of nongovernmental organizations attended to express their views. Here, one of the leaders of the International Indigenous Commission is interviewed by a reporter.*

## The Trusteeship Council

The Trusteeship Council supervises the administration of the UN trust territories, which are former colonies that have not yet gained independence. The former colonies located in Africa and the Pacific—originally 11 in number—were either inherited from the League of Nations mandate system, were nations defeated in World War II, or were states that voluntarily placed their territories under UN authority.

The Trusteeship Council asks countries that administer these trust territories to give detailed reports every year about the steps they are taking to promote self-government and education. The Trusteeship Council also considers letters and petitions

*Members of the Trusteeship Council inspect one of the hospitals in the U.S. Trust Territory of the Pacific in 1953.*

*The emblem of the International Court of Justice.*

from individuals and groups within the trust territories about complaints they may have and sends missions to the territories to study economic and social conditions in order to assess how the people are being prepared for self-government. The council then reviews and evaluates the information it has received and passes it on to the General Assembly.

The membership of the Trusteeship Council consists of states that administer trust territories, permanent members of the Security Council, and enough additional members to equalize the number of states on the council that administer and do not administer these territories. The council meets once a year, and its recommendations are decided by majority vote.

Ironically, the Trusteeship Council is the victim of its own success. By 1975, 10 of the original 11 UN trust territories in Africa and the Pacific had gained their independence or had freely joined neighboring countries. With the remaining trust territory—the U.S. Trust Territory of the Pacific—recently removed from the system as well, the work of the Trusteeship Council has been completed. (For more about the work of the Trusteeship Council, see Chapter 9.)

## International Court of Justice

The UN Charter recognizes the International Court of Justice (ICJ) as one of the six principal organizations of the United Nations, even though it functions as a semi-independent body outside the UN framework. The ICJ, or World Court, is the successor to the Permanent Court of International Justice of the League of Nations (which existed from 1922 to 1946), and it too is located in The Hague in the Netherlands.

The General Assembly and the Security Council, voting separately, elect fifteen judges to serve on the court for nine-year terms. Every three years five judges are elected, with sitting judges eligible for reelection. No country can have more than one judge on the World Court at the same time.

The court's jurisdiction extends to all disputes that contending parties submit to it. The court also gives advice on legal questions submitted to it by other UN bodies, such as the General Assembly and the Security Council. Cases are decided by majority vote; a quorum (or minimum attendance) of nine is needed for voting.

The World Court rules on a wide range of cases, many of them involving boundary disputes on land and at sea. For example, when Canada and the United States could not settle their dispute about fishing rights in the Gulf of Maine in the early 1980s, they submitted their dispute to the World Court. After examining the competing claims of the two countries about the location of their respective continental shelves, the ICJ issued a ruling that settled the matter in 1984. (For more about the International Court of Justice, see Chapter 10.)

A UN staff member from Pakistan gets a haircut at the barbershop at UN headquarters in New York.

## The Secretariat

The Secretariat is the staff of international civil servants who do the day-to-day work of the United Nations. They administer agencies and departments, prepare budgets, type reports, translate meetings and documents, and arrange conferences for the UN throughout the world. More than 25,000 full-time employees of the Secretariat carry out the policies and programs of the UN at its headquarters in New York, at UN offices in Geneva, Vienna, Nairobi, and at hundreds of other places around the world where the UN is at work.

The UN secretary-general, whom Article 97 of the charter designates as "the chief administrative officer of the Organization," is head of the Secretariat. On the recommendation of the Security Council, the secretary-general is chosen for a five-year term of office by a two-thirds vote of the General Assembly. His responsibility, according to Article 99, is to be guardian of international peace and security by bringing to the attention of the Security Council "any matter which in his opinion may threaten the maintenance of international peace and security."

Under the leadership of the secretary-general the Secretariat initiates formal and informal mediation efforts to resolve international conflicts, administers UN peacekeeping operations, and monitors the extent to which UN decisions are carried out. The Secretariat also surveys world economic and social trends, prepares studies on human rights and other issues, informs the world about the work of the UN, and translates documents into the official languages of the United Nations—English, French, Spanish, Russian, Chinese, and Arabic. The Secretariat is composed of people from more than 150 countries with diverse backgrounds, beliefs, attitudes, and languages.

The UN Charter underscores the neutrality of the Secretariat by stating that "the Secretary-General and the staff shall not seek or receive instructions from any government or from any authority [outside] the Organization." Likewise, UN member states are required "to respect the exclusively international character of the responsibilities of the Secretary-General and the staff and not to seek to influence them in the discharge of their responsibilities." All UN staff members take an oath not to seek or receive instructions from any country or outside authority.

The secretary-general is the only person in the United Nations capable of speaking for the entire organization. Thus far there have been six secretary-generals: Trygve Lie of Norway (1945–1953); Dag Hammarskjöld of Sweden (1953–1961); U Thant of Burma, now Myanmar (1961–1971); Kurt Waldheim of Austria (1972–1981); Javier Pérez de Cuéllar of Peru (1982–1991); and Boutros Boutros-Ghali of Egypt, who took office on January 1, 1992.

Trygve Lie of Norway, the first secretary-general, demonstrates the UN's earphones for simultaneous translation to his three-year-old grandson.

# A MARTYR FOR PEACE

On September 17, 1961, United Nations Secretary-General Dag Hammarskjöld was killed in a plane crash in Africa, where he had gone to try to resolve a crisis in the Congo. His death was a tragedy for the UN and for the world. Hammarskjöld had been a quiet, tactful, but highly active and effective secretary-general. His tireless efforts on behalf of peace around the world had increased the influence of the UN and the prestige of the office of secretary-general.

The son of a former Swedish prime minister, Hammarskjöld entered government service in 1930. After serving as head of the Bank of Sweden and deputy foreign minister, he went to the UN as a Swedish delegate in 1951. In 1953 he was elected the second secretary-general of the United Nations, succeeding Trygve Lie, and in 1957 he was reelected for a second term.

As secretary-general, Hammarskjöld personally expanded the reach of the UN by leading peace missions to the Middle East, China, and other places around the world. In 1960, shortly after disorder broke out in the newly independent Republic of the Congo (now Zaire) and after Belgium sent troops to its former colony, Hammarskjöld directed a vigorous UN response to the crisis. At the time of his death, he was on his way to what was then Northern Rhodesia (now Zambia) for talks about settling the conflict.

*At the airport in Salisbury, Southern Rhodesia, an honor guard escorts Dag Hammarskjöld's body onto a plane for the journey to his hometown in Sweden.*

Secretary-General of the United Nations Boutros Boutros-Ghali commands wide respect for his diplomatic skill and international experience and knowledge. At the time of his unanimous appointment by the General Assembly to a five-year term, he was deputy prime minister of Egypt for foreign affairs, a tenured professor of international law, a Fulbright scholar at Columbia University, and the author of more than 100 publications about regional and international affairs, law and diplomacy, and political science.

As a member of the Egyptian Foreign Service, Boutros-Ghali helped negotiate the 1979 peace treaty between Egypt and Israel (the Camp David accords) and mediated a number of disputes among African nations. He has led numerous delegations to meetings of the Organization of African Unity and the Movement of Non-Aligned Countries. In 1990 he helped win the release of African National Congress leader Nelson Mandela from a South African prison.

Boutros-Ghali has stated that his goals are to make UN peacekeeping efforts more effective through preventive diplomacy, to narrow the gap between rich and poor nations, to promote sustainable development (progress that does not damage the environment), and to make the UN Secretariat more efficient and productive.

Boutros-Ghali's predecessor, Secretary-General Javier Pérez de Cuéllar, said, "I am enormously happy to be able to leave my delicate post in the hands of an Egyptian intellectual and diplomat of notable skill and courage."

The Boutros-Ghali era at the UN got off to a fast start. On January 31, 1992, the heads of state of the Security Council—the

5 permanent members and the 10 rotating members—met for the first time in history at the summit level to discuss the future of the United Nations. In response to their request, Boutros-Ghali produced a report several months later in which he recommended ways to strengthen the peacemaking, peacekeeping, and diplomatic work of the UN. (For more about the report—called *An Agenda for Peace*—see the Epilogue.)

On February 7—one week after the Security Council summit meeting—Boutros-Ghali announced his plan to restructure the Secretariat. The first phase of the ongoing process involved cutting a number of top posts and putting the management of the Secretariat in the hands of assistants called undersecretaries-general.

The vast array of agencies and programs that the Secretariat operates is testimony to the worldwide scope of the work of the United Nations. The UN headquarters in New York and the three main UN offices in Geneva, Vienna, and Nairobi are but the administrative focal points of a vast international operation that reaches into every corner of the globe.

*While on a diplomatic mission to Cambodia, UN Secretary-General Boutros Boutros-Ghali (second from left), holds a press conference in the Throne Room of the Royal Palace in Phnom Penh.*

# CHAPTER 3

# Keeping Peace

The UN was less than five years old when it faced its first major international crisis. On June 25, 1950, North Korean troops attacked South Korea, setting into motion a bloody war that ravaged the Korean peninsula for three years and threatened to draw the cold war superpower rivals—the United States and the Soviet Union—into a nuclear conflict.

Shortly after the war started, President Harry S. Truman sent U.S. troops stationed in Japan and Okinawa to Korea to support the South Korean government. "The attack upon Korea," Truman said, "makes it plain beyond all doubt that communism has passed beyond the use of subversion to conquer independent nations and will now use armed invasion and war."

At the time of the invasion, the Soviet delegate was refusing to attend Security Council meetings, to protest the fact that the Chinese seat on the council was filled by the government of nationalist China (on the island of Formosa) rather than communist China, which controlled the mainland in the wake of its defeat of the nationalist forces. Free from the threat of a Soviet veto, the Security Council acted quickly on the request of the United States for military assistance to South Korea to reinforce the U.S. troops President Truman had already dispatched.

On July 7—two weeks after the North Korean invasion—the Security Council called on UN member states to supply troops to a unified UN command under the authority of the United States. When the Soviet delegate returned to the Security Council in August, the Korean issue was moved to the General Assembly, out of reach of the Soviet veto.

The Allied military campaign in the Korean War was more of a joint U.S.–South Korean effort than a United Nations operation. Although the unified command reported to the UN, the United States decided what it reported. Also, the vast bulk of the Allied forces were either American or South Korean. The United States supplied more than half the ground forces, 85 percent of the naval forces, and almost the entire air force. South Korea provided most of the rest. Although 16 UN member states sent troops and 5 supplied medical units, less than 10 percent of the Allied forces came from countries other than the United States and South Korea.

In the early stages of the war the UN General Assembly acted decisively, but eventually Chinese intervention, a military

*The Korean War presented the UN with its first major international crisis. Throngs of Korean refugees crowd this road in search of safety away from the fighting.*

*UN military observers talk to a young South Korean refugee.*

stalemate, and nervousness about the possibility of World War III eroded Allied unity. With the armistice that stopped the fighting on July 27, 1953, the United Nations succeeded in meeting the first major challenge to its ability to protect international peace and security.

After the armistice, the United Nations established the Commission for the Unification and Rehabilitation of Korea, which remained in Korea until 1973. The United Nations Command, which the armistice created to police the truce, still operates in Korea and will most likely continue to do so until the opposing sides resolve the political issue of troop withdrawal and the unification of North and South Korea.

In 1993, new tensions developed between North and South Korea when Director-General Hans Blix of the International Atomic Energy Agency (IAEA), an autonomous organization affiliated with the UN, declared that the IAEA could no longer verify that North Korea's nuclear activities were strictly for peaceful purposes. The North Korean military denied the existence of a nuclear weapons program, stating "we have neither the intention nor the capacity to develop" such weapons.

When North Korea signed the nuclear Non-Proliferation Treaty in 1985, it agreed

to let the IAEA inspect its facilities. Until the end of 1992, North Korea allowed the IAEA to inspect its nuclear sites and install surveillance cameras at several locations. In 1993, however, the North Korean government suddenly blocked IAEA inspectors from visiting two possible nuclear waste depositories and announced its intention to withdraw from the nuclear Non-Proliferation Treaty. Although North Korea later reversed its decision about the treaty, it continued to limit IAEA inspections, and in 1994 it once more threatened to withdraw from the treaty.

## Charter Provisions

The driving force behind the creation of the United Nations was the determination to establish a world where peace, not war, would reign. The victorious Allies wanted to make sure that the massive destruction of World War II never happened again. The UN Charter made this intent quite clear in the first two articles. Article 1 states that the central purpose of the United Nations is "to maintain international peace and security" and to that end "to take effective collective measures for the prevention and removal of threats to the peace." Article 2 declares that all United Nations member states "shall refrain in their international relations from the threat or use of force against the territorial integrity or political independence of any state, or in any other manner inconsistent with the Purposes of the United Nations."

The charter further discusses "effective collective measures" the Security Council can take against aggressors. These may include "complete or partial interruption of economic relations and of rail, sea, air, postal, telegraphic, radio and other means of communication, and the severance of diplomatic relations." If these measures are not

Soldiers from Norway (left), Canada (center), and India get acquainted on their flight to Kamina in the Congo in 1960.

## UN Peacekeeping Operations

Because the charter does not provide for peacekeeping operations specifically, the United Nations has had to improvise ways to contain conflicts. The first time the UN used the term *peacekeeping* was in connection with the United Nations Emergency Force that the General Assembly created during the 1956 Arab-Israeli War. The term has been used extensively since then to describe UN-sponsored military operations designed to control conflict.

United Nations peacekeeping operations try to contain or halt conflicts long enough to allow opposing sides to enter negotiations toward a lasting peace. To do this, UN peacekeeping missions have performed a variety of roles. They have observed border violations, monitored cease-fire and truce lines, served as a buffer between opposing sides, and maintained order within a territory during transition periods. UN peacekeeping forces are sent only where they can operate with the consent of the host government and usually with the consent of the other parties to the conflict as well. UN operations are not supposed to interfere in the internal affairs of the host country, and they must not favor one side over the other in the conflict.

sufficient, the Security Council can "take such action by air, sea, or land forces as may be necessary to maintain or restore international peace and security." Member states are called on "to make available to the Security Council . . . armed forces, assistance, and facilities, including rights of passage, necessary for the purpose of maintaining international peace and security."

The cold war atmosphere that followed World War II made the use of such collective military action difficult, if not impossible, since both superpowers could veto any such attempt. As a result, the military clout that a permanent standby UN military force might have provided never came into being.

The emphasis in the charter on peace and security is so strong that it even defines UN functions not connected to the prevention and containment of military conflict in terms of their potential contribution to peace. Since the United Nations recognizes the important role economic and social conditions play in creating instability and conflict, it seeks to reduce national, regional, and international tensions by tackling poverty, hunger, social injustice, environmental destruction, international drug trafficking, crime, terrorism, and other problems.

A UN jeep passes through a checkpoint to enter the Jerusalem headquarters of the UN Truce Supervision Organization. UNTSO was established in 1948 to monitor the cease-fire reached after the Arab-Israeli War of 1948.

The United Nations tries to keep dangerous situations from breaking out into armed conflict by encouraging the opposing sides to talk rather than fight. The UN does this by providing peacekeeping forces, observers, and fact-finding and good-office missions (neutral visits by UN personnel to judge what is happening in a country or region). It also offers election and plebiscite supervision (a plebiscite is typically a vote on a constitution or on the establishment of a new form of government) and mediation of disputes. Under the UN Charter, member states are obligated to "agree to accept and carry out the decisions of the Security Council." The recommendations of the General Assembly and other UN bodies are also influential as expressions of international opinion.

UN member states provide troops for peacekeeping operations on a voluntary basis. Usually, UN military observers do not carry weapons, but soldiers in UN peacekeeping units are allowed to have light defensive arms such as rifles and pistols. They are not authorized to use them, however, except in self-defense. Because UN peacekeepers do not impose their will on contending parties and their use of force is limited to self-defense, their effectiveness for the most part depends on the cooperation of the host countries and the parties to the conflict. To remain in a trouble spot, UN peacekeepers depend on the support of the Security Council, which authorizes their stay, and on member states, which supply the troops.

## First Missions

The first uses of UN peacekeeping forces occurred in Greece, Indonesia, Kashmir, and Palestine in the late 1940s, although at the time the term *peacekeeping* was not yet used for these missions. From 1947 to 1949, the UN Special Committee on the Balkans kept a small team of observers along the northern border of Greece. The job of the observer team, which never exceeded 20 people, was to monitor border violations by Eastern European, Soviet-bloc states who were supporting communist guerrillas in the Greek civil war. The war ended in 1949 with the defeat of the communists and the restoration of the Greek constitutional monarchy.

Another small UN mission operated in Indonesia from 1947 to 1951. The UN Commission for Indonesia assigned military observers to help the peacemaking efforts of the Security Council in the Indonesian war for independence from the Netherlands. The observers monitored the Indonesian cease-fire and later the Dutch troop withdrawal.

The other two UN observer missions turned out to be more than temporary. The first was created in response to the Middle East conflict between Jews and Arabs over the future of Palestine. The problem was placed before the UN in 1947 when Great Britain, which administered Palestine under a mandate from the League of Nations, was having trouble managing the demands for independence from both Jews and Arabs.

The United Nations Special Committee on Palestine put before the General As-

*A UN observer team in the Indian state of Kashmir in 1955.*

sembly a plan to divide Palestine into a Jewish state, an Arab state, and a small internationally administered zone that included Jerusalem. On November 29, 1947, the plan won the support of the necessary two-thirds of the member states of the General Assembly, including the United States and the Soviet Union. Britain abstained, and the Arabs walked out in protest.

On May 14, 1948—the day that Britain relinquished its mandate over Palestine—the Jews in Palestine proclaimed the state of Israel. The surrounding Arab states immediately attacked the new Jewish state. After the Security Council called for a truce, which was broken, a new cease-fire went into effect on July 18. Under the guidance of United Nations mediator Ralph Bunche, Israel and four Arab countries—Egypt, Jordan, Lebanon, and Syria—signed armistice agreements to halt the war in early 1949.

The Security Council had created the United Nations Truce Supervision Organization to supervise the cease-fire. This group of military observers, whose number eventually rose to almost 700, stayed on to supervise the armistice agreements and has been in the area ever since, monitoring cease-fires following the Arab-Israeli wars of 1956, 1967, and 1973.

The United Nations Military Observer Group in India and Pakistan is the other early UN observer mission still in place. The conflict between India and Pakistan over the Indian state of Kashmir caused the Security Council to establish a United Nations Commission for India and Pakistan in 1948 to investigate and help the two sides resolve the crisis. The Security Council recommended that the commission go to the Indian subcontinent and use observers to stop the fighting in Kashmir.

When a cease-fire went into effect on January 1, 1949, the commission sent the

Military Observer Group to supervise it. In July 1949, with the help of the Commission for India and Pakistan, both warring parties agreed to a cease-fire line in Kashmir. This small observer group, which at one time reached 102 members, has been deployed ever since to watch over the cease-fire along the India-Pakistan border.

*Members of UNTSO (top) inspect a machine gun found in the countryside in Palestine. A UN military observer in the Indian state of Kashmir (bottom) uses a donkey for his patrol in 1955.*

## United Nations Emergency Force

The Arab-Israeli war of 1956 was the reason the United Nations Emergency Force was created. The war was sparked by Egypt's nationalization of the Suez Canal in July 1956. Egyptian President Gamal Abdel Nasser set up the Egyptian Canal Authority to replace the existing privately owned company of English and French investors. In

August, Nasser expelled British oil and embassy officials. These actions led to an Israeli invasion of Egypt, with British and French support, in October. When action by the Security Council was blocked by the British and French veto, the General Assembly, meeting in emergency special session, called for a cease-fire and the withdrawal of Israeli, British, and French forces from Egyptian territory.

The General Assembly authorized UN Secretary-General Dag Hammarskjöld to prepare a UN emergency force. Because of the size of the opposing armies involved and the expanse of the territory to be monitored, the UN fielded a force of 6,000 troops from 10 countries. Earlier UN missions had been concerned mostly with observing and reporting, but this emergency force was given the broader goal of serving as a buffer between the opposing sides and a peacekeeping force in the areas under its control. In terms of size and function, the Suez emergency force was far more ambitious than any previous UN peacekeeping operation.

After the emergency force supervised the troop withdrawals, it was moved to the Egyptian side of the border to act as a buffer between the Egyptian and Israeli forces. For more than ten years it patrolled the border and succeeded in keeping the area relatively quiet. The emergency force continued to perform its responsibilities until shortly before the 1967 Arab-Israeli war, when Egypt requested that the 3,400 UN troops be withdrawn.

## The Congo

The next challenge the United Nations faced was in Africa. Shortly after the Belgian colony of the Congo gained its independence as the Republic of the Congo (now Zaire) on June 30, 1960, rioting, tribal disorders, and mutiny in the Congolese army

The UN responded to the crisis in the Congo by sending peacekeeping forces along with food and relief supplies. A member of the UN's Food and Agriculture Organization supervises the mixing of powdered milk for distribution to the hungry (top). Members of the UN's peacekeeping force receive medals for their service in the Congo (bottom).

erupted. Belgium sent in its troops on July 8 to protect the lives and property of Belgian citizens. Three days later the province of Katanga, which had strong economic ties to Belgium, declared its independence from the central Congolese government.

Faced with internal disorder, outside intervention, and secession by regions within its own country, the Congolese government requested military assistance from the UN to help it protect its sovereignty and territory. The Security Council called on Belgium to withdraw its troops from the Congo and approved Secretary-General Hammarskjöld's plan for military and technical assistance to the Congolese government. Less than 48 hours after the council authorized an operation for the Congo, UN peacekeeping troops arrived, followed by civilian experts sent to assist in the operation of essential public services.

The orders given to the UN peacekeeping force in the Congo were to help the Congolese government establish its political independence, defend its territorial integrity, maintain domestic peace, and put into effect a long-range program of technical assistance.

To achieve these goals the United Nations assembled the largest force it had ever put together. At its peak the peacekeeping force numbered nearly 20,000 troops from 29 countries. The cost of operating it came to more than $400 million over four years.

When the United Nations sided with the central government in its struggle to prevent the secession of Katanga, the UN peacekeeping force was no longer able to maintain its nonfighting role because the Katanga secessionists (who wanted to form their own nation) and their foreign mercenaries (paid soldiers) had to be suppressed by force. As a result, the UN force suffered many casualties and Dag Hammarskjöld himself died in a plane crash while trying to resolve the conflict.

In February 1963, after Katanga failed to break away from the Congo, the UN force there began to be phased out. However, even after the force's departure in June 1964, UN assistance to the Congo continued in what turned out to be the single largest UN aid program to that time. In 1963–64, 2,000 UN civilian aid experts were at work in the Congo.

Although the UN force had to operate in very difficult circumstances, its work was successful. Belgian troops, mercenaries, and foreign military advisers left the Congo, the secession of Katanga and other parts of the Congo was prevented, and law and order were for the most part restored. The civilian side of the UN operation kept essential public services —transportation, health, education, communications, and public administration—functioning. It also supplied emergency relief and technical training to Congolese throughout the country.

## West New Guinea

While the Congo operation was still in progress, the United Nations sent a peace-keeping force to West New Guinea. The root of the problem there was a dispute between the Netherlands and Indonesia. The Netherlands had granted Indonesia independence in 1949, but the status of the territory of West New Guinea (now called West Irian) remained unresolved. Indonesia took the dispute to the United Nations in 1954, claiming the territory as its own.

The Dutch defended their continuing presence in the territory, contending that since the Papuans of West New Guinea were not Indonesian they should have the right to determine their future when they were ready to do so. Tensions increased after Indonesia sent troops to the territory and the Dutch denounced the move as an act of aggression. Indonesia claimed it was simply entering its own territory, which the Dutch were occupying by force.

UN Secretary-General U Thant persuaded the two sides to negotiate. After years of resisting Indonesian claims to the disputed territory, the Dutch government finally relented to growing anticolonial

*In October 1962 UN troops were sent to keep the peace in West New Guinea when tensions between Indonesia and the Netherlands over control of the island threatened to erupt.*

As part of the agreement between Indonesia and the Netherlands, the Netherlands turned over administration of West New Guinea to the UN Temporary Executive Authority, which served as a transitional government. UNTEA took control of all aspects of the territory, including issuing these postage stamps.

opinion and agreed to give up its claim to West New Guinea. Indonesia and the Netherlands reached an agreement on August 15, 1962, that committed the Netherlands to turn over the administration of the territory to a group called the United Nations Temporary Executive Authority (UNTEA), which was to govern the territory as a transitional government.

The agreement granted the UN full authority to administer the territory, protect the rights of the inhabitants, and maintain order using a United Nations force to bolster the existing Papuan police force. The UN Temporary Executive Authority was to transfer political control to Indonesia after May 1, 1963, on the condition that the native Papuans retained the right to determine their political future by a plebiscite no later than the end of 1969.

On October 1, 1962, UNTEA took over the administration of West New Guinea from the Dutch. The UN raised its flag and flew it next to the Dutch flag. The UN security force supervised the cease-fire, enforced UN administrative decisions, and trained the local police force. For seven months the United Nations governed the territory—something it had never done before. The UN Temporary Executive Authority built roads, supervised the withdrawal of Dutch forces, assisted local government, and reestablished the judiciary.

On December 31, 1962, UNTEA replaced the Dutch flag with the Indonesian flag, which now flew next to the UN flag. The UN Temporary Executive Authority spent the final four months of its administration easing the transfer of power to Indonesia. On May 1, 1963, the UN officially transferred control of the territory to a representative of the Indonesian government and, in a closing ceremony, took down the UN flag. The UN left West New Guinea with its mission fully accomplished.

## Arab-Israeli Conflict

During the cold war the Middle East was the world's most unstable region. With the two superpowers facing each other on opposite sides of the Arab-Israeli conflict—the United States in support of Israel, the Soviet Union backing the Arabs—every new outbreak brought the world dangerously closer to nuclear war.

On June 5, 1967, when fighting broke out between Israel and Egypt, Syria, and Jordan, the UN Security Council called for an immediate cease-fire. The war lasted only six days. After it was over, Israel occupied the Sinai Peninsula, the Gaza Strip, the West Bank of Jordan, including East Jerusalem, and part of the Golan Heights. At the request of the Security Council the secretary-general stationed UN observers in the Golan and Suez Canal areas to supervise the cease-fire.

On November 22, 1967, the Security Council unanimously adopted Resolution 242, which called on Israel to withdraw from the territories it captured during the war. It called on all states in the area to respect the sovereignty, territorial integrity, and political independence of every other state in the region and their right to live in peace within secure and recognized boundaries. The resolution also called for a guarantee of free navigation in international waterways and for a just settlement of the refugee problem. A UN special representative for the Middle East began talks with Egypt, Jordan, and Israel (Syria did not accept Resolution 242) in hopes of bringing peace to the region, but there was no significant progress.

Six years later, on October 6, 1973, the Middle East erupted again when the armies of Egypt and Syria launched a surprise attack on Israeli positions. Egyptian forces crossed the Suez Canal and advanced past the posts of UN observer forces, which had been created during the 1948 Arab-

*UNTSO's Major Arnold Wouters of the Netherlands at his post in the Golan Heights in Syria.*

Israeli war. Simultaneously, Syrian forces attacked the Israelis on the Golan Heights. On both fronts the Israelis were caught by surprise and driven back. However, after initial Arab advances, the tide of the war turned, and Israeli forces pushed the Arabs back across the boundary lines that were in place when the war began.

The improved performance of the Egyptian and Syrian forces this time surprised Israel and went a long way toward restoring Arab self-respect, which had been badly shattered by the 1967 rout. "In 1967 they threw their guns down and ran," said one Israeli commander. "This time they fought."

The United States and the Soviet Union arranged a cease-fire, which the Security Council adopted as Resolution 338. Egypt and Israel accepted the cease-fire right away. The Security Council authorized a UN emergency force to supervise the cease-fire and the troop disengagement on the Egyptian front and later to control the UN buffer zone between the two sides. By early 1974 the number of troops in this emergency force reached 7,000.

On the Syrian front the hostilities continued until May 1974 when U.S. Secretary of State Henry Kissinger arranged for Syria and Israel to sign a peace agreement. Because the agreement provided for UN observers to supervise the disengagement and patrol the border area, the Security Council established another United Nations observer force for the Golan Heights area.

Both observer forces supervised the buffer zones between the opposing sides and succeeded in keeping the hostile incidents to a minimum. Improved relations between Egypt and Israel led to the 1978 Camp David Accords and a formal peace treaty between the two countries that was concluded in March 1979. The treaty—the first political settlement between Israel and an Arab country—called for the withdrawal of Israeli forces from the Sinai Peninsula in three stages and the reestablishment of Egyptian control there. After the completion of the Israeli withdrawal from the Sinai in 1982, the UN military force was withdrawn, leaving only a small unit of UN observers.

Most of the 259 UN observers presently in the Middle East are in the Sinai monitoring the Egyptian-Israeli frontier. The Security Council has renewed the UN force that monitors the Syrian front every six

*UNTSO officers take time to talk with some local children in Jerusalem. As of 1990, UNTSO had 300 observers scattered through-out the Middle East monitoring cease-fires, facilitating communication between hostile parties, and assisting other peacekeeping operations in the area.*

months. It continues to keep peace on the Golan Heights along a 47-mile-long corridor between Israeli and Syrian forces.

Although the United Nations has provided various peacekeepers and observers to monitor cease-fires, it has for the most part been on the diplomatic sidelines in the struggle between Israelis and Palestinians, which many see as the heart of the Arab-Israeli conflict. One of the reasons for the inability of the UN to bring peace to the Middle East has been Israeli distrust of the United Nations because of its support for the Palestinians.

Since the 1967 Arab-Israeli war, the General Assembly has consistently championed the Palestinian cause. In 1974 the General Assembly included "the question of Palestine" on its agenda as a separate item for the first time and invited the Palestine Liberation Organization (PLO) to participate in the proceedings as an observer.

After the Camp David Accords and the 1979 peace treaty between Egypt and Israel, the General Assembly condemned "all partial agreements and separate treaties" that violate the rights of the Palestinian people and claim to determine their future. When

the Israeli Knesset (Parliament) passed a law in 1980 that proclaimed a united Jerusalem the Israeli capital (including East Jerusalem, which Israel captured in the 1967 war), the General Assembly declared the law null and void.

The United Nations has also focused on economic and social issues that affect Palestinians. What began as short-term emergency aid to Palestinian refugees after the 1948 Arab-Israeli war grew into long-term development assistance. The UN body most involved in aiding the Palestinians is the United Nations Relief and Works Agency for Palestine Refugees in the Near East (UNRWA). The General Assembly created the Relief and Works Agency in 1949 to provide humanitarian assistance to refugees who lost their homes and livelihood as a result of the 1948 war.

This agency provides a wide range of welfare services to about 2.8 million Palestinian refugees in Jordan, Lebanon, Egypt, Syria, and the occupied territories of the West Bank and Gaza Strip. More than one-third of the Palestinians who receive assistance through the UN Relief and Works Agency live in refugee camps. UNRWA has

# HOPE FOR PALESTINIAN YOUNG PEOPLE

Fadia, Rula, and Leila are sisters, 3 of the 13 girls who live at the Beit Fatayat home on the West Bank. The home is one of several that Dr. Francis Azraq established in 1988 for troubled children.

The three sisters, who are now in their teens, grew up in the Shu'fat refugee camp under difficult circumstances. When they were very young, their parents separated. "Our father was a zero," says Fadia, the oldest of the three. "And our family life was a catastrophe." Fadia, who felt overwhelmed by her problems, was not interested in her studies, rebelled against authority, and frequently got into fights.

Helped by a social worker who knew of Azraq's program, the sisters began a new life at the Beit Fatayat home two years ago. The home provides

Dr. Viveca Hazboun, one of the heads of UNRWA's mental health program.

warmth and support for the 13 girls who live there with 5 social workers chosen and trained by Azraq.

Francis Azraq, a Palestinian from Jerusalem with a Ph.D. in psychotherapy from the University of Paris, heads UNRWA's mental health program on the West Bank with Dr. Viveca Hazboun, an American-born Palestinian with a Ph.D. in psychiatry from the University of San Francisco. Every day they visit a different UNRWA clinic in the refugee camps. Funded and managed by UNRWA, the program provides psychotherapy to Palestinian refugees.

According to Azraq, many Palestinians "are faced with problems of drug abuse, severe depression, pervasive developmental retardation, aggressive behavior and posttraumatic symptoms." These problems have a number of causes, "including the underlying atmosphere of violence which Palestinian children and adults have to cope with every day of their lives." These are compounded by family problems and divorces, which occur in every society, he notes.

The most important result of the intensive psychotherapy provided by the UNRWA mental health program in the refugee clinics and the homes supervised by Azraq is that many of the children undergoing treatment gain a new sense of hope. A girl from the Shu'fat camp says she wants to be a lawyer so she can "defend my people and their rights," while a teenager from the Tulkarm camp wants to be a social worker "to help other children as unlucky in life as I was."

17,000 employees, which makes it the largest operation in the UN system.

The Relief and Works Agency often has difficulty servicing refugees, however, because of political tensions and violence in the area. The Arab-Israeli wars, the Lebanese civil war in the late 1970s and 1980s, and the Palestinian uprising (called the *intifadah*) that began in the Israeli-occupied territories (West Bank and Gaza Strip) in 1987 have disrupted its programs, damaged agency facilities, and endangered both clients and workers. In Lebanon alone 26 UNRWA workers have been killed since 1982. Since the start of the Palestinian uprising, 7 UNRWA workers have been killed in the occupied territories and 64 detained by Israeli military authorities.

In its early years, the agency provided mostly food, shelter, and clothing to the refugees, but later it concentrated more on education and health care. Today almost half of the agency's budget goes to education for refugee children, and more than 20 percent goes to health services. The UN Relief and Works Agency provides education to 393,000 Palestinian children in 641 schools in Jordan, Lebanon, Syria, and the occupied territories. It also runs 8 vocational and technical training institutes and offers 750 university scholarships a year to young Palestinian refugees.

With guidance from the World Health Organization, UNRWA provides health care services to Palestinian refugees that emphasize preventive medicine, immunization, health education, mother and child care, supplementary feeding of young children, and improvement of sanitation. The UNRWA health care centers receive more than 6 million patient visits each year.

*Israeli soldiers withdrawing from their position on the Golan Heights. In accordance with the terms of the cease-fire worked out between Syria and Israel in 1974, UN troops served as a buffer between the two countries.*

*Palestinian refugees attend class at a UNRWA school.*

Although the Palestinian uprising put pressure on the Israelis to pay more attention to Palestinian demands for self-determination, little progress was made until American secretary of state James Baker succeeded in breaking the diplomatic logjam by convincing all the parties involved in the conflict—Israel, Syria, Lebanon, Jordan, and the Palestinians—to gather in Madrid in October 1991. With the United States and the Soviet Union serving as cohosts, the Madrid Conference became the formal opening to a series of direct negotiations between Israel and the Arabs in Washington, D.C.

In 1993 a dramatic breakthrough occurred when secret talks between Israel and the Palestine Liberation Organization resulted in the signing of a peace accord on the White House lawn and a handshake between PLO chairman Yasir Arafat and Israeli prime minister Yitzhak Rabin. The accord granted the Palestinians self-rule in Gaza and Jericho and the prospect of greater control in the rest of the occupied territories.

During the cold war (1950s–1980s) UN peacekeeping operations were generally limited to situations in which the interests of the two superpowers—the United States and the Soviet Union—were not involved directly (Cyprus, West New Guinea, and the Congo) or in which the superpowers were involved so heavily that any conflict could lead to a wider war (the Middle East, for example). The end of the cold war era paved the way for a fuller range of UN peacekeeping efforts in the late 1980s and 1990s.

# CHAPTER 4

# A Hunger for Peace: Peacekeeping Since the 1980s

The end of the cold war changed the atmosphere at the United Nations. The collapse of communism in Eastern Europe and the Soviet Union, which reduced international tensions, paved the way for a new spirit of cooperation and provided the UN with new opportunities and increased responsibilities. With the threat of a superpower veto no longer hanging over its proceedings, the Security Council functioned more effectively and more in keeping with the original intention of the UN's founders.

Nowhere was the new effectiveness more in evidence than during the Persian Gulf crisis. Following the Iraqi invasion of Kuwait in August 1990, the Security Council moved swiftly to condemn the Iraqi attack and spearhead international opposition to it. In the months following the invasion, the council passed a series of resolutions condemning Iraq and supporting Kuwait that finally led to its approval of an international military operation against Iraq.

As a result of its new effectiveness in the 1990s, the United Nations is now more in demand than ever. It has been called on to resolve major conflicts in Afghanistan, El Salvador, Cambodia, Somalia, the former Yugoslavia, and many other troubled areas around the world. The UN has launched more peacekeeping operations since 1989 than it did in all the years between 1945 and 1989. In a single 18-month period in the early 1990s, the number of UN peacekeepers around the world jumped from 11,000 to 93,000.

Besides these new peacekeeping operations, the United Nations has been

*UN troops from Australia land in Cambodia in November 1991. The Australians' arrival marked the beginning of UN peacekeeping efforts in the war-torn country.*

*A UN official stands in front of posters urging Nicaraguans to vote and reminding them that their vote is secret. The UN has increasingly been called on to monitor and guarantee fair elections.*

called on to perform tasks that it traditionally had been unwilling to assume. For example, developing nations are increasingly requesting assistance with such internal nation-building matters as the supervision and guaranteeing of fair elections. In re-

sponse, the United Nations has monitored elections in Nicaragua, Haiti, Cambodia, Angola, Eritrea, and many other places.

So great has been the demand for electoral help that in 1992 the UN held a conference on the coordination of international assistance for elections, in Ottawa, Canada. A special unit dedicated to this specific purpose has been set up to handle requests for help with elections. It reviews all requests for electoral verification from around the world before channelling them to the appropriate UN agency.

These new opportunities and responsibilities have raised hopes around the world that the full potential of the UN and the en-

# REFERENDUM IN ERITREA

Early in 1993 UN observers began arriving in Eritrea to monitor a referendum on whether Eritreans wished to become independent from Ethiopia. UN monitors met with local religious and political leaders and helped election officials demonstrate voting procedures. Later a much larger team of international monitors—UN officials, diplomats, and election experts—arrived to oversee the three-day referendum itself.

Across the country, and in Addis Ababa and the Sudan, where hundreds of thousands of Eritrean refugees displaced by the 30-year struggle for independence from Ethiopia lived, UN observers reported an enthusiastic turnout. For most Eritreans it was their first chance ever to exercise their vote in a secret ballot. "This is the happiest day for everybody here in Eritrea," said first-time voter Mohammed Bashir. "This is the day of freedom in Eritrea."

The final result of the referendum was an overwhelming majority—more than 95 percent—in favor of independence from Ethiopia. A few months later—on May 28, 1993—Eritrea joined the United Nations and proudly took its place in the family of nations.

ergy and dedication of its staff will help make the world a better place. When UN peacekeepers were honored with the Nobel Prize in 1988, Secretary-General Pérez de Cuéllar called the award "a tribute to the idealism of all those who have served the organization."

### The Iran-Iraq War

The Iran-Iraq war began in 1980 when Iraq invaded Iran to gain complete control of the Shatt-al-Arab waterway, which forms the border between the two countries for 60 miles and is at the head of the Persian Gulf. Iraq hoped to overturn by force the Algiers Accord of 1975, which gave the two countries joint control of the Shatt.

Secretary-General Kurt Waldheim and the Security Council immediately called on Iraq and Iran to stop fighting and use the offices of the United Nations to negotiate a settlement. The Security Council adopted resolutions and issued statements calling for a cease-fire, troop withdrawal, prisoner exchange, freedom of navigation in international waters, and efforts by the secretary-general to find a just settlement.

In 1985 Secretary-General Pérez de Cuéllar traveled to Teheran and Baghdad in hopes of getting the two sides to stop fighting. He also dispatched a number of UN missions between 1984 and 1988 to investigate claims by both Iraq and Iran about the use of chemical weapons, attacks on civilian populations, and mistreatment of prisoners. The Security Council condemned the use of chemical weapons and called for strict observance of the 1925 Geneva agreement that banned the use of such weapons. A UN investigative team reported that Iraq used chemical weapons repeatedly.

On July 20, 1987, the Security Council unanimously adopted Resolution 598, which called for an immediate cease-fire "on land, at sea and in the air." The UN resolution condemned the continuation of the war, advocated an investigation into responsibility for the war, and threatened an arms embargo—a cutoff of military aid from outside countries—against any country that contributed to the continuation of the war with its huge loss of life, estimated at more than 1 million soldiers and civilians. When both sides finally accepted the resolution a year later, the eight-year war ended.

The Security Council sent a 350-member peacekeeping force to super-

*Brigadier General Venky Patil (center), commander of the UN Iran-Iraq Military Observer Group, confers with UNIIMOG officers in Basra. UNIIMOG was set up by the Security Council to verify, confirm, and supervise the Iran-Iraq cease-fire and the withdrawal of troops to the internationally recognized boundaries.*

vise the cease-fire, which went into effect along the 740-mile front on August 20, 1988. Negotiations between the two countries followed in Geneva and New York, but little progress was made toward a final settlement. Though the "no war, no peace" period that followed the war did not produce a peace treaty, the UN-sponsored cease-fire did succeed in ending the fighting.

## Afghanistan

Shortly after the Soviet Union invaded Afghanistan in late December 1979, 52 member states of the United Nations requested an immediate meeting of the Security Council. Six council members drafted a resolution that condemned the invasion and called for an immediate withdrawal of foreign troops from Afghanistan. The Soviet Union vetoed the resolution. To get around the Soviet obstacle the Security Council called for a special emergency session of the General Assembly.

The General Assembly passed a resolution that deplored "the recent armed intervention in Afghanistan" as a violation of the UN Charter and called for an immediate and total withdrawal of foreign troops from

Afghanistan "in order to enable its people to determine their own form of government and to choose their economic, political and social systems free from outside intervention, subversion, coercion or constraint of any kind whatsoever."

The negotiations involving the foreign ministers of Pakistan and Afghanistan, which the secretary-general began in Geneva in 1981, led seven years later to the signing of a treaty—on April 14, 1988—that provided for the withdrawal of Soviet troops, the use of UN military observers, and the return of refugees. The full withdrawal of Soviet troops from Afghanistan, completed on February 15, 1989, was monitored by the 40-member United Nations Good Offices Mission in Afghanistan and Pakistan.

In May 1989, in response to the General Assembly's call for the secretary-general to assume a higher political profile, Javier Pérez de Cuéllar appointed a personal representative to make contact with different segments of the Afghan population inside Afghanistan and among the 6 million Afghan refugees in Pakistan and Iran. For the first time in UN history the General Assem-

*UN Under Secretary-General Diego Cordovez (right) traveled to Pakistan in January 1988 to meet with the leaders of the Afghan rebels.*

## AFGHAN ORPHAN

In 1992 thirteen-year-old Mahmud had lived in an orphanage in Kabul for eight years after his parents were killed in the civil war. In the ruined building where the children lived, conditions are appalling. There was no electricity or running water. Food was scarce—a little rice and some stale bread from a nearby bakery. Mahmud was but one of millions of Afghans struggling to survive.

Mahmud and his fellow orphans tried to keep warm during the winter by moving around the gutted building. Like the many other Afghans living on the edge of survival, Mahmud took life one day at a time, waiting for the help he hoped was on the way. After the fall of the Najibullah government Mahmud began seeing hopeful signs—more food, a peace that was holding, and the first relief workers in Kabul. With evidence that the civil war was really over, life was finally returning to normal, Mahmud began thinking about going to school.

The UN now hopes to help Afghanistan recover, rebuild, and cope with millions of refugees trekking home to their villages and communities and with the many other Afghans like Mahmud who survived the war without leaving the country.

bly authorized the secretary-general to get involved in a country's internal affairs. UNICEF and dozens of other UN and nongovernmental relief organizations are providing emergency care, but relief work in the refugee camps has been hampered by the interference of the armed militias who control them.

Most observers assumed that the Soviet pullout would lead to the immediate fall of the government of President Mohammed Najibullah to the Afghan guerrillas who drove the Soviets out of Afghanistan. The Najibullah government, which fell in 1992, lasted longer than expected. But because of disagreement between the various guerrilla factions, no stable central government has yet taken its place.

Since the signing of the Afghan treaty, there has been little progress in dealing with the devastation the Soviet invasion and 15 years of civil war brought to Afghanistan. Nearly 10 percent of the Afghan population—1.5 million people—died as a result of the fighting. Three-quarters of the country's 22,000 villages were destroyed by bombs and shelling. The six million Afghans in Pakistan and Iran constitute the world's largest refugee population.

By 1994 the country's religious, tribal, and geographical divisions appeared almost impossible to solve, and the breakup of Afghanistan into unconnected regions governed by warlords seemed more probable than ever.

### The Gulf War

Iraq's invasion of Kuwait in August 1990 and the Gulf War that followed in early

1991 challenged the United Nations like no other crisis since the Korean War 40 years earlier. The Security Council reacted to the Iraqi invasion swiftly and decisively. On the day of the attack—August 2—the council unanimously adopted a resolution condemning the invasion and demanding that Iraq withdraw immediately. The council further called on Iraq and Kuwait to enter into negotiations to discuss their differences.

Four days later—on August 6—the Security Council voted again unanimously to impose sanctions on Iraq. Acting under Article 51 of the UN Charter, the council placed a full trade embargo, or ban, on all Iraqi exports and imports, except medicine and food, which meant that UN member nations were prohibited from trading with Iraq. On August 9, the council unanimously declared "that annexation of Kuwait by Iraq under any form and whatever pretext has no legal validity, and is considered null and void."

The day after the invasion the United States and the Soviet Union issued a joint statement condemning the invasion and suspending Soviet arms shipments to Iraq. On August 5 President Bush declared that Iraq's "brutal, naked aggression will not stand." Shortly afterward American troops were sent to Saudi Arabia as the first wave of what would be a large military buildup of American and allied forces. The buildup was designed to defend Saudi Arabia while preparing for a military offensive to drive the Iraqis out of Kuwait.

In August and September the Security Council passed more resolutions approving the use of force to enforce trade sanctions and beginning a full sea and air transport blockade of Iraq. Working with the United Nations, President Bush succeeded in isolating Saddam Hussein and having his actions condemned by most of the governments of the world. Bush's reliance on the Security

Teams of U.S. troops board helicopters in Saudi Arabia in January 1991. Security Council Resolution 678 authorized the UN to use "all necessary means" to oust Iraq from Kuwait—only the second time in UN history that it used military force to counter armed aggression.

*Iraqi soldiers set this Kuwaiti oil well on fire before Allied troops drove them from the country. After the war, Secretary-General Javier Pérez de Cuéllar dispatched a special mission to Kuwait to assess the damage done to the country by the Iraqi invasion.*

Council and Soviet cooperation created powerful international pressure to get Iraq out of Kuwait.

Late in 1990 the Security Council adopted its most important resolution. After three weeks of intense discussion, on November 29, the council adopted Resolution 678 by a vote of 12 to 2 to 1 (Cuba and Yemen voted against; China abstained). Resolution 678 authorized the United Nations to use "all necessary means" to restore international peace and security in the area if Iraq did not withdraw from Kuwait by January 15, 1991. The threat of force marked only the second time in UN history the Security Council used its power under the UN Charter to permit the use of military force to counter armed aggression (the Korean War was the first).

The January 15 deadline created a flurry of last-minute peace proposals to head off a war in which 680,000 allied troops, including 410,000 Americans, were squared off against 545,000 Iraqi troops in Kuwait and southern Iraq. None of these attempts was successful, and on January 16 the war

began with a prolonged and intense aerial bombardment of Kuwait and Iraq, conducted mostly by U.S. warplanes and missiles.

The bombardment, designed to pave the way for a massive land attack on Kuwait, targeted Iraq's nuclear, chemical, and biological weapons factories and Iraqi army headquarters. The massive aerial assault damaged Iraqi tanks and artillery and destroyed the morale of the Iraqi troops in Kuwait. Iraq retaliated against the bombardment by launching Soviet-made SCUD missiles at Israel and Saudi Arabia. Although most of the Iraqi missiles missed populated areas, one slammed into an Israeli apartment building and another hit a U.S. Marine barracks in Saudi Arabia, killing 28 and wounding 97.

The land war that began on February 25 lasted 12 days. The allied military coalition, which included army units from Egypt, Syria, and other Arab countries, defeated the Iraqi army decisively and drove its surviving units back into Iraq. After Kuwait was liberated, President Bush halted the as-

*Security Council Resolution 687 outlined the council's peace terms for Iraq. They included the elimination of Iraq's weapons of mass destruction. A UN worker wearing a gas mask inspects an Iraqi bomb (left), while a UN weapons inspector (right) takes a sample from an Iraqi facility suspected of making biological weapons.*

sault and declared a cease-fire on March 2, leaving allied troops in control of a large piece of Iraqi territory south of the Euphrates River. Immediately after the Iraqi defeat, Iraqi Shiites in southern Iraq and Iraqi Kurds in the north rebelled, but Saddam Hussein ruthlessly put down these revolts.

After the Gulf War the Security Council passed three more resolutions. One demanded Iraq pay Kuwait for damages done by the war, set free Kuwaitis and other foreign citizens held in Baghdad, and arrange for an immediate release of prisoners of war. Another condemned the arrest, torture, and killings of Iraqi civilians "most recently in Kurdish populated areas" and called for respect for "the human and political rights of all Iraqi citizens." In consultation with the UN High Commissioner for Refugees, allied troops mounted a relief effort in northern Iraq to assist Kurdish refugees. This effort was later taken over by the UN.

In April 1991 the Security Council adopted Resolution 687, which defined the Security Council's peace terms for Iraq. The resolution demanded that Iraq accept the prewar border with Kuwait and make payments to repair the psychological and physical damage its occupation caused to Kuwait. The resolution also established a demilitarized zone along the Iraq-Kuwait border to be monitored by a 1,400-member UN Iraq-Kuwait Observer Mission (UNIKOM).

The resolution called for UN supervision to ensure that Iraq reduced its military force and destroyed most of its weapons, including its nuclear, chemical, and biological arsenals. The resolution also continued the international trade embargo on Iraq. When Iraq reluctantly accepted what it called the "unjust" terms of the resolution in order to prevent a resumption of allied attacks, the cease-fire became official.

This comprehensive Security Council resolution marked a major turning point for the United Nations. By making itself re-

# DRAWING A BOUNDARY
# IN THE SAND

Thanks to a historic action by the UN, a row of 106 concrete pillars resembling tombstones stretches across 240 kilometers of desert between Iraq and Kuwait. The markers, which define the border between the two countries, are the result of two years of work by the UN Iraq-Kuwait Boundary Demarcation Commission. The five-member commission was created in 1991 by Security Council Resolution 687, which set the terms of the cease-fire for the Gulf War.

"The initial problem was the enormous amount of unexploded materials in the area," said Miklos Pinther, the UN's chief cartographer (mapmaker) and secretary of the commission. "Things like mines, grenades, and leftover stuff from the war. They were scattered all over the place. The wind would blow and the sand would cover them."

Canadian engineers cleared mines for the survey team, and the UN Iraq-Kuwait Observation Mission (UNIKOM) supplied transportation and a camp site. "The logistics of moving pillars through the area were horrendous," said Pinther. "In many places ground conditions were very poor. Cranes would get stuck in the sand."

Although the heat was oppressive, the team remained in high spirits because "everyone understood they were making history," according to Pinther. This was the first time the UN was ever called on to demarcate an international boundary, but it most likely will not be the last. Similar requests are expected from newly formed nations in Eastern Europe.

*Members of UNIKOM in front of one of the concrete pillars placed in the desert to mark the boundary between Iraq and Kuwait.*

sponsible for the reduction of the size and power of Iraq's armed forces, the UN agreed to involve itself in the internal affairs of a country to an unprecedented degree. Iraq made the UN's task even more difficult by resisting its work every step of the way. This was especially true of the International Atomic Energy Agency missions to monitor the dismantling of Iraq's nuclear arms facilities and stockpiles and missions by UN ballistic-missile experts to supervise the destruction of Iraqi missiles. The Iraqi pattern of resistance has been to protest UN efforts, obstruct its missions, and then back down at the last minute for fear of punishment.

## Nicaragua

During the 1980s the Sandinista government of Nicaragua complained to the United Nations on several occasions about American policy. In the Security Council it charged that the United States was threatening its right to rule the country by arming and training antigovernment rebels and by waging economic warfare.

The United States countered that Nicaragua was interfering in the affairs of its neighbors, especially El Salvador, with aggressive behavior designed to destabilize their governments. In 1984 Nicaragua charged that the United States was laying explosive mines in its ports and submitted its case to the World Court. The Security Council drafted a resolution that condemned the practice, but the resolution was never adopted because the United States vetoed it.

The General Assembly also criticized U.S. policy toward Nicaragua. On October 25, 1988, the assembly adopted a resolution by a vote of 89 to 2 that demanded the United States comply with the 1986 ruling of the World Court, which condemned U.S. support for Contra rebel attacks against Nicaragua. (The Contras, who got their name from the Spanish word *contra*, which means *against*, were backed by the United States and sought to overthrow the Sandinista government, which was named after the early-20th-century Nicaraguan patriot Augusto Sandino.) On December

*Nicaraguan president Daniel Ortega addresses his supporters at a rally in Managua before the February 1990 elections.*

20, the assembly voted by the same margin to express its disagreement with the U.S. trade embargo against Nicaragua.

In 1987 five Central American countries (Costa Rica, El Salvador, Guatemala, Honduras, and Nicaragua) put forward a peace plan for the region—called the Esquipulas peace plan—that called for domestic reforms inside Nicaragua (the right to vote, freedom of the press, respect for human rights), negotiations to end the civil war, and a halt to outside support for guerrillas attacking from neighboring countries.

As a result of agreements reached in the first half of 1989, the Central American governments called on the United Nations to put into effect important parts of the plan by sending UN observers to the region. Nicaragua requested the UN to monitor its election scheduled for February 1990, and the Central American presidents called on the UN and the Organization of American States (OAS) to help with the disbanding and return to civilian life of the Contra rebels.

On July 5, 1989, the UN secretary-general and the Nicaraguan government agreed to the creation of the UN Observer Mission for the Verification of the Elections in Nicaragua, known by its Spanish acronym ONUVEN. The operation began in late August with the arrival of 18 officers in the Nicaraguan capital of Managua to monitor voter registration. In December, 22 more UN election monitors were sent to oversee the campaign and make sure all candidates and parties were allowed to campaign freely. Additional UN and OAS monitors were sent just before the February election to observe the voting, say whether or not the vote was fair, and then either approve or reject the results.

The UN-monitored Nicaraguan election brought to power a new government headed by President Violeta Barrios de Chamorro and led to the disarming and return to Nicaragua of rebel forces and other refugees with the help of the UN High Commissioner for Refugees. The election of the new government and the disbanding of the Contras, which was completed on June 28, 1990, thus marking the end of the Nicaraguan civil war, stood as an important diplomatic victory for the UN. The success of the United Nations in Nicaragua and other countries led to increased demand for UN electoral assistance in the 1990s.

## Cambodia

In the 1970s Cambodia was ravaged by a civil war that brought to power Pol Pot, whose brutal Khmer Rouge government was responsible for the deaths of more than 1 million Cambodians (out of a population of 7 million). Hundreds of thousands more fled their homes to seek safety in Thailand or in the Thai-Cambodian border area.

In December 1978, Vietnam invaded Cambodia and overthrew the Pol Pot government. In January 1979, the Security Council met at the request of the Pol Pot government, which charged Vietnam with aggression. The council drafted a resolution calling for the withdrawal of Vietnamese troops from Cambodia, but Vietnam's ally, the Soviet Union, vetoed the resolution and a similar one drafted two months later.

The Vietnamese installed a new government in the Cambodian capital, Phnom Penh, and the Khmer Rouge fled to the border with Thailand to regroup. In February 1979, China attacked northern Vietnam to "teach Vietnam a lesson" and supported Khmer Rouge attacks on Vietnamese troops in Cambodia and on troops of the people's Republic of Kampuchea, as the new Vietnamese-backed government was now called.

In 1979 the General Assembly also called for an immediate cease-fire and the

*Nicaraguan president Violeta Barrios de Chamorro, winner of the UN-monitored election, addresses the General Assembly in September 1993.*

*In June 1992, weary Cambodians return to their native country from refugee camps in Thailand aboard a UNHCR train.*

withdrawal of all foreign forces, proclaiming that the people of Kampuchea had the right to choose their government democratically without outside interference or threats. In July 1981, the General Assembly invited all the parties to the conflict to an international conference on Kampuchea in New York. The conference, which Vietnam chose not to attend, adopted a Declaration on Kampuchea, which called for negotiations to achieve a comprehensive political settlement and established a special committee to find a solution to the conflict. The assembly also called on all nations and international organizations to provide humanitarian relief to Cambodian civilians.

In 1982 Secretary-General Javier Pérez de Cuéllar became actively involved in the issue, mostly through his special representative for humanitarian affairs in Southeast Asia. The secretary-general pressed for negotiations and dialogue between the contending parties and appointed a coordinator of humanitarian relief operations to supervise relief assistance. Most of the UN humanitarian work was carried out by the United Nations Children's Fund, the Food and Agriculture Organization, the World Food Program, the World Health Organization, and the UN High Commissioner for Refugees, as well as by various nongovern-

mental organizations that became active in Cambodian relief.

By 1982 China and the members of the Association of Southeast Asian Nations (ASEAN) had joined forces to try to isolate Vietnam and the Cambodian government it supported. With the encouragement of the United States, China and ASEAN formed and supported the Coalition Government of Democratic Kampuchea, which consisted of the Khmer Rouge and two noncommunist resistance groups. Later in the 1980s improved relations between the Soviet Union, China, and the United States and the withdrawal of Soviet aid to Vietnam led to a joint effort to secure a political settlement.

In the meantime, the UN provided relief to hundreds of thousands of displaced Cambodians living near the Thai border. The United Nations Border Relief Operation assisted close to 300,000 refugees, while the office of the UN High Commissioner for Refugees provided relief for another 14,000.

In 1989 the five permanent members of the Security Council drafted a detailed peace plan for Cambodia, and the four Cambodian factions met in several Asian cities to discuss and react to the plan that was taking shape. Negotiations led to a breakthrough agreement to end the war and hold elections, which the Cambodian parties signed in Paris on October 23, 1991. The Paris agreement called for an initial UN unit that was to go to Cambodia immediately to set the stage for the most ambitious and complex peacekeeping operation in UN history.

The agreement created a large UN team to supervise a cease-fire and organize and conduct an election for a national assembly that would form Cambodia's future government and move the country down the road to national reconstruction. Though the agreement stated that during the transition to a new government the Supreme National Council, composed of the four factions who signed the agreement, would rule Cambodia, it gave the UN team extensive power over many functions of the government, such as police work and the administration of government departments.

In November 1991, the UN advance unit arrived to begin supervising the cease-fire and prepare for a larger group to follow. Within months the UN was engaged in a full-scale transformation of Cambodia—moving refugees into Cambodia from camps on the Thai border, disbanding 70 percent of each faction's military forces, administering the Cambodian government and civil service, repairing the country's roads and bridges, retraining former soldiers, clearing mines, and registering voters.

Despite the attempts of the Khmer Rouge to disrupt the election and obstruct the work of the 22,000 UN peacekeepers (70 lost their lives), the election took place in late May 1993 with 20 parties competing for assembly seats and with 90 percent of those eligible to vote casting their ballots. The Paris agreement called for UN peace-keepers to relinquish authority to a new Cambodian government three months after the elections. But given the extent of Cambodia's devastation and the enormous task of reconstruction it faces, it is likely the United Nations will be involved with Cambodia's development for years to come.

**The Former Yugoslavia**

The continued fighting between Serbs, Croats, and Muslims in the former Yugoslavia is one of the most difficult challenges the United Nations faces in the 1990s. In this war, the participants are concerned primarily with terrorizing, displacing, and killing unarmed civilians. Although the ethnic hatred that fuels the fighting is centuries old, the main drive behind the war is Serbian determination to expel Muslims and Croats from territory Serbs claim belongs to them. "It is in the Serbian interest to terrorize civilians," says Andreas Khol, an Austrian politician who visits Yugoslavia frequently. "It is part and parcel of the plan for a 'Greater Serbia.'"

Each new round of shellings, forced expulsions, mass executions, rape, torture,

*As part of the cease-fire agreement worked out by the UN, these soldiers of the National Army of Independent Kampuchea turned in their weapons to the UN Transitional Force in Cambodia.*

and murder brings with it new cries for revenge. "They killed my husband and son," said one tearful Bosnian refugee. "They burned our home. But they can never rest easy, because one day we will do the same to them, or worse. My children will get their revenge, or their children."

The ethnically mixed communist state of Yugoslavia—a federation of six republics (Serbia, Croatia, Bosnia-Herzegovina, Macedonia, Slovenia, and Montenegro) and two autonomous provinces (Kosovo and Vojvodina)—had been held together since World War II by the iron fist of Marshal Tito (1892–1980) and his successors. However, after the fall of the Berlin Wall in 1989 the changes that swept through Eastern Europe also shook Yugoslavia and fragmented it into five separate republics— Yugoslavia (Serbia and Montenegro), Croatia, Slovenia, Bosnia-Herzegovina, and Macedonia.

Serbia had wanted to preserve Yugoslavia in the form of a federation under its

*Ambulances from the British contingent of the UN Protection Force drive through the destroyed Croatian city of Vukova.*

leadership, but Croatia and Slovenia declared their independence on June 25, 1991, followed by Bosnia-Herzegovina and Macedonia. (All were eventually admitted to the UN—Croatia, Slovenia, and Bosnia-Herzegovina on May 22, 1992; Macedonia on April 8, 1993, as "the former Yugoslav Republic of Macedonia," pending the settlement of a dispute with Greece about the use of the name "Macedonia," which is the name of one of the Greek provinces.) As the former Yugoslav republics declared their independence, what had begun as a civil war became a conflict between sovereign states.

Serbia demanded that the maps of the republics be redrawn to allow Serbia to include areas where Serbs lived into a "Greater Serbia." When the Republic of Croatia refused to go along with the plan, Serbia attacked it to bring it into line. United Nations involvement in the former Yugoslavia began with its support of the efforts of the European Community to reach a negotiated settlement. In September 1991 the Security Council clamped an arms embargo on the whole of former Yugoslavia on the grounds that the Yugoslav war was a threat to international peace and security.

At the request of the Security Council, Secretary-General Javier Pérez de Cuéllar appointed former U.S. Secretary of State Cyrus Vance to be his personal representative on Yugoslavia. In February 1992 the first peacekeeping force—the UN Protection Force—was sent to Croatia to monitor the cease-fire negotiated by Vance and to separate the two armed forces and demilitarize the areas of conflict. Relief workers followed. By the end of 1992 an estimated 22,500 UN soldiers, policemen, and civilian administrators were in Croatia and Bosnia—more than the previous UN record of peacekeepers sent to the Congo in 1960.

In late May 1992 the Security Council imposed wide-ranging sanctions on the Federal Republic of Yugoslavia (Serbia and Montenegro). By that time newly independent Bosnia-Herzegovina had replaced Croatia as the target of Serbian aggression. Serb forces surrounded the Bosnian capital of Sarajevo and shocked the world with their policy of "ethnic cleansing," which involved killing and raping Muslims and destroying their homes. More than 1.6 million Bosnians were forced to flee their homes—the largest number of refugees in Europe since World War II. Seeing their own chance to grab more territory, the Croatians joined the Serbs in attacking Bosnian towns and villages.

The 6,000 UN peacekeepers stationed in Bosnia were unable to curb the fierce fighting. Cease fire after cease-fire collapsed. The UN had more trouble delivering food and medicine to needy areas. Diplomatic pressure and stiffer economic sanctions against Serbia failed to get the Bosnian Serbs to curb their aggression.

In January 1993, negotiators—headed by Cyrus Vance for the United Nations and Lord David Owen for the European Community—convened the three sides in the Bosnian conflict—Muslims, Serbs, and Croats—for peace talks in Geneva. There they unveiled a plan for dividing Bosnia-Herzegovina into 10 ethnically defined provinces, but the plan failed because it lacked the

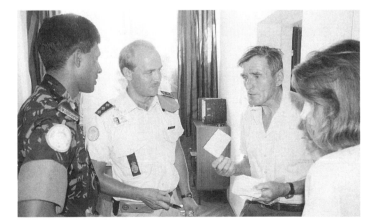

*A Croatian villager (second from right) asks officers from the UN Civilian Police Force to help him contact his relatives in another city.*

# WARRIOR FOR PEACE

Major General Lewis MacKenzie is a veteran of nine peacekeeping missions, but his most difficult and dangerous assignment by far was his five-month tour of duty in the former Yugoslavia as chief of staff to UN forces in 1992.

MacKenzie, a 52-year-old native of Nova Scotia in eastern Canada, arrived in Sarajevo in March shortly before fierce fighting among Croats, Muslims, and Serbs erupted throughout Bosnia. Although he moved the UN headquarters to the Serbian capital of Belgrade, he returned to Sarajevo with 1,600 UN peacekeepers, including 800 Canadians. His success in negotiating control of the airport allowed up to 250 tons of food and medicine to be airlifted each day into the besieged Bosnian capital, where the fighting never stopped.

During his time in Sarajevo, MacKenzie was the target of hostility from all sides. He was fired on by mortars, taken hostage, and received death threats by telephone and fax. The fax machine allowed him to send messages back inviting the people making the threats to visit him and talk over their complaints, but he said, "Nobody ever took up the offer."

The day that stands out most in the general's mind is Sunday, May 10, when Serbian soldiers took Bosnian President Alija Izetbegovic hostage. MacKenzie was able to negotiate the president's release in exchange for the freedom of the city's Serbian commander and some of his men who were being held by Bosnian troops.

MacKenzie and his UN troops were taking the Serbs in a convoy to be released when Bosnian soldiers stopped the convoy, took out several Serbian officers, and executed them in front of MacKenzie. The Bosnians took 200 other Serbs prisoner. MacKenzie is certain the presence of UN peacekeepers was what prevented further bloodshed. "If we hadn't been there," he said, "it would have been a massacre."

Before he left the city in August, MacKenzie said he would like to return to Sarajevo someday when peace is restored. "I moved into this city when it was still a beautiful place," he said. "I've watched it, stone by stone, wall by wall, building by building, deteriorate into enclaves of people trying to kill the people next to them." However, he does not expect peace to come to Sarajevo soon. When he returns, he says, "I just hope I'm young enough to enjoy it."

"People are horrified when I say Bosnia was probably the five best months of my life," MacKenzie says. "But to go into a situation where you can use professional military combat skills to try and stop other people from fighting is, we think, a pretty honorable undertaking."

*Refugees in a gymnasium being used as a temporary shelter in Croatia.*

*UN Secretary-General Boutros Boutros-Ghali (center) meets at UN headquarters in New York with the co-chairs of the Conference on the Former Yugoslavia, Cyrus Vance (left) and David Owen.*

support of both Bosnian Serbs and the Bosnian government, which opposed the plan because it rewarded Serbian aggression and ethnic cleansing.

In the meantime, the Bosnian tragedy continued. In April 1993 a convoy of UN relief trucks reached the besieged town of Srebrenica, where 40,000 Bosnian refugees had been trapped for more than a year. Thousands rushed the trucks in order to be evacuated to the safer Muslim enclave of Tuzla 60 miles away. After each truck unloaded its sacks of flour and supplies, up to 200 desperate refugees squeezed into the empty truck. Families were separated in the pandemonium as thousands of refugees shoved, shouted, and fought for a place on the trucks for themselves or their children.

"I thought I would die of hunger or be killed," said Aida Salehovic, who reached Tuzla, leaving her mother and two brothers behind in Srebrenica. Many frantic parents sent their children away without good-byes. "They threw babies up onto the trucks just to get them out," said Kenneth Thorstensson, the Danish leader of the convoy. "We left in a hurry—it was panic."

Three trips by the convoy to Tuzla brought out more than 5,000 civilians, many of them sick and wounded. However, at least 9 people, including 7 children, suffocated or were trampled to death while trying to escape.

Hatija Hukic, 14, who saved her 7-year-old sister from being crushed, had to

watch helplessly as the crowd pressed in on her cousin. "People were pushing and someone fell on her, and then more people fell on her," she remembered tearfully. "After an hour, she died."

The unchecked fighting in Bosnia presented the United Nations, as well as Europe, the United States, and the rest of the world, with one of the most difficult diplomatic challenges in the post–cold war era. As correspondent Paul Lewis wrote, "A failure in Yugoslavia would represent a setback for the hopes expressed by Boutros Boutros-Ghali and others that UN peacekeepers can gradually come to play a more aggressive role in enforcing peace and civilized standards of behavior."

### Somalia

Somalia, with a population of 7 million, was once a colony of Britain and Italy, but during the cold war it became a pawn of the superpowers, courted first by the Soviet Union, then by the United States. By the early 1990s, after years of drought, famine, and dictatorial rule, Somalia was in a state of crisis. The overthrow of Somalia's dictator, Mohamed Siad Barre, led to clan warfare, widespread destruction, and social chaos. It was so dangerous in the Somali capital of Mogadishu that foreign embassy staff and almost all UN workers had to be withdrawn.

By late 1992 Somalia had no functioning government, its roads, phone system, and other public works were all but destroyed, and thousands of Somalis were dying of starvation every day. International relief efforts to feed the starving Somalis were hampered by fighting and theft. Organizations like the International Red Cross were forced to resort to bribing warlords and armed gangs with money or food

*Admiral Jonathan T. Howe (second from right), special representative of the secretary-general for Somalia, visits a UN-supported feeding center in Baidoa run by CONCERN, a nongovernmental organization.*

to continue their relief work. More than half the food sent to Somalia was stolen, while massive starvation continued in the countryside.

The Security Council had trouble responding, in part because governments were unwilling to send personnel into such a place and UN rules did not permit relief workers to operate in dangerous areas. Secretary-General Boutros Boutros-Ghali publicly scolded the Security Council for allocating too many resources to a "rich man's war in Yugoslavia" while turning "a blind eye on a crisis because it takes place in Africa." By that time the United Nations had committed $630 million and 22,500 UN troops to the former Yugoslavia, while the UN operation in Somalia had a budget of $23 million and a peacekeeping force of 500 soldiers, many of whom felt frustrated because they could not carry out the UN objective of feeding millions of starving Somalis.

President Bush responded to the Secretary-General's appeal for outside help by dispatching 30,000 U.S. troops to Somalia. The mission succeeded in stabilizing the Somali capital and main cities, restoring the supply lines, and getting food to the coun-

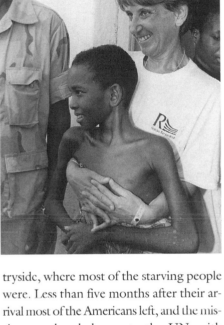

*A young Somali boy, a patient at a hospital run by the International Committee of the Red Cross, with a hospital staff member.*

tryside, where most of the starving people were. Less than five months after their arrival most of the Americans left, and the mission was handed over to the UN, with 4,000 U.S. soldiers remaining as part of the UN operation. By May 1993, the mission was in the hands of a UN military command that included Pakistani, Italian, and American forces.

CHAPTER 5

# Stepping Back: Disarmament and Arms Control

The nuclear age began at 8:15 A.M. on August 6, 1945, when an American Air Force plane dropped an atomic bomb on Hiroshima, Japan. Two weeks earlier Truman, Stalin, and Churchill, who were meeting at Potsdam, Germany, to finalize their postwar plans following the defeat of Nazi Germany, had issued an ultimatum to the Japanese that if they did not agree to surrender unconditionally they would suffer "complete and utter destruction."

When Japan ignored the warning, President Truman decided to use a new secret weapon—a recently developed bomb with the explosive force of 20,000 tons of TNT. The atomic bomb completely destroyed the center of the city and instantly killed more than 71,000 people. Five years

after the Hiroshima blast the number of deaths due to direct exposure to the bomb reached 200,000. In the decades that followed, thousands more survivors died from leukemia, long-term anemia, and other effects of radiation sickness.

Three days after the Hiroshima bombing, when the Japanese still refused to surrender, the United States dropped another atomic bomb, on the port city of Nagasaki. No longer able to hold out, Japan finally agreed to surrender unconditionally. On September 2, 1945, the surrender became official in a formal ceremony aboard the battleship *Missouri* in Tokyo Bay. The most terrible war in human history was over.

In the wake of the war that devastated Europe and large parts of Asia, the United States and the Soviet Union emerged as the two most powerful nations in the world. They had cooperated as allies during the

*The atomic bomb dropped over Nagasaki on August 9, 1945, produced this tremendous mushroom cloud. These Japanese boys (inset) are survivors of the bombing. The bomb dropped on Hiroshima three days earlier killed 71,000 people instantly. Over the next five years, 200,000 people died from the effects of the bomb.*

war, but prospects for keeping friendly relations faded quickly as differences in political beliefs and national ambitions pulled the two superpowers apart, producing an era of intense struggle that came to be known as the cold war.

Tensions between the two superpowers increased in the late 1940s when communists seized power in Eastern Europe with the help of the Soviet army. The United States countered the threat of Soviet expansion by launching the Marshall Plan to rebuild war-torn Europe and by sending aid to Greece and Turkey. In 1948, when the So-

viet Union blockaded West Berlin, the United States airlifted supplies into the city.

In 1949 the Communists under Mao Zedong seized control of mainland China. The same year the Soviet Union exploded its first atomic bomb, signaling the start of the nuclear arms race.

### Early UN Disarmament Efforts

Before the United Nations was created in 1945, disarmament negotiations always had limited objectives—an arms "freeze" or reduction, the prohibition of specific types of weapons, or the removal of troops and weapons from a specific area. However, the atomic bomb that exploded over Hiroshima demonstrated to the world a capacity for destruction far greater than anything ever before imagined, making the need for large-scale disarmament and arms control all the more urgent.

Third World nations (the poor nations of the world, often called "developing nations"), alarmed by the growing threat of nuclear destruction, found the United Nations a ready forum to express their concern and urge the superpowers to curb their nuclear arms race. As the cold war intensified in the 1950s, arms reduction no longer seemed enough. In 1960, the General Assembly declared by unanimous vote that the goal of the United Nations was "general and complete disarmament."

The framers of the UN Charter did not make disarmament an important part of its central goal of international peace and security. One reason is that they were unaware of the nuclear bomb American scientists were secretly preparing to test at the very time the charter was being written. Another reason is that their vision of a UN military force to maintain peace and security made them unenthusiastic about pursuing disarmament goals that they considered unrealistic.

*An Allied checkpoint into West Berlin. The cold war between the two superpowers came dangerously close to growing into a hot war when the Soviet Union blockaded the city in 1948. The United States kept the city supplied with an around-the-clock airlift. The Soviet blockade was lifted in May 1949.*

Unlike the League of Nations Covenant, which called for arms *reduction,* the United Nations Charter called only for arms *regulation.* The framers of the UN Charter thought an international ceiling on armaments—an agreement that would allow nations to possess only so many weapons—would reduce the fear many nations had of being attacked by surprise and would allow the Security Council and other UN agencies to pursue their goals of international peace and security.

The charter assigned responsibilities for arms control to both the General Assembly and the Security Council. Under Article 11 of the UN Charter, the General Assembly may propose plans to keep international peace and provide security, "including . . . disarmament and the regulation of armaments," and may make "recommendations [about these ideas] to the Members or to the Security Council."

The very first resolution the General Assembly adopted—on January 24, 1946—established the UN Atomic Energy Commission. The assembly called on the commission to create a plan to promote the peaceful use of atomic energy, eliminate atomic weapons and other weapons of mass destruction, and establish an inspection and enforcement system to safeguard against violations.

In the spring of 1946, at the first meeting of the Atomic Energy Commission, Bernard Baruch, the American representative, proposed a plan that would have eliminated atomic weapons and promoted the peaceful use of nuclear energy. Under the plan the UN would have been allowed to inspect nuclear facilities anywhere in the world to make sure no country was secretly making bombs. Permanent members of the Security Council would also have had to give up their veto power over UN decisions having to do with atomic energy.

The United States promised to destroy its own stockpile of atomic weapons if such an international control system were put into effect. The Soviet Union rejected the American plan. Deeply suspicious of the West and its strong influence on the United Nations, the Soviets were unwilling to allow UN inspectors into the Soviet Union, and they did not want to give up their veto power on the Security Council.

Instead, the Soviets presented a plan of their own that called for the United States to destroy its nuclear weapons. When the United States refused to agree, the Soviet Union continued to develop its own nuclear weapons. In 1949, when the Soviet Union successfully tested its first atomic bomb, it became the world's second nuclear power. Great Britain joined the "nuclear club" in 1952, followed by France and China in the early 1960s.

To control the nuclear arms race, the UN created a number of discussion and negotiation committees—some within the UN framework, others outside—to seek agreements on disarmament and arms control. A second UN disarmament commission—the Commission for Conventional Armaments—was created in 1947 to regulate and reduce the world's armaments and armed forces under an international system of control and inspection. When neither one of the commissions made sufficient progress, the General Assembly brought them together into a single Disarmament Commission in 1952. The assembly asked the new commission to prepare a complete program for the regulation, limitation, and gradual reduction of all armed forces and armaments.

Even though most cold war disarmament negotiations have taken place in a sporadic and piecemeal fashion among the nuclear powers, the United Nations Disarmament Commission served as an important place for arms control discussions. Although

On June 12, 1982, nearly one million demonstrators converged on New York City's Central Park to express their support for a nuclear freeze.

the Disarmament Commission met only occasionally and failed to produce tangible results, it did explore approaches not taken by the superpowers. Eventually the General Assembly decided that its First Committee, which works on political and security matters and is composed of all members of the United Nations, should function as the UN Disarmament Commission.

## Antinuclear Demonstrations

Against the backdrop of the disarmament talks at the UN, a small but determined number of people in the West, including the English philosopher Bertrand Russell, began demonstrating against nuclear weapons. Russell, winner of the Nobel Prize for Literature in 1950, was in his 80s when he became the world's leading spokesman for nuclear disarmament. In 1954 he made his famous "Man's Peril" broadcast on BBC radio, in which he condemned the U.S. hydrogen bomb tests on Bikini Island in the Pacific Ocean.

In 1958 Russell led the Campaign for Nuclear Disarmament, but he resigned from it in 1960 to form the more militant Committee of 100, whose goal was to incite mass civil disobedience. When the 89-year-old Russell and his wife led an anti-nuclear protest march in London, the authorities arrested him and charged him with inciting the public to civil disobedience. They sentenced him to two months in prison, although for health reasons he only had to serve seven days.

Even when a "ban the bomb" demonstration did not draw a large number of protesters, it usually made news. For example, in 1961 a determined group of 100 demonstrators from all over Great Britain went to Holy Loch in Scotland to protest the presence of U.S. Navy nuclear submarines offshore. To publicize the event, some of the demonstrators walked the entire 350 miles from London to Holy Loch.

When they blocked the pier and chanted, "We shall not be moved," 50 Scottish constables began to clear them out. The

English philosopher Bertrand Russell was a strong opponent of nuclear weapons.

demonstrators did not resist. They sat or lay down flat and let their bodies go limp. Every time the constables dragged one demonstrator away, another one moved in to take his place.

The protestors wanted to keep sailors from servicing the U.S. submarine supply ship *Proteus*. Earlier they had used a fleet of 13 canoes and kayaks, a lifeboat, and a motorized houseboat to try to reach the *Proteus* and board it. Although British police boats and U.S. frogmen kept them at bay for three hours, some of the demonstrators did get close enough to the supply ship to touch its side. Sailors on the *Proteus* turned the ship's fire hoses on the invaders to keep them from climbing on board.

Although the demonstration failed to keep the *Proteus* from supplying the nuclear submarines, protest leader Pat Arrowsmith claimed a moral victory. "At least," she said, "we have made people think."

In the 1980s antiwar demonstrations took place in Europe, especially in West Germany, involving people worried that the presence of intermediate- and short-range missiles in Western and Eastern Europe made Europe the most likely place for a nuclear confrontation. "Limited nuclear war," wrote one European newspaper, "means nuclear war limited to Europe."

In 1985, the work of the International Physicians for the Prevention of Nuclear War was recognized when the private Boston-based organization headed by two heart doctors (one American, one Russian) won the Nobel Peace Prize. Dr. Barnard Lown, of the Harvard School of Public Health, and Dr. Yevgeny Chazov, chief physician to the Kremlin, flew to Oslo, Norway, to accept the prize on behalf of the peace group with more than 135,000 members in 41 countries.

"We cannot keep silent knowing what the final epidemic—nuclear war—can bring to humankind," said Chazov in his acceptance speech. "The bell of Hiroshima rings in our hearts not as a funeral knell but as an alarm bell calling out for actions to protect life on our planet."

*In 1984, more than 50,000 people gathered in Moscow for a government-sponsored anti-nuclear protest.*

# ON THE BRINK

In October 1962 a confrontation over the presence of Soviet nuclear missiles in Cuba brought the United States and the Soviet Union to the brink of nuclear war.

When Soviet premier Nikita Khrushchev promised in 1960 to defend Cuba with Soviet arms, he assumed that the United States would not try to prevent the installation of Soviet missiles on the island. However, the U.S. government became concerned in 1962 when photographs taken by American U-2 spy planes flying over Cuba revealed the construction of medium-range ballistic missiles.

President John Kennedy called a secret meeting of his top advisers to decide what to do about this nuclear threat less than 100 miles off the coast of the United States. They discussed launching air strikes against the missile sites, but in the end they chose to impose a naval "quarantine," or blockade, around Cuba to prevent the further shipment of Soviet weapons to the island.

At seven o'clock on Monday evening, October 22, 1962, the President, in a TV and radio broadcast from his White House study, told the country and the world about the Soviet missiles and called on Khrushchev "to halt and eliminate this clandestine, reckless and provocative threat to world peace." Kennedy warned that "any nuclear missile launched from Cuba against any nation in the Western Hemisphere" would be deemed "an attack by the Soviet Union on the United States, requiring a full retaliatory response upon the Soviet Union."

That same evening at the United Nations, Adlai Stevenson, the U.S. ambassador to the United Nations, submitted a formal request to Ambassador Vale-

*President John Kennedy (with his back to the camera) confers with his top aides at the height of the Cuban Missile Crisis.*

rian Zorin of the Soviet Union to call the Security Council into emergency session. At the same time Stevenson proposed a resolution calling for the immediate dismantling and removal of Soviet missiles and bombers from Cuba under UN observation. The proposal also called for negotiations between the United States and the Soviet Union about the issue and an end to the quarantine once the missiles were gone.

In the late afternoon of the next day—Tuesday—Stevenson presented the American case before the Security Council. Zorin countered by rejecting the "false accusation" that his country had placed offensive weapons in Cuba and offered his own resolution that condemned "the actions of the government of the United States aimed at violating the United Nations Charter and at increasing the threat of war."

As Soviet ships headed across the Atlantic for Cuba and U.S. ships waited to intercept them, the threat of nuclear war increased with each passing hour. On Thursday, when the Security Council met again to discuss the crisis, the mood was somber. Stevenson's speech restating the American position was calm and reasonable, but Zorin's was harsh and contemptuous. He accused Stevenson of shifting his position because the U.S. lacked evidence that offensive missiles were in Cuba and because the world and the UN did not support the American action.

Stevenson listened intently, jotting down a note from time to time. When he rose to reply, he said, in a rare display of anger, "I want to say to you, Mr. Zorin, that I do not have your talent for obfuscation, for distortion, for confusing language and double-talk. And I confess to you that I am glad that I do not!" He then went on to counter Zorin's charge that he lied and that offensive missiles "do not exist, or that we haven't proved they exist."

"All right, sir," he said, looking hard at Zorin, "let me ask you a simple question: Do you, Ambassador Zorin, deny that the U.S.S.R. has placed and is placing medium- and intermediate-range missiles and sites in Cuba? Yes or no? Don't wait for the translation. Yes or no?"

"I am not in an American courtroom, sir," Zorin shot back, "and therefore I do not wish to answer a question that is put to me in the fashion in which a prosecutor puts questions. In due course, sir, you will have your answer."

"You are in the courtroom of world opinion right now and you can answer yes or no. You have denied that they exist and I want to know whether I have understood you correctly."

"Continue with your statement. You will have your answer in due course."

"I am prepared to wait for my answer until hell freezes over, if that's your decision."

But Stevenson did not wait. Immediately, he displayed to the council and to the world a series of enlarged photographs of the missile sites taken by air reconnaissance, explaining in detail what each photograph showed. The evidence was damning.

"As to the authenticity of the photography," he said to the Soviet ambassador, "I wonder if the Soviet Union would ask its Cuban colleague to permit a United Nations team to go to these sites. If so, Mr. Zorin, I can assure you that

*In a dramatic showdown at the UN, Adlai Stevenson, U.S. ambassador to the UN, confronted his Soviet counterpart with photos that showed the Soviets were building missile sites in Cuba.*

we can direct them to the proper places very quickly."

Stevenson paused, then said he hoped they could now "get down to business."

"We know the facts and so do you, sir, and we are ready to talk about them," Stevenson concluded. "Our job is not to score debaters' points. Our job, Mr. Zorin, is to save the peace. And if you are ready to try, we are."

After this dramatic showdown at the UN, Khrushchev sent Kennedy a letter proposing to dismantle the missiles and ship them back to the Soviet Union under UN supervision, provided the United States promised not to invade Cuba. A second letter from Khrushchev was more demanding, proposing that the U.S. dismantle its bases in Turkey in exchange for the dismantling of Soviet bases in Cuba. Kennedy wisely decided to ignore the second letter and accept the first, thus easing the crisis and pulling the world back from the edge of nuclear catastrophe.

Subsequent negotiations led to the withdrawal of the missiles, the destruction of the launching sites, and the removal of the Soviet bombers, under UN supervision.

In the United States a nuclear freeze movement—a campaign to get both superpowers to freeze their production of nuclear weapons—gained ground in the early 1980s. By the fall of 1982, 1,500 peace groups across the country were backing a nuclear freeze, and 9 states, 50 cities, and more than 500 towns had endorsed freeze resolutions. In June 1982, nearly a million antinuclear demonstrators gathered in New York's Central Park to show their support for the freeze.

During the cold war these antinuclear demonstrations provided a sense of urgency to the issue of the nuclear arms race and helped put pressure on world leaders to solve the problem. While that sense of urgency decreased after the end of the cold war, concern about the threat of nuclear weapons remains strong.

### Special Sessions on Disarmament

In an effort to slow or even reverse the arms race, the UN General Assembly convened a series of special sessions on disarmament in 1978, 1982, and 1988. Devoted entirely to disarmament and arms control, the sessions were meant to impress upon the nations of the world, especially the superpowers and their allies, the urgency of the issue and to provide them with a place to discuss their ideas and proposals.

The first General Assembly special session on disarmament was held in New York from May 23 to July 1, 1978. At the session—the largest, most complete gathering of nations ever assembled to address the issue—the community of nations agreed, for the first time in history, on an overall strategy for disarmament, which it declared in the session's final document.

The final document stated that "genuine and lasting peace can only be created through the effective . . . security system pro-vided for in the Charter of the United Nations, and the speedy and substantial reduction of arms and armed forces . . . leading ultimately to general and complete disarmament under effective international control."

By emphasizing the importance of disarmament to international peace and security and by stating the primary responsibility of the United Nations, the final document gave the disarmament issue more attention and publicity than it had ever been given before. It also emphasized that disarmament planning needed to include countries from all parts of the world.

The final document, which served as the guide for later UN disarmament efforts, also declared that "disarmament and arms limitation agreements should provide for adequate measures of verification satisfactory to all parties." The session also established what is now called the UN Department for Disarmament Affairs, which supports disarmament studies, trains diplomats, organizes conferences, and distributes the *United Nations Disarmament Yearbook*.

The General Assembly convened a second special session on disarmament from

As part of a worldwide campaign to call attention to the second special session on disarmament in 1982, the UN sponsored a competition for a poster design on the theme of disarmament. The winning entry was created by a man from the German Democratic Republic.

June 7 to July 10, 1982. The assembly had declared the 1980s the Second Disarmament Decade, but when it quickly became obvious that arms control negotiations were stalled on every front and spending on weapons was rising throughout the world, the General Assembly decided it was time for another special session on disarmament.

Nineteen heads of state and 50 foreign ministers were among the representatives of more than 140 nations who attended. Although international tensions prevented the session from achieving any significant new breakthroughs, it did unanimously reaffirm the validity of the first special session's final document and the General Assembly's World Disarmament Campaign.

The purpose of the World Disarmament Campaign was to seek public understanding and support for UN arms control and disarmament goals. The campaign sought to enlist community leaders, elected

representatives, professionals, academics, and others around the world as disarmament activists. It also sought the help of the international media, nongovernmental organizations, colleges and universities, and research institutions.

To further the goals of its World Disarmament Campaign, the General Assembly established three centers in different parts of the world—the Regional Center for Peace and Disarmament in Africa (in Togo), the Regional Center for Peace, Disarmament and Development in Latin America and the Caribbean (in Peru), and the Regional Center for Peace and Disarmament in Asia (in Nepal). The General Assembly also declared that each year the week of October 24 was to be designated Disarmament Week.

The General Assembly convened its third special session on disarmament from May 31 to June 25, 1988. The 159 UN member states who attended considered a wide range of issues—conventional disar-

*The General Assembly proclaimed the 1970s the Disarmament Decade. This UN stamp was issued in 1972 to commemorate the decade.*

mament, naval armaments, chemical weapons, nuclear weapons in outer space, how to check on countries that promise they are not making nuclear or chemical weapons, and the role of the UN in arms control and disarmament.

Although the atmosphere at this third special session was less confrontational than at the second—because of the improved relations between the Soviet Union and the United States—strong national and regional interests kept UN member states from reaching an agreement that would have produced a worthwhile final document.

The recommendations of these UN special sessions did not end the arms race, but they did generate public interest and create an international stage for arms control proposals. The sessions also helped convince the members of the UN that disarmament had to be a joint undertaking of *all* countries, not just the superpowers.

At its regular sessions, the General Assembly sought to put into action the decisions and recommendations of its special disarmament sessions. For example, the assembly called for a nuclear test-ban treaty that included all nations, nuclear-weapon-free zones in the Middle East and South Asia, a strengthening of the security of non-nuclear countries against the threat of nuclear attack, a ban on chemical weapons, and a reduction of conventional arms. It also called for the prevention of an arms race in outer space, the prohibition of the development of new weapons of mass destruction, a reduction of military budgets, and the transfer of money from the military to economic and social development. Although the ultimate UN goal of complete disarmament remained as far away as ever, several important arms control agreements were concluded.

## Limiting Nuclear Weapons

In Moscow, on August 5, 1963, Great Britain, the United States, and the Soviet Union signed the Treaty Banning Nuclear Weapons Tests in the Atmosphere, in Outer Space and Underwater—called the Partial Test-Ban Treaty because it did not ban underground tests, which at the time were thought to be too difficult to detect. U.S. President John F. Kennedy told the American people the treaty was "an important first step—a step toward peace—a step toward reason—a step away from war." While he acknowledged the limited nature of the treaty, he saw it as a chance "to slow down the perilous arms race."

After the United States and the Soviet Union signed the Partial Test-Ban Treaty, they stopped testing in the atmosphere, although both countries continued to conduct underground tests. France and China, which did not sign the treaty, conducted tests in the atmosphere, although neither country did so after 1980. The 1963 Partial Test-Ban Treaty was the first international agreement to regulate nuclear arms. It helped reduce international tensions, limited radioactive pollution, and created an ex-

*Antinuclear activist Jerry Rubin (center) presents a 400-yard-long petition to a representative of the UN second special session on disarmament.*

ample for further nuclear arms control agreements to follow.

Throughout the 1970s the UN Disarmament Commission called for a comprehensive, or complete, test-ban treaty, believing that the halt of all nuclear testing would curb the nuclear arms race and reduce the likelihood of nuclear weapons being used. Although negotiations for such a treaty ended in 1980, the UN goal continued to be a total ban on all nuclear testing.

Intensive debate and negotiations in the UN Committee on Disarmament and in the General Assembly's First Committee led to the Treaty on the Non-Proliferation of Nuclear Weapons, which the assembly approved in 1968. The main purpose of the treaty was to stop the spread of nuclear weapons to nations that do not already possess them. The treaty also stated that each nonnuclear state must enter into an agreement with the International Atomic Energy Agency (IAEA), the successor of the Atomic Energy Commission. The IAEA provides for inspections that check to see if nuclear material has been diverted from peaceful uses to nuclear weapons. Other treaty provisions called for all countries to have access to nuclear technology for peaceful purposes and for nuclear nations to promote nuclear disarmament.

After the General Assembly's approval of the Non-Proliferation Treaty, the challenge was to get as many nations as possible to sign it. The last two nuclear holdouts, France and China, agreed to sign the treaty in the early 1990s. However, as of 1994, a number of smaller states with the potential to develop nuclear weapons had yet to sign.

Like some other nations that signed the Non-Proliferation Treaty, Iraq tried to find ways to evade international inspections and secretly develop nuclear weapons. However, the Gulf War and Resolution 687, which the Security Council passed after the war, stopped Iraq in its tracks. The resolution declared that Iraq must "unconditionally agree not to acquire or develop nuclear-weapons-usable material" and place all its "nuclear-weapons-usable materials

*A mushroom cloud forms over a small, uninhabited island in the Pacific after the explosion of a nuclear bomb by France in the 1970s.*

under exclusive control, for custody and removal, of the International Atomic Energy Agency (IAEA)."

The Security Council also called on the secretary-general to develop a plan to monitor Iraq's compliance with the resolution. A UN Special Commission (UNSCOM), now headed by the Swedish diplomat Rolf Ekeus, was created for this purpose. UNSCOM and the IAEA discovered just how far Iraq had gone toward acquiring and deploying weapons of mass destruction—nuclear, chemical, and biological—and ballistic missiles. While Iraq tried to obstruct the inspections and repeatedly failed to comply with UN resolutions, on-site inspections on short notice uncovered large weapons stockpiles and an intricate network of research, development, and production facilities.

The most surprising and disturbing findings had to do with nuclear weapons. Following its initial denials that it was pursuing a nuclear weapons program, Iraq admitted in July 1991 that it had three undeclared uranium-enrichment programs. That led the Security Council to declare on August 15 that Iraq had violated international standards by failing to subject its uranium-enrichment program to IAEA standards.

After the IAEA discovered more operations that violated Iraq's obligations under the Non-Proliferation Treaty, the agency removed or destroyed most of these materials and facilities. It also forced Iraq to destroy the nuclear complex at al-Athir, where much of the research and development work relating to Iraq's nuclear program took place.

In early January 1993, when Iraq barred a flight of UNSCOM weapons inspectors, tensions between Iraq and the Security Council boiled over. On January 13, British, French, and American planes blasted missile sites and their radar bases in southern Iraq. In a second raid four days later, U.S.

Navy ships fired 40 Tomahawk cruise missiles at the Zaafaraniya industrial complex in a Baghdad suburb—a site the Special Commission had visited and identified as a precision computer-aided tool shop capable of making crucial parts for Iraq's banned nuclear weapons program.

As a result of these military and diplomatic rebukes, Iraq grudgingly complied with the Security Council's demands for dismantling its nuclear, biological, and chemical weapons programs and for demolishing its missiles with a range greater than 150 kilometers (about 90 miles). Ambassador Ekeus of UNSCOM was confident that the special commission had the necessary tools it needed to do the job it was assigned. "Given the resources to carry out the control system, and as long as the arrangements under the cease-fire stand," he said, "we will be able to prevent Iraq from rebuilding its capability."

## Nuclear-Weapon-Free Zones

The United Nations has long regarded the establishment of nuclear-weapon-free zones as an effective way to limit the proliferation of nuclear weapons and protect nations that do not possess nuclear weapons. In 1959, 12 countries, including the United States

*After Iraq's defeat in the Gulf War in 1991, Security Council Resolution 687 required Iraq to cooperate in the UN-supervised identification and destruction of its nuclear, biological, and chemical weapons. Here, an Iraqi army bulldozer, under UN supervision, destroys SCUD missiles at a military camp in Baghdad.*

*In 1992, a UN Special Commission inspection team, set up under the terms of Security Council Resolution 687, destroyed this building, believed to be used by Iraq in building missiles.*

and the Soviet Union, signed the Antarctic Treaty, which declared that Antarctica was to be used only for peaceful purposes. The treaty, which prohibited military activity, nuclear explosions, and radioactive waste disposal anywhere in Antarctica, was the first arms control agreement to emerge after World War II. It was also the first international agreement that prohibited nuclear weapons in a specific area. The provisions of the treaty have been strictly followed ever since.

The 1967 Treaty for the Prohibition of Nuclear Weapons in Latin America (the Treaty of Tlatelolco) created the first nuclear-weapons-free zone in a densely populated area. It was also the first arms control agreement that set up a permanent system for international supervision of its terms. The group that enforces this treaty—the Agency for the Prohibition of Nuclear Weapons in Latin America—works in coordination with the International Atomic Energy Agency. The Latin American countries that have signed the treaty have agreed to prohibit nuclear weapons in their territories and to use their nuclear materials and facili-

ties only for peaceful purposes. When Argentina and Brazil agreed to abide by the treaty, Cuba was left as the lone holdout in the region.

In 1961 the General Assembly requested all nations to "consider and respect the continent of Africa as a denuclearized zone." Three years later the Organization of African Unity adopted a Declaration on the Denuclearization of Africa. Although many African governments supported it, there was enough resistance by some African countries to prevent the idea from being implemented. Other proposals to establish nuclear-weapon-free zones in the Middle East, South Asia, the Balkans, the Mediterranean, central and northern Europe, and the Indian Ocean have been presented in General Assembly sessions or developed by regional groups.

## Superpower Talks

From the beginning, the United Nations has known that direct talks between the nuclear superpowers were the best way to make progress in arms control. Though

General Assembly disarmament organizations and conferences could address the issues and urge nuclear disarmament, only the superpowers had the power to limit the arms race. Nonetheless, the international pressure and encouragement provided by the United Nations played an important part in superpower negotiations.

In 1964, at a meeting of the UN Committee on Disarmament, the United States suggested that both superpowers explore ways to freeze the expansion of their nuclear weapons systems. At the signing of the UN-sponsored Treaty on the Non-Proliferation of Nuclear Weapons in 1968, the two nuclear superpowers agreed to begin negotiations, known as the Strategic Arms Limitation Talks (SALT), which started in late 1969 in Helsinki, Finland. (Strategic arms are the long-range rockets carrying nuclear bombs possessed by both the United States and Soviet Union, now Russia.) The objective was to reach agreement on the control of strategic nuclear warheads, rockets, and other offensive and defensive weapons systems through uninterrupted negotiations. These face-to-face superpower negotiations

resulted in several agreements to limit defensive anti-ballistic weapons (missiles that are designed to shoot down other missiles). One of the agreements produced by the SALT I talks was the Treaty on the Limitation of Anti-Ballistic Missile Systems (the ABM Treaty), which the United States and the Soviet Union signed in Moscow in May 1972. In the ABM Treaty, both sides agreed not to put into place movable anti-ballistic missiles and agreed to limit ABM systems to two fixed sites in each country.

The second round of SALT talks, which began in November 1972 and had as its goal a long-term treaty to limit offensive weapons (missiles with nuclear bombs that are launched against another country), led to a full treaty signed in Vienna in 1979. The Treaty on the Limitation of Strategic Offensive Arms (SALT II) put limits on missiles, bombers, and the number of nuclear warheads. Although neither side went on to approve the treaty officially, both parties agreed to abide by its provisions as long as the other did.

In 1982 the United States and the Soviet Union resumed a new round of arms

*This Titan II missile is being removed from its silo on a military base in Arkansas. During the late 1980s, the United States and the Soviet Union reached agreements on reducing the size of each nation's nuclear arsenal.*

control negotiations, which they called the Strategic Arms Reduction Talks (START). The emphasis of this new round of talks was on reducing, not just limiting, the size of each nation's nuclear arsenal.

The beginning of the end of the cold war began in March 1985, when Mikhail Gorbachev became general secretary of the Communist party and chief political leader of the Soviet Union. Quickly consolidating his power by retiring scores of aging and incompetent high party officials and hiring younger, more vigorous replacements, he took immediate steps to revive the stagnant Soviet economy.

In 1987 and 1988, Gorbachev took even bolder steps to reform the Soviet economic and political system under his policy of *glasnost* ("openness") and *perestroika* ("restructuring"). Freedom of the press was permitted and encouraged, and elections were allowed for some party and government posts. To stimulate the economy, industries and collective farms were given more decision-making responsibility instead of taking their orders from Moscow. Small-scale businesses were also legalized and encouraged.

In foreign affairs Gorbachev improved the international climate by seeking friendlier ties and more trade with other nations. In 1988–89 he withdrew Soviet troops from Afghanistan after their nine-year occupation. He extended his country's moratorium on nuclear testing three times, and in 1987 he and President Ronald Reagan of the United States signed an agreement for their two countries to destroy all existing stocks of medium-range, nuclear-tipped missiles.

On December 7, 1988, Gorbachev addressed the UN General Assembly—the first Soviet head of state to do so since 1960. In his historic speech, he announced a unilateral withdrawal of Soviet troops from Eastern Europe and a substantial reduction

*Mikhail Gorbachev, premier of the Soviet Union, addresses the General Assembly on December 7, 1988.*

of armed forces and weapons over the next two years.

His speech and the political changes that swept Eastern Europe created a new, more peaceful international climate such as the world had not known for four decades. In July 1991, President George Bush and Gorbachev signed the START treaty, which had been under negotiation for more than nine years. According to the treaty, both sides agreed to reduce their long-range offensive nuclear forces by 30 to 35 percent.

One year later in Washington, Presidents Bush and Boris Yeltsin of Russia signed a new arms-reduction agreement that called for the two sides to cut their nuclear forces to 3,000 to 3,500 weapons each within a decade. This unprecedented call for a 70 percent cut in nuclear weapons on both sides took the steam out of the nuclear arms race and marked the end of the cold war.

Throughout the course of these superpower talks during the cold war, the UN offered its support and encouragement and regularly asked for reports on the progress of the negotiations. It continually urged the two superpowers to consider not just their own national interests, but also the interests of the entire world.

## Biological and Chemical Weapons

In 1925 the United States and Soviet Union signed the Geneva Protocol, prohibiting the use in war of poisonous and bacteriological gases. This treaty was the result of strong reaction to the devastation and suffering caused by the use of biological and chemical weapons (such as mustard gas) in World War I. However, since the Geneva Protocol prohibits the use of such weapons but not their production or stockpiling, during the cold war both superpowers built up substantial arsenals.

Since 1969 the General Assembly has put the issue of biological and chemical weapons on its annual agenda. In 1972, the assembly adopted an agreement calling for a prohibition on the development, production, and stockpiling of deadly biological weapons. This agreement has since been signed by more than 100 countries and was the first authentic international disarmament agreement because it actually called for the *destruction* of existing weapons.

Since 1972 the General Assembly has also been trying to create an agreement that would prohibit chemical weapons—their development, production, stockpiling, and use—as well as the supervised destruction of existing supplies and production plants. After both the United States and Soviet Union agreed to cease the production of chemical weapons and seek the large-scale reduction and eventual destruction of their stockpiles, the completion of a chemical weapons treaty was assured.

Discussions in the Conference on Disarmament and the General Assembly about changing the environment for military purposes led to an agreement in 1977 against the military use of techniques to modify the environment during war. The agreement prohibits tampering with the earth, air, or water during wartime in ways that would have severe environmental effects, such as earthquakes, tidal waves, or changes in the weather or climate.

## Outer Space

From the beginning of the space age the United Nations has sought to prevent the military exploitation of outer space. Shortly after the Soviet Union launched the first earth satellite in 1957, the UN Disarma-

*Members of the UNSCOM team in Iraq inspect Iraqi artillery projectiles that could have been used for chemical weapons.*

*An American astronaut steps onto the surface of the moon. After years of negotiations, the General Assembly approved the Outer Space Treaty in 1967, which declared that outer space was to be used only for peaceful purposes.*

ment Commission proposed inspections to make sure objects sent into outer space were used solely for peaceful purposes, and the General Assembly established the Committee on the Peaceful Uses of Outer Space.

The committee developed a set of principles to guide countries in their exploration and use of outer space. In 1963 the General Assembly supported the committee's recommendations by unanimously adopting the Declaration of Legal Principles Governing the Activities of States in the Exploration and Use of Outer Space (known as the Outer Space Treaty). This document sought to make outer space and the other planets in our solar system an international zone, not the territory of any single country.

After 10 years of negotiations aimed at avoiding a military space race, the General Assembly approved the Outer Space Treaty. The treaty came into force in 1967 after the United States, Soviet Union, and 82 other nations signed it.

The treaty declared that outer space is to be used only for peaceful purposes and that space exploration is for the benefit of all countries. The treaty prohibits placing nuclear weapons and other weapons of mass destruction in orbit around the earth, on the moon, or on any other celestial body. It also bans military installations on the moon and other planets and rejects as invalid any national claims in outer space.

## Conventional Weapons

The United Nations has long been concerned with the control of conventional as well as nuclear weapons. (Conventional weapons are any kind of device such as a bomb, bullet, rifle, tank, machine gun, or mine that does not have a nuclear, chemical, or biological capability.) In 1978 the General Assembly declared that negotiations on the reduction of armed forces and conventional weapons should be pursued with as much determination as negotiations on nuclear disarmament.

In 1980 a United Nations conference in Geneva worked out an agreement that banned or restricted the use of certain kinds of conventional weapons, such as mines, booby traps, and incendiary and fragmentation bombs, that cause great injury, especially to civilians.

In 1992 the General Assembly adopted a resolution that established a Registry of Conventional Arms. The registry records information supplied by member states on their arms imports and exports during the preceding year, information that makes it easier to keep track of international arms transfers. The resolution specifies that information be included about tanks, armored vehicles, artillery, combat aircraft and helicopters, warships, and missiles.

CHAPTER 6

# *Global Development: Promise and Pain*

The French photojournalist Maya Vidon went to Somalia in 1992 to cover a famine that threatened 4.5 million people with starvation. One September morning she saw something she would never forget. A starving man by the name of Mohammed Osman collapsed under a tree at a feeding center in Baidoa. Attempts to get him to drink a few drops of milk were unsuccessful.

"As Mohammed's breathing became increasingly uneven," reported Vidon, "I kept myself at a distance, not daring to invade this man's intimacy in his last minutes." Suddenly he turned his eyes in her direction. "I was pierced by his stare," she said. She took his picture. Five minutes later Mohammed Osman died.

During her three-week stay in Somalia, Maya Vidon witnessed many horrible scenes—shootings, looting, starvation, and death. "It was like the end of the world," she said, "which made me forbid myself to think, to feel." To shield herself from the suffering that surrounded her, she used her camera to "detach and see the picture only." Her photographs became part of the words and images that went out from Somalia to alert the world to the magnitude of the tragedy.

On September 14, 1992, while Vidon was in Somalia, UN Undersecretary-General for Humanitarian Affairs Jan Eliasson announced that UN agencies were launching a large-scale 100-day plan to speed up international relief efforts to Somalia. Since the ouster of the Somali president in January 1991, the country had been torn apart by a civil war that pitted clan against clan. It destroyed the country's economy and social fabric and crippled humanitarian relief efforts. When Secretary-General Boutros Boutros-Ghali reported that Somalia was "a divided country, fragmented on clan and family lines, without any recognized channels for political action," the Security Council acted.

In April 1992 the council authorized the United Nations Operations in Somalia

*A crowd of Somalis gathers to welcome Admiral Jonathan T. Howe, special representative of the secretary-general for Somalia.*

(UNOSOM). Initially UNOSOM was dispatched to monitor a cease-fire in the Somali capital of Mogadishu, but the number of UNOSOM peacekeepers quickly grew as it set up headquarters in four different parts of the country to provide security for relief operations.

When the main warring factions in Somalia agreed not to interfere with the international relief efforts during the emergency operation, UN agencies acted quickly to move massive supplies of food, seed, clean water, building materials, and basic health services to the areas hardest hit by the famine.

The UN's World Food Program airdropped food supplies to remote Somali villages, the United Nations High Commissioner for Refugees helped Somali refugees who had fled to neighboring countries, and the United Nations Development Programme restored basic services. The United Nations Children's Fund and the Food and Agricultural Organization were also part of the massive humanitarian effort by the United Nations and other international relief organizations.

## UN Development Decades

From the beginning the United Nations believed international peace and economic progress were linked. This is why the new organization committed itself to the promotion of "higher standards of living, full employment, and conditions of economic and social progress and development." To achieve these goals, the member states of the United Nations have committed themselves to solving on a global scale problems of health, economic development, and social injustice.

In the first years of its existence, immediately after World War II, the UN concentrated its efforts on the plight of war refugees, reconstruction of war-torn areas, and caring for children in countries devastated by the war. As these problems were solved, the UN turned its attention to the needs of poorer countries, often called developing countries because their economies are not yet industrialized. The United Nations has since expanded its economic and social activities so that today 80 percent of its money and staff work go to economic and social programs in developing countries.

To keep the focus of the United Nations on its commitment to help the underdeveloped parts of the world, the General Assembly has proclaimed four successive United Nations Development Decades. In the First Development Decade (1961–70) the General Assembly launched a major effort to build economies and modernize societies in the developing world. In the succeeding Development Decades—the Second (1971–80), the Third (1981–90), and the Fourth (during the 1990s)—the assembly continued to strengthen these policies and goals through the adoption of new declarations, programs, and development strategies.

During the 1960s many developing countries increased their economies as measured by their gross national product (the total value of the items and services produced in a country each year), but these gains were offset by population growth, unfavorable balances of trade (when money paid to other countries for imports exceeds

the money received for the goods the home country sends abroad, called exports), and large debts. But instead of growing and progressing, many of these countries found themselves falling further behind economically and socially, and their problems only got worse in the 1970s and 1980s. In 1970 the General Assembly unanimously adopted a strategy for the Second Development Decade—called the International Development Strategy—that pledged to close the gap between rich and poor nations. It aimed to create a just world order by encouraging cooperation between developed and developing countries "in all spheres of economic and social life."

The International Development Strategy proposed a plan whose goal was to double the standard of living in the developing world between 1970 and 1990. The plan called for economically advanced countries to transfer to developing countries every year financial resources equal to at least 1 percent

*Farmers on a corn cooperative in Ecuador. The UN Development Programme has helped farmers such as these by providing tractors, fertilizers, and new and better seeds.*

of their gross national product, most of it in the form of long-term, low-interest development loans.

To help with the implementation of this new economic order, the General Assembly adopted the Charter of Economic Rights and Duties of States in 1974. The charter declared that every nation has the right to fully control its own natural resources; to regulate foreign investment within its borders; and to nationalize, or seize control of, foreign-owned property. However, the charter also declared that in the case of the nationalization of foreign property, the nation taking the property should in some way compensate the company or other nation whose property has been taken.

The International Development Strategy for the Third Development Decade, which the General Assembly adopted in 1980, reaffirmed the urgent need for the rapid development of the world's less developed countries. The strategy set specific goals for progress in international trade, finance, science and technology, energy, the environment, and transportation.

In 1990 the General Assembly prepared a new strategy for the last decade of the 20th century— the Fourth Development Decade (1991– 2000). While the new strategy aims for accelerated development, its goals are broader and more comprehensive than those of its predecessors. The United Nations still seeks to spur economic progress in underdeveloped countries, but the development it now promotes—called human development—has more to do with poverty, hunger, environmental degradation, and the living conditions of people than with governments and large corporations.

An experimental windmill being constructed in Colombia by UNDP staff. Developing alternative sources of energy to oil and other fossil fuels is a priority for the UNDP. A conference on new and renewable energy sources was held in 1981 at UN headquarters in New York. The symbol for the conference is shown below.

## United Nations Development Programme

Created in 1965, the United Nations Development Programme (UNDP) administers and coordinates most of the UN development programs around the world. These include projects in virtually every economic and social sphere— farming, mining, manufacture, transportation, communications, housing, fishing, forestry, electrical power, trade, tourism, health, sanitation, education, environmental protection, social welfare, public administration, and community development. In the 1990s UNDP has also become involved in helping countries hold elections and studying the effect of the worldwide HIV-AIDS epidemic on the work force in developing countries.

The UNDP headquarters is in New York, but more than 80 percent of its staff works in its 124 field offices around the world. Its current annual budget of $1.5 billion comes from contributions to its various funds

# NEW POLICE IN EL SALVADOR

After the UN brokered the 1992 peace accord that ended the 12-year civil war in El Salvador, it moved quickly to put the accord into practice and provide assistance to the war-ravaged country.

At a camp in the provincial town of Aguacayo, former guerrilla fighter Jose Maria Lennon is part of an ambitious UN plan to replace the former national police with a new 6,000-strong force. Lennon, who is temporarily being supported by a UNDP emergency program, hopes to contribute to El Salvador's peaceful future. "My objective is to join the national police force," he says, "to serve the country's security forces."

Lennon is enrolled in a special program at the camp that stresses human rights. It is part of a plan to bring ex-fighters up to the ninth-grade level required for admission into the National Police Academy.

Once a major violator of human rights, the police today represent hope for law and civilian rule. Currently the academy accepts more than 300 students each month, with 40 percent of the places reserved for former guerrillas and government soldiers. For the first time, women are also accepted.

In September 1993 Secretary-General Boutros Boutros-Ghali urged other countries to help El Salvador get back on its feet; two-thirds of its population live in poverty, one-third "in extreme poverty." The country's economy was devastated by the civil war, which caused more than $1.5 billion worth of damage.

The secretary-general also reported that El Salvador was "the most densely populated country of the Americas" and had the highest degree of soil erosion, the most polluted water system, and the highest rate of deforestation in Latin America. Despite these many problems and obstacles, the country seems well on its way to achieving national reconciliation and a better life for its people.

*A UN project in the Caribbean helped train local fishermen to use modern fishing methods. Here, a trainee is instructed in the proper use of a navigational device called a sextant.*

and programs. The total number of ongoing UNDP projects is now close to 6,000.

Since the 1990 publication of its first annual *Human Development Report,* the UNDP has been stressing the importance of the human factor in its development planning. Human development puts people rather than economic plans or governmental projects at the center of development programs.

The UNDP's new human development approach has prompted it to increase its partnerships with nongovernmental organizations, promote the inclusion of women in development plans, and encourage free enterprise, political freedom, respect for human rights, and fair and free elections. In 1992 alone more than 30 developing countries asked the UNDP for electoral assistance, two-thirds of them African nations holding elections for the first time.

A growing number of developing countries are asking the UNDP to help them apply the human development approach to their development plans so they can improve the lives of their people. Of 93 UNDP country programs approved for 1992–96, 79 focus on human development.

## OTHER UN DEVELOPMENT AGENCIES

- **UN Capital Development Fund** provides grant assistance for the reduction of poverty in the least-developed countries.

- **UN Sudano-Sahelian Office** helps 22 African nations combat drought, the spread of deserts, and land degradation.

- **UN Fund for Science and Technology for Development** helps developing countries make use of the latest advances in science and technology.

- **UN Revolving Fund for Natural Resources Exploration** funds mineral exploration and mining projects.

- **UN Conference on Trade and Development** promotes international trade policies designed to speed up the economic growth of developing countries.

- **UN Development Fund for Women** provides financial and technical assistance to low-income women in developing countries.

- **UN Volunteers** recruits volunteers to work on UN development projects throughout the world.

## Population

With the number of people inhabiting the earth expected to exceed 6 billion by the year 2000, the issue of the world's population and the earth's resources that will be required to sustain it are of urgent concern to the United Nations.

UN involvement in population issues began in 1947, when the Population Com-

mission—the first international body to deal with population problems—was set up as one of the working commissions of the UN Economic and Social Council. The commission prepared population estimates and projections, improved statistics that were incomplete or lacking in many parts of the world, and advised the Economic and Social Council and other UN bodies on the effect

*A group of West African children gathers in front of a billboard encouraging family planning. The UN has been concerned with population issues since its inception.*

of population policies on economic and social development.

In 1966, after the General Assembly recommended a more active role for the UN in population research, planning, data collecting, and information and advisory services, the secretary-general established a trust fund, called the United Nations Population Fund, to help the UN respond more effectively to countries seeking help with their population problems.

To heighten awareness about population issues the United Nations convened international population conferences in Bucharest (1974), Mexico City (1984), and Cairo (1994). Nongovernmental organizations, which played a major role in planning the 1994 International Conference on Population and Development, were present in Cairo in full force to discuss the topics of health for pregnant women and babies, rights of women and children, elimination of unsafe abortions, the status of women, aging, urbanization, education, AIDS, international migration, and refugees.

According to Dr. Nafis Sadik, executive director of the United Nations Population Fund, by the end of the century 90 percent of the world's population growth will be in developing countries. The additional strain on land, air, and water resources will be a threat to the survival of future generations. In the Arab Republic of Yemen, for example, the population is increasing at more than 3 percent a year, which means the country's 12 million people will double in less than 20 years. With the blessing of the country's religious leaders, Yemen has introduced a voluntary family planning program and has begun educating people about birth control. With the help of the government and the UN Population Fund, the Yemeni Family Care Association provides family planning and a wide range of services to mothers and children, as well as ex-

pectant mothers, in this traditional Muslim society.

"Slowly, by lectures, meetings with religious and educational leaders, and through radio and TV, and by nurses and midwives talking to groups of people at all levels," said a Yemeni social worker, "we have succeeded, somehow, in convincing people that contraceptives are not religiously forbidden."

## Human Settlements

The United Nations is also involved with the issue of housing and human habitat. The UN Conference on Human Settlements held in Vancouver in 1976 affirmed the right of people to freedom of movement and settlement within countries, the right to be part of decisions affecting their homes and communities, and the right to decent shelter, sanitation, clean water, and a satisfactory physical environment.

On the recommendation of the conference, the General Assembly established the United Nations Center for Human Settlements (UNCHS), known as Habitat, in 1978. Headquartered in the Kenyan capital of Nairobi, Habitat promotes the planning, financing, and managing of better housing. It seeks to improve human settlements in developing countries through low-income housing construction, energy conservation, the renovation of slums and

The official emblem for the UN Conference on Human Settlements, held in Vancouver in 1976. The circle represents the world, the triangle within the circle represents shelter, and the figure in the center represents humanity.

*A low-cost housing unit in the suburbs of Dakar, the capital of Senegal.*

squatter settlements, urban and regional planning, low-cost building technologies, and better sanitation and water supply systems.

Habitat receives its overall direction and policy guidelines from the Commission on Human Settlements, which meets every two years unless a special session is convened. The commission has a membership of 58 countries, each elected for a four-year term by the Economic and Social Council, with the following regional representation: 16 members from Africa, 13 from Asia (including the Pacific), 10 from Latin America (including the Caribbean), 6 from Eastern Europe, and 13 from Western Europe and North America.

Habitat's programs and projects in more than 100 countries are generally initiated at the request of the governments concerned. In many cases, Habitat is involved in the very early stages of the project, preparing plans that can then be implemented when funding becomes available. Habitat stresses the importance of using local materials and workers in its projects.

In Costa Rica, Habitat is promoting the use of bamboo rather than wood as a building material in order to provide low-cost housing and reduce dependence on wood from the country's rapidly diminishing rain forest. Bamboo provides an additional environmental advantage because bamboo reforestation helps combat soil erosion, a costly result of the loss of the country's rain forest. In Singapore, Habitat is helping the government centralize its various land databases and information systems into a single Land Data Hub Network that will improve the country's policy planning and administration.

Habitat is also active in Africa. For example, it is providing low-cost housing through the use of local "building brigades" in Zimbabwe, constructing urban public housing in Burundi, and restoring the historic Stone Town section of Zanzibar City in Tanzania.

In the 1980s, in cooperation with the UNDP, the United Nations Capital Development Fund, and the government of Malawi, Habitat launched the Rural Housing Project to provide decent housing to the people of Malawi. The ambitious project used native materials, identified and trained local builders and artisans, built demonstration houses, established a sound rural housing credit system, and adopted the idea of "the house that grows." This concept involved putting up a basic unit that could later be extended and enlarged when and if the owner chose to invest more time and money.

## Food

The United Nations famine relief effort in Somalia is an example of the fight the UN wages around the world against hunger, malnutrition, and starvation. When famine and drought strike in Africa and in other parts of the world, UN agencies work with both governments and nongovernmental organizations to feed the hungry and help farmers protect their livelihood.

The first direct encounter of the United Nations with mass starvation came shortly after it dispatched peacekeepers and civilian experts to the newly independent nation of the Congo in 1960. The famine, which hit the headlines in early 1961, had been developing for some time. Members of the Baluba tribe had been moving westward into the territory of the Lulua tribe, and

when independence came, the Lulua turned on the Baluba, fearful they would try to take control of the area.

About 280,000 Baluba people set off on a 300-mile trek toward their tribal homeland without food to eat, water to drink, or seeds to plant. Then they stopped because they simply had no more strength to continue. By that time thousands were little more than walking skeletons. The weakest, mostly children, were dying at the rate of 200 a day.

In November 1960 when Secretary-General Dag Hammarskjöld appealed for funds within the UN system, the United Nations Children's Fund (UNICEF) came up with $150,000 for emergency relief. However, getting supplies into Bakwanga, the main local town, was complicated by the problems of distance and terrain and by co-tribesmen of the Baluba who had seceded from the central government and set up their own government in the area.

In early December, Albert Kalonji, "president" of the new government, agreed

*A UN worker offers a lesson in nutrition to these African villagers in Upper Volta.*

to let in a special UN unit. The airlift began, a fleet of trucks was enlisted, and distribution centers were set up. By this time the area's two hospitals and handful of dispensaries were overwhelmed by thousands of starving people.

Many children could no longer digest ordinary food. Dr. Melson, a British medical officer attached to a Ghanaian military unit, tried to cope with 1,000 patients in a 150-bed hospital in the village of Miabi. He and a colleague from the World Health Organization made "cookies" from maize flour, powdered milk, and sugar and gave them to those most in need. Gradually, a system of food distribution was set up, so that by mid-January 60 of the 150 tons of food needed daily were being delivered.

The Oxford Famine Committee (Oxfam), a British charity which contributed money to the UN relief effort and to the Congolese Red Cross before the famine became front-page news, appealed to the public for help. The response was overwhelming. Oxfam had to hire a church hall so its 30 volunteers, working in shifts, could process all the donations that poured in. In towns all over England regional organizers were swamped with demands for collecting tins and Congo literature.

By January 21, Oxfam's Congo Appeal collected £104,000 (about $290,000), while about the same amount was donated to two other charities, the British Red Cross and the War on Want. Oxfam's Leslie Kirkley flew to the Congo to visit the famine area. Conditions were still severe, with about 40 deaths a day, but thanks to the UN emergency relief effort and Oxfam's prompt response with cash, the worst of the crisis was over.

Although the image of the starving Congolese child soon faded from public consciousness and the famine (which resulted in about 10,000 deaths) paled in

comparison with later African famines, the world witnessed the tragedy of hunger and poverty in Africa and learned how the UN and private charities like Oxfam, working together, could make a difference. Their cooperation set a precedent for later joint UN-NGO relief efforts.

In response to a rash of droughts and crop failures in the early 1970s, the UN General Assembly convened the World Food Conference in Rome in 1974. Attended by representatives from 133 nations, the conference succeeded in focusing international attention on the crisis and the early relief efforts.

The Universal Declaration on the Eradication of Hunger and Malnutrition, which the conference adopted, stated that "every man, woman, and child has the inalienable right to be free from hunger and malnutrition in order to develop fully and maintain their physical and mental faculties." The declaration emphasized the responsibility of governments to provide food for their own people and stressed the need of developing countries for technical and financial assistance to help them feed their citizens.

At the request of the Rome Conference the General Assembly established the World Food Council. Headquartered in Rome, the Food Council often meets in dif-

*In 1970 the Food and Agriculture Organization held its Second World Food Congress at The Hague in the Netherlands. Delegates from 100 countries met to discuss ways to reduce hunger, malnutrition, and starvation.*

ferent parts of the world at the invitation of UN member states. Although it does not actually run its own projects, the World Food Council works closely with the UN World Food Program and UN specialized agencies—the Food and Agriculture Organization and the International Fund for Agricultural Development. In 1980 the council helped focus world attention on the food crisis in Africa. In concert with other UN agencies it successfully promoted the creation of a food credit mechanism in the International Monetary Fund to help countries finance food imports in times of crisis.

Another UN food agency is the World Food Program. Created jointly with the Food and Agriculture Organization in 1963, the program provides food for economic and social development projects as well as emergency food aid. Its food assistance is used as a partial substitute for cash wages to workers engaged in mining, industry, forestry, irrigation, soil erosion control, land rehabilitation, construction, and other development projects.

## United Nations Environment Programme

In 1972 the UN convened a Conference on the Human Environment in Stockholm. Representatives from 112 countries around the world called attention to the damage being done to the environment and the threat this damage posed to future generations. The conference issued a Declaration on the Human Environment, a series of rules it hoped the international community would follow, and adopted a plan of action that called on governments, UN agencies, and other organizations to take steps to stop the destruction of the environment.

June 5—the opening day of the Stockholm Conference—is now observed each year as World Environment Day. The General Assembly has urged all member states and UN bodies to mark the day with activities that feature concern for the environment.

Following the Stockholm Conference, the UN created the United Nations Environment Programme (UNEP), the group that coordinates the environmental policies

*These eucalyptus trees were planted in Senegal, with the assistance of the UNDP, to help stop the desertification brought on by drought.*

# DESERTIFICATION IN MALI

Drought, which has plagued much of western Africa since the late 1960s, has brought desertification (the spread of deserts) inexorably southward. The desertification problem is worldwide, affecting about one-quarter of the earth's land area and one-sixth of the world's population.

Before it dried up, Lake Fagubine in Mali was one of the biggest lakes in West Africa. As fishing and farming collapsed, 60,000 people were forced to leave the area.

One of the keys to fighting back the desert is the Niger River. Malian aid worker Drissa Coulibaly came up with an idea about how to get the waters of the Niger to bring Lake Fagubine back to life. Because there is a nine-meter drop in height between the Niger River and the dried-up lakes of Tele and Fagubine, his plan was to connect the river and Lake Tele with a channel. He figured once Niger water reached Lake Tele, it would flow easily into Lake Fagubine.

Working under the auspices of the UN Sudano-Sahelian Office, Coulibaly's army of workers labored under the blazing sun for more than nine months to dig millions of cubic meters of sand with nothing more than hand tools. When the channel was completed and water flowed into Lake Tele and started returning to Lake Fagubine, villagers and their herds began returning. When the water stopped short of many fields, workers kept digging to restore the lake and the communities it supported.

and activities of all the UN agencies. Often called "the environmental conscience of the UN system," the Environment Programme works with governments, nongovernmental agencies, and business and scientific groups to increase awareness of environmental issues. Headquartered in Nairobi with another office in New York, the UN Environment Programme was the first agency whose headquarters the United Nations placed in a developing country.

More nations have come to recognize that environmental degradation is an international problem. Mostafa Tolba, executive

director of the Environment Programme, says worry about the environment is a unifying force "because everybody knows that in the environment they are all connected, they are all partners in it." In cooperation with the UN Development Programme and the World Bank, the UN Environment Programme seeks to solve problems such as the pollution of international waters, global warming, depletion of the ozone layer, and loss of plant, insect, reptile, and animal species (often called biodiversity).

Thanks to an UNEP initiative started in September 1992, rhinoceroses are no longer teetering on the brink of extinction. Rhino populations have increased in Namibia, South Africa, Malaysia, India, and Kenya, whose black rhino population increased since 1986 from about 340 to 420.

UNEP pressure resulted in the enforcement of bans on the sale of rhino products in Yemen and the United Arab Emirates. China banned the export of medicines containing rhinoceros horn, following a visit by a UNEP representative. In too many places, however, rhinos are still endangered. Since 1989 poachers have reduced Zimbabwe's black rhino population from 2,000 to 400. In late 1992 and 1993, at least 18 rhinos were illegally killed in Nepal.

Other activities of the Environment Programme include maintaining the International Register of Potentially Toxic Chemicals, which supplies important information about chemical safety, as well as the International Referral System (Infoterra), a world-wide register of environmental data. One of UNEP's most interesting projects is its Earthwatch Program, which uses satellites and other high-tech devices to measure pollution and the healthiness of the Earth's atmosphere in 142 countries.

UNEP is also a major force in the creation of important environmental conventions and treaties. The Montreal Protocol, negotiated with the help of the Environment Programme in 1987, seeks to reduce chemical damage to the ozone layer, which shields the earth from harmful ultraviolet rays. In 1989 the Environment Programme negotiated the Basel Convention, which sets controls on the international movement and disposal of hazardous wastes.

The Environment Programme is also active in efforts to stop the spread of deserts in Africa and other places and promote water conservation and environmental education. It is now working with other UN agencies to preserve tropical forests and with the World Meteorological Organization to limit global climate changes. The Environment Programme works with developing countries to help them preserve their forests, animals, soil, and water and to bring the ideas of conservation and environmental protection into the development plans of these countries.

## The Rio Conference

The United Nations Conference on Environment and Development —better known as the Earth Summit—was held in Rio de Janeiro in June 1992. Attended by the leaders of more than 170 nations, thousands of government negotiators, 1,500 accredited nongovernmental observers, and 8,000 journalists, the conference was the largest meeting of its kind ever held. In addition to the conference itself another 30,000 private citizens—environmentalists, church groups, women, young people, indigenous peoples, scientists, and business executives—turned out for other events, including the '92 Global Forum, which hosted several hundred separate meetings.

Organized by Canadian businessman Maurice Strong, the summit was the result of a lunch meeting he had had six years earlier with the prime minister of Sweden, Ingvar Carlsson. Concerned that the world's environmental problems were getting worse, despite progress in some areas, the two decided to use the 20th anniversary of the 1972 Stockholm Conference, which Strong had also organized, to renew the world's pledge to clean up the planet. Carlsson proposed the idea to the UN General Assembly, which gave its approval to a conference on both the environment and development to be organized by Strong.

Strong was used to challenges. The son of an assistant railway station manager from Oak Lake, Manitoba (population 350), he left home at age 14 to become a

UNITED NATIONS CONFERENCE ON ENVIRONMENT AND DEVELOPMENT
Rio de Janeiro 3–14 June 1992

*Thousands of people and groups—including indigenous peoples (below)—gathered at the Earth Summit in Rio de Janeiro. Despite the wide range of opinions about how best to clean up the planet, the participants at the Earth Summit developed comprehensive plans to protect the environment and promote sustainable development.*

merchant seaman and apprentice fur trader. After he got his start in business as a securities analyst in Winnipeg and Calgary, Strong went on to become a multimillionaire industrialist, serving as president of Power Corporation of Canada and chairman of Petro-Canada. In 1966 he established the Canadian International Development Agency, his country's foreign aid body. Besides organizing the Stockholm and Rio environment conferences, Strong served as a UN under-secretary-general from 1985 to 1987.

Held 20 years after the 1972 Stockholm Conference and after two and a half years of negotiations about how to cure the failing health of the planet, the Rio Conference came at a crucial time in the history of the world. During the 1980s the earth lost about

154 million hectares of rain forest—an area about the size of Ecuador and Peru combined, or three times that of France. Asia alone was losing 1.1 percent of its forest every year. Each year about 50,000 species become extinct, 25 billion tons of topsoil gets washed away, more than 8.2 billion tons of carbon dioxide are released into the atmosphere, and 6.5 million tons of refuse get dumped into the ocean. Moreover, the population of the world is growing by 100 million every year, most of the increase taking place in the poorer countries least able to cope with more people.

One of the two major documents the conference adopted was a 700-page blueprint for environmental renewal called Agenda 21, so named because it is intended to provide a list of environmental

*One of the treaties signed at the Earth Summit was the Convention on Biological Diversity. Here, the delegate from Angola signs the document, as Dr. Mostafa Yolba, UNDP executive director (right), and other delegates look on.*

goals for the 21st century. It is a detailed, comprehensive plan of action to promote sustainable development (meaning economic progress without environmental destruction). Its 40 chapters cover almost all aspects of the relationship between economic development and the environment and present more than 2,500 national and international actions to be taken in areas ranging from eliminating poverty to dealing with radioactive wastes. Strong called Agenda 21 "the most comprehensive, the most far-reaching and, if implemented, the most effective program of international action ever sanctioned by the international community."

The second document the conference adopted was the Rio Declaration on Environment and Development. Its 27 principles seek the establishment of "a new and equitable global partnership" and affirm the importance of human beings in sustainable development. According to the declaration, while nations have the right to develop their own natural resources, they also have a responsibility to ensure that their activities do not damage the environment within or beyond their borders.

At the Rio Conference more than 150 governments also signed international treaties on climate change and biological diversity. One of the most important commitments made at the conference was the promise to reduce national emissions of carbon dioxide and other gases that accumulate in the atmosphere and trap the heat of the sun, thereby contributing to global warming.

Another result of the conference was the adoption of an agreement known as the Forest Principles. These principles call on all nations to "green the world" by protecting and expanding forest cover in ways that are sound ecologically, economically, and socially. To the disappointment of many experts, the Forest Principles were watered down by developing countries seeking to protect their right to develop their national resources.

Maurice Strong was pleased that the Rio conference won political approval and worldwide attention for many of its goals, although he wishes the commission which the UN set up to monitor the implementation of Agenda 21 had been given authority to enforce its provisions. He sees the Earth

Summit he organized as a great opportunity. "Rio helped to set direction and energize the political process. But its promise will not be realized unless people make it happen where they are—in corporations, in communities, in their own lives."

One offshoot of the 1992 Rio Earth Summit was a world conference held in Barbados from April 25 to May 6, 1994, to consider the special problems of small island developing states (called SIDS). The SIDS conference addressed the question of ways to promote economic growth without harming the environment.

Most people imagine that tropical islands are trouble-free paradises with palm trees and warm breezes. But that is not the whole story. Because many SIDS depend on a single industry, often tourism, they are especially vulnerable to fluctuations in the world economy. They often have to pay extremely high passenger and freight rates because they are located outside major transportation routes. Some are situated on geological fault lines where earthquakes or volcanic eruptions occur, or they lie in the path of tropical hurricanes, cyclones, and tidal waves.

The prospect of global warming is especially worrisome to inhabitants of low-lying islands, which will be most affected by higher temperatures and melting glaciers. The fragile ecosystem of a small island is subject to epidemics caused by the introduction of human diseases or new plants or animals.

What these small islands most need are better markets for their exports, more regional cooperation, training in environmental law and management, and sustainable levels of development that respect the fragility of island ecosystems.

# CHAPTER 7

# Helping Hands

For two days in late September 1990, 71 heads of state and representatives from 152 countries assembled at UN headquarters for the largest gathering of world leaders ever—the World Summit for Children. Proposed by the leaders of Canada, Egypt, Mali, Mexico, Pakistan, and Sweden, the historic meeting had as its purpose "to bring attention and promote commitment, at the highest political level, to goals and strategies for . . . the survival, protection and development of children as key elements in the social development of all countries and human society."

The climax of the two-day summit was the signing of the World Declaration on the Survival, Protection and Development of Children and the plan of action for putting the declaration into effect by the year 2000. This bold new move placed the needs of children at the top of the international political agenda. Among its goals were saving the lives of at least one-third of the 14 million children under the age of five who die each year, reducing by half the malnutrition of children under five, making sure all children have clean water to drink, and providing basic education to all children by the end of the century.

The declaration is yet another sign of the new UN focus on human development. Putting the quality of people's lives ahead of the numbers that for so long were the accepted measure of economic progress, the human development approach recognizes the rights of children to "first call" on their nations' resources.

The world leaders who signed the declaration promised to create national programs to meet the summit's 27 child welfare goals by the year 2000 and to report back to the UN Children's Fund about their plans. Many of them expressed the hope that children would be the first to benefit from any money governments were expected to save as the result of arms reductions at the end of the cold war.

In the General Assembly hall, Canadian prime minister Brian Mulroney, co-chair of the summit, told the world leaders that what was most needed to wage war on child suffering was political will. "Today may represent the beginnings of a change in the lives of the world's children," he said. "Today in this hall, they may finally have found the voice and the friends they have long been seeking."

Secretary-General Javier Pérez de Cuéllar told the summit that the main enemies of children, whom he described as

*The heads of state of 71 countries gather for a group picture during the World Summit for Children, held in New York in September 1990.*

"the world's most precious resources," were poverty, hunger, disease, illiteracy, and despair. "Children personify the world's future," he said. "In ensuring their welfare, we transcend all divisions of the present. We participate in the shaping of human destiny. This unique occasion should serve as inspiration to that end."

Although children were not delegates to the summit, they did have a role at the opening and closing ceremonies. While 25 children (ages 8 to 11) from the United Nations International School sang during the entrance of the heads of state into the General Assembly hall, each world leader was escorted to his seat by children from his country. At the closing ceremony, more than 160 children from around the world served as witnesses to the signing of the Summit Declaration and Plan of Action by the world's leaders.

Shortly before the world summit, 200 young adults (ages 17 to 30) from 110 countries and 20 international youth organizations, representing 275 million members, met for four days in Geneva to discuss their role in advancing the agenda of the world's young people and implementing the Convention on the Rights of the Child.

An event specifically for children and young people—the World Summit of Children—is planned in San Francisco in June 1995 in conjunction with events marking the 50th anniversary of the signing of the UN Charter. Conceived by Nina Lynn of the Heart's Bend World Children's Center in Newfane, Vermont, the World Summit *of* Children takes place nearly five years after the World Summit *for* Children that was held in New York in 1990.

### United Nations Children's Fund (UNICEF)

The United Nations Children's Fund—which was awarded the Nobel Peace Prize in 1965—is as old as the UN itself. At its opening session in 1946, the General Assembly established the United Nations International Children's Emergency Fund (UNICEF) to help children in Europe and China who were desperately in need of food, clothing, and medicine after World War II. Four years later, the assembly redirected the fund's efforts toward long-term programs on behalf of children in developing countries. The General Assembly changed the fund's name to the United Nations Children's Fund but kept the acronym UNICEF.

UNICEF is the only UN agency devoted exclusively to the needs of children. It assists developing countries with projects that protect children and encourage them to develop their talents to their fullest. UNICEF programs help countries train teachers, health-care workers, nutritionists, and child-welfare specialists. UNICEF also provides supplies and equipment for the construction of schools, health clinics, and sanitation and water plants. Although most UNICEF programs are long-term, the agency is also capable of acting swiftly when children are victimized by natural disasters, famine, epidemics, or civil war.

UNICEF, with national and regional offices in 120 countries, is completely dependent on voluntary contributions to finance its programs. More than three-quarters of its budget comes from contributions from governments. The rest comes from private organizations, individual donors, fund-raising campaigns, and the sale of greeting cards.

In 1976—which UNICEF proclaimed the International Year of the Child—the agency launched a broad new campaign to help governments plan, build, and expand low-cost, community-based services that promote health care for mothers and children, special services for women and girls, clean water, better nutrition, sanitation, education, and responsible parenthood.

UNICEF actively participated in the working group of the Commission on Human Rights that drafted the Convention on the Rights of the Child, which the General Assembly adopted unanimously on November 20, 1989. The convention establishes the universal legal and moral obligation of adults toward all children to ensure their basic rights to survival, protection, and development.

Support for the convention was so immediate and strong that it entered into force only eight months after it was opened for signature—record time for a human rights treaty. By 1992 the parliaments and congresses of 120 countries had voted in favor of this convention. Its ratification by the vast majority of the nations of the world is helping place children's issues at the top of many national agendas.

For example, the government of Bangladesh, which ratified the Convention on the Rights of the Child in 1990, has issued a decree that makes primary school compulsory. Most children did not go to school because they helped their parents at home and in the fields and because there were not enough teachers and schools. The decree is in compliance with Article 28 of the convention, which affirms the right of all children to a primary education. With UNICEF's encouragement and support, the government has made education free for girls as well as boys up to the eighth grade as a way to encourage them to go to school. It was widely assumed girls did not need

*Namibian children enjoy a game at their school. UNICEF provides vital assistance to developing countries by helping to train teachers and build schools.*

# "A SAINT IN SHIRTSLEEVES"

UNICEF staff members work in dangerous places, such as Somalia, where British-born Seán Devereux was killed in January 1993 at the age of 28. Idealistic and dedicated to helping children, Devereux had worked for UNICEF in Liberia before going to Somalia.

Caroline Tanner, a colleague and friend in both Liberia and Somalia, remembers the time she told Devereux that she was not comfortable wearing a UN hat or T-shirt because she was afraid it would make her a target. But Devereux disagreed. "No," he said, "the UN is important. We've got to stick up for what we work for. We've got to stick up for what we believe."

Tanner was with Devereux in Kismayo the night he was killed. "It was about seven o'clock at night. Seán was at the office. It was decided we'd go on an assessment mission to an area where we hadn't been able to get access before, with a military escort. The trucks were due to meet very early the next morning so he had to organize a lot of stuff. So he stayed behind late. He was walking back to the compound. I was inside the house. There were four other people with me. I was just coming outside and I heard the shots."

Seán Devereux was remembered in New York on June 30, 1993, at a film screening and tribute in the Dag Hammarskjöld Auditorium at the UN headquarters. A BBC-produced documentary called "Mr. Seán" showed his work with children in Liberia and Somalia. Before the screening, Karin Sham Poo, deputy executive director of operations for UNICEF, read a message from the UNICEF staff in Somalia that expressed their determination to continue Devereux's "crusade to bring hope, health, and happiness to the children of Somalia."

Devereux's family established the Seán Devereux Liberian Children's Fund, which will help provide temporary homes for war-affected children, rebuild schools and medical centers in Liberia, and support two schools in the Liberian capital of Monrovia.

"Seán embodied what UNICEF is about," said Tanner. "Children are our future. He felt that. He lived that. He did it. Some people have called him a saint. A saint in shirtsleeves. Who knows what a saint is. Nobody can really say. He had a very special something about him."

school since they could best learn their future role as homemaker and mother at home working with their mothers.

As a result of the government's decree, 12-year-old Rahena Khatun returned to school in January 1993 after an absence of almost six years. She is now studying in an all-girl class at the Jafrabad Government Primary School in Sadar, Rangpur District.

Rahena had dropped out of school to help her mother take care of her three younger sisters after her older brothers and sisters married and left home. When her mother died in 1992, Rahena became the "mother" of the family at age 10.

Her father is a landless rickshaw driver who is having trouble finding work because of his failing health. He and his children live in a one-room straw hut that belongs to a neighbor. They share the neighbor's water pump but have no sanitation facilities. All they own is a few pots and bedclothes, which they spread out at night on mats that cover the dirt floor.

Every morning before she goes to school, Rahena cooks for her father and sisters. After school she airs the bedding, sweeps the floor, washes the dishes at the pump, and prepares supper. Her father is glad Rahena has gone back to school. "She will be able to make a better marriage," he says. "I'll be able to write letters," says Rahena.

In Bangladesh the low status of girls and women is reflected in their low literacy and school enrollment rates and high malnutrition and mortality rates. However, attitudes are changing. With increasing landlessness and male migration to cities, the need for additional family income is having an effect on traditional roles.

A study conducted jointly by UNICEF and the University of Bangladesh in 1992 found that women viewed the future role of girls more as income earners

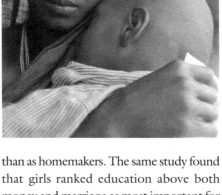

*A young mother holds her sick baby as she waits to see the doctor at a clinic in Bangladesh.*

than as homemakers. The same study found that girls ranked education above both money and marriage as most important for success in life.

UNICEF is supporting Bangladesh's efforts to achieve universal primary education (the government's goal is to reach a primary school enrollment rate of 85 percent by 1995). With girls like Rahena attending school, the enrollment gap between girls and boys is closing. By 1992, about 45 percent of all the primary school students in Bangladesh were girls.

Another result of this increased focus on the needs of children is the Expanded Immunization Program, a UN effort sponsored jointly by UNICEF and the World Health Organization. Recently the program reached its five-year goal of providing immunization against six deadly childhood diseases for 80 percent of the world's children under the age of one—a truly remarkable achievement. One UNICEF official described the Expanded Immunization Program as the largest peacetime health operation ever mounted.

## AMBASSADOR OF THE
## WORLD'S CHILDREN

For Danny Kaye, the comedian and actor whose movies made millions of people laugh, it was just another benefit show. In 1957 UN Secretary-General Dag Hammarskjöld wanted to give a party for his hard-working crew at the UN headquarters in New York. He invited an impressive list of entertainers, among them Kaye, opera basso Ezio Pinza, and contralto Marian Anderson.

At the end of the evening, when Dag Hammarskjöld and UN Undersecretary-General Ralph Bunche thanked him for his performance, Kaye offered to help with other UN projects. The next day the secretary-general and Maurice Pate, executive director of the United Nations Children's Fund (UNICEF), called Kaye and asked to meet with him. Knowing that he was on his way to South Africa for a tour, Pate asked him to photograph UNICEF installations in the southern part of Africa.

"What's UNICEF?" asked Kaye.

The secretary-general explained that the initials stood for the United Nations Children's Fund.

"Gee, that sounds like a fine idea," he said. "If I can help kids, I'm all for it."

Kaye's enthusiasm quickly turned the UN's simple request that he take some pictures in southern Africa into an around-the-world film project. He convinced Paramount Studios in Hollywood to supply the project with the latest in camera equipment and a camera crew of two. He made arrangements for them to return to Hollywood at the end of the tour by way of Asia—at Kaye's expense. Pate was overwhelmed, Hammarskjöld delighted.

Danny Kaye, who knew nothing about suffering in other parts of the world, was shocked to learn that at that time—the 1950s—two-thirds of the world's nearly billion children lacked adequate food, shelter, and protection from disease.

*Danny Kaye (left) shakes hands with Maurice Pate, executive director of UNICEF. Standing between them is UN Secretary-General Dag Hammarskjöld.*

*UNICEF ambassador-at-large Danny Kaye shows a child a UNICEF greeting card, produced by the organization to raise money.*

Kaye's first trip for UNICEF, which was to take him and his crew to 24 countries and cover 40,000 miles, started in a tiny village in India, selected as a typical example of UNICEF's tuberculosis (TB) vaccination program at work. UNICEF workers had circulated leaflets telling villagers about the program and inviting mothers to bring their children to the village square on the day the UNICEF team was to arrive.

Kaye was there primarily to film the work being done, but he was not used to staying on the sidelines. "As soon as a small crowd assembled in the square I began to do what I could to entertain them. No one there had ever heard of a guy named Danny Kaye. I don't think anyone there had ever seen a movie. They didn't speak my language. I didn't speak theirs."

Kaye quickly overcame the language barrier by doing what came naturally. "I jigged through a couple of dances, shouted a couple of songs, got the children clapping their hands in accompaniment, and pretty soon the crowd doubled, redoubled, and redoubled again. Kids came flocking from all over the village to find out what all the commotion was about. They stayed to receive a lifesaving injection of TB vaccine, courtesy of UNICEF."

That was what he found most satisfying. "The long lines at the vaccination center are probably the most rewarding tribute I have ever received for my peculiar ability to make funny faces. After all, what's the use of being a comic if you can't amuse children?"

Danny Kaye reached the world's children as only he could. He played ball with children who were learning to catch with the stumps of their arms, he ran races with other physically handicapped children, and he danced and laughed with lepers.

"At first the children, shy of us strangers, often tried to hide from the cameras. I would make an unexpected funny face, wink or make some comic gesture that would intrigue them. Then another face or two, and I would get them laughing. We would start clapping hands, and before long we would be playing follow-the-leader down the lanes, all over temples and pagodas. They would let me hold them, even feel their tummies for the telltale malaria-enlarged spleen. Children are the same the world over. They ought to have a chance to live."

Danny Kaye believed in UNICEF and remained a children's ambassador for the rest of his life. "You cannot bring health and happiness to a million children by talking about it, signing a paper, or waving a wand. It has to be child by child. It has to be done personally and with love. And that's the way UNICEF works."

## Youth

The United Nations is also concerned with the welfare of the 15-to-24 age group. In 1965 the General Assembly adopted the Declaration of the Promotion among Youth of the Ideals of Peace, Mutual Respect, and Understanding between Peoples. Five years later the 1970 World Youth Assembly, held at the UN headquarters in New York and attended by 650 young people from around the world, was the first such meeting of young people ever organized by the United Nations. The World Youth Assembly gave the young people the chance to discuss peace, development, education, the environment, and the work the UN was doing in these areas.

The General Assembly proclaimed 1985 as International Youth Year and set up the UN Youth Fund to support projects that involve young people in the development of their countries. The Youth Fund is administered by the Center for Social Development and Humanitarian Affairs in Vienna, which is responsible for UN youth policies and programs.

The UN agency with the most active outreach program to young people is the United Nations Environment Programme (UNEP), which seeks to involve the world's youth in the environmental movement. As its contribution to International Youth Year, UNEP organized a regional meeting of African youth leaders at its Nairobi headquarters and sent its recommendations to the first African Ministerial Conference on the Environment in Cairo, Egypt, in December 1985.

To raise the environmental awareness of young people and increase their effectiveness, UNEP created a Global Youth Environment Network for exchanging information about what young people were doing in different parts of the world to protect the environment. The network is run by 12 trained youth leaders who serve as bridges between UNEP and youth groups around the world. By 1993, the Global Youth Environment Network had established contacts with youth groups in 136 countries.

Another aspect of UNEP's outreach to young people is its Global Youth Forum. Held yearly since 1988, the forums have provided opportunities for hundreds of young people to share their experiences and inspire each other with their work. As the

*In honor of International Youth Year (1985), these young musicians from England performed at the UN headquarters in New York.*

# SAVING SEA TURTLES

*Christian Miller addresses the Global Youth Forum in New York in 1994.*

Christian Miller was shocked when he moved to Florida and found a dead turtle on the beach near his house. He had grown up on a farm where he learned to love animals, so when he found more dead turtles, he decided he had to do something about it.

Sea turtles come up on the beach only to lay eggs. When baby turtles hatch, they crawl out of their nests under the sand, head for the ocean, and swim away. However, many baby turtles never make it. They are killed by predators—raccoons, dogs, or crabs—or are stolen by poachers who take the eggs so they can sell the shells for jewelry. Some baby turtles never make it out of the nest, so they suffocate or die from heat.

When Christian told the organizer of the local beach cleanup program that he was concerned about the turtles, he was referred to the Florida Department of Natural Resources. The department, in turn, put him in touch with other volunteers, who spent a year teaching Christian how to rescue turtles. And rescue turtles he did. Over a six-year period he saved more than 12,000 baby turtles, and in 1990 alone he rescued more than 3,500 of them.

After a giant sea turtle lumbers up on the beach and lays its batch of 100 to 150 eggs, Christian marks the nest. Then he watches and guards it. After the babies hatch, he rescues any that remain trapped in the nest and releases them in the ocean.

Every day Christian gets up early so he can walk the beach looking for tracks that signal the location of nests. When he finds them, he marks the area with stakes so people will not step on them. Then he digs sand out of the hole until he finds the eggs. "Usually I find a hatched baby turtle that didn't escape with the others," he says. "I carry it to the water and let it swim away." He then covers the unhatched eggs up again.

After he patrols the beach, he records the number of turtles rescued from each nest, the number that died before he could help them, and the number of hatched, unhatched, and fertilized eggs. He enters the data into his computer at home. At the end of each nesting season, he sends the information to the state Department of Natural Resources.

"It's amazing how one thing leads to another. I've helped the sea turtles, and they've helped me. I've done two research projects for my school's science fair based on them," said Christian.

Christian Miller received the 1990 Palm Beach Chamber of Commerce Board of Directors Special Award in honor of his work. He has also attended UNEP Global Youth Forums in New York, where he and other young people from around the world share their stories of what they are doing to help the earth.

world's largest assembly of young environmentalists, the Global Youth Forum fosters environmental leadership and provides an international forum for young activists.

Until 1992, the forums were held at the UN headquarters in New York. Global Youth Forum '92 drew 1,600 young people from nearly 50 countries. Global Youth Forum '93 in Boulder, Colorado, produced a plea to help the earth, written by two groups of young people (those under 12 and those 12 and older), called the Boulder Declaration.

These forums showcase outstanding young leaders and projects. For example, an Australian from Brisbane, 13-year-old Beth Hamilton, spearheaded the campaign to clean up a local creek and became an environmental leader in her school and community. Marcos Calderia, an 18-year-old from Brasilia, Brazil, helped draft a children's environmental handbook and set up a new waste-reduction and recycling campaign for his city of more than 400,000 people. A group of young people organized by Canadian engineering student Trevor Dagilis

raised funds that financed the sending of more than 25 engineering students to South America to work at water purification facilities in order to improve the local water.

Youth projects have included a successful effort by American students to win the support of their county for their campaign to save 68 acres of cypress trees in Coral Springs, Florida. Thirty young people in Rostov-on-Don in Russia set up a waste management program, placing trash cans around the city to make the streets cleaner. In Sioux Falls, South Dakota, handicapped young people at the Crippled Children's Hospital organized a successful recycling program.

In 1992 UNEP launched its Global 500 Youth Environment Awards at its World Environment Day celebrations (June 5) at the Rio Earth Summit to honor young people between the ages of 6 and 25 who have made outstanding contributions to the protection of the environment. The award is a division of UNEP's Global 500 Roll of Honor for Environmental Achievement.

*Children from around the world fill the seats of the General Assembly for Global Youth Forum '92. The meeting, sponsored by the UNEP's Outreach Programme, was an occasion for young people to discuss environmental issues and how they could deal with these issues in their own areas.*

*Members of
ECOSOC's First
Sub-Commission on
the Status of Women
gather for a meeting
in May 1946.*

## Women

The United Nations Charter affirms the rights of women in its preamble, which declares that the peoples of the United Nations are determined "to reaffirm faith in fundamental human rights, in the dignity and worth of the human person, in the equal rights of men and women."

In 1946 the Economic and Social Council established the Commission on the Status of Women. The responsibility of the 32-member commission is to report on ways to help women find a larger voice in public life and make recommendations on urgent matters concerning women's rights.

The commission drafted two important statements that the General Assembly adopted—the Convention on the Political Rights of Women (1952) and the Convention on the Elimination of All Forms of Discrimination against Women (1979). The 1979 convention states that women should have civil, political, social, and economic rights equal to those of men. It also outlines steps governments need to take to improve the conditions under which women live and work. To achieve this goal, the UN recommended ending discrimination against women in public life, politics, education, employment, health care, marriage, and family life. Countries who sign the convention must be willing to bring their national legislation into line with its principles.

The UN proclaimed the year 1975 as International Women's Year. Its focal point was a world conference on women's issues held in Mexico City that called on governments to promote the equality of women and support their right to participate fully in society. After the Mexico City conference the General Assembly declared the next 10 years (1976–85) the United Nations Decade for Women.

World conferences followed in Copenhagen (1980) and Nairobi (1985). The Copenhagen Conference emphasized that equality for women means equal participation in development. It urged governments to support women's groups and organizations and to increase the number of women in public office. Conference resolutions urged legislation to improve women's rights with respect to ownership and control of property, inheritance of property, and child custody.

# A WOMEN'S CENTER
# IN CAMEROON

Each day at a women's center in the Cameroon capital of Yaoundé, 300 mothers and infants receive health services and instruction in child care and preventive medicine. In classes supported by the UN Population Fund they learn about family planning, and the center makes contraceptives available at minimal cost.

As a result of what she has learned in her classes at the center, Anastasie Neutchap wants to have only three children. She is opposed to large families "because when you have too many children, you can't take care of them properly. Someone might take them away."

The UN World Food Program and UNICEF are helping provide the center and 23 others like it in Cameroon with food and kitchen utensils. Mothers learn to prepare nutritious food from commonly available ingredients. Too many children in Cameroon are malnourished, not because there is not enough food but because it is not used efficiently.

The center also offers a three-year course in dressmaking. The young women sell the clothes they sew and embroider. Ten percent of the income is put aside to help them start their own small businesses. It is an important step in helping them become self-sufficient.

The 1985 Nairobi Conference reviewed the achievements of the UN Decade of Women and advanced a plan called Forward-Looking Strategies for the Advancement of Women to the Year 2000, which the UN has adopted as its official guide for national and international action. In 1990 the Commission on the Status of Women concluded that "the pace of [putting these strategies into action] must be improved in the last decade of the twentieth century since the cost to societies of failing to [do so] would be high in terms of slowed economic and social development, misuse of human resources and reduced progress for society as a whole." The International Year of the Family (1994) focused on the status of women in the home and the problem of domestic violence, which is important to all UN bodies that deal with human rights.

Other UN bodies also address women's issues. In 1976, on the recommendation of the Mexico City conference, the General Assembly established the International Research and Training Institute for the Advancement of Women (INSTRAW) as an independent research organization within the UN system. The institute collects and distributes information worldwide to promote women as key agents of development and to document their underrecognized contributions to economic growth.

Margaret Shields, director of INSTRAW, believes that exploited women around the world are the unrecognized heroes of economic development. For example, African women, who produce, process, store, and sell more than 80 percent of Africa's food for family consumption, receive little in the way of credit for the work they do. "Women own one percent of the world's land," Ms. Shields points out, "but do far more than fifty percent of the world's work."

The UN Development Fund for Women (UNIFEM), created in 1976, provides financial and technical support for projects that assist poor women in developing countries, with special emphasis on giving them access to training and credit. Work-

ing in partnership with the UN Development Programme, which administers most of its projects, UNIFEM has assisted tens of thousands of poor women in Africa, Asia, and Latin America.

The United Nations is currently embarked on a campaign to improve the status of women inside the UN itself. The campaign began in 1970 when the General Assembly urged that women be given equal opportunity for employment at the Secretariat. It declared that nondiscrimination on the basis of gender was a fundamental UN principle and appointed a panel to investigate charges of discrimination. UN efforts to increase the proportion of women serving in professional positions in the Secretariat have for the most part not been very successful. The General Assembly has set 1995 as the date by which 35 percent of professional staff of the UN should be female.

*Women work alongside men in India's Nilgiri Hills, observed by a curious elephant.*

*These elderly Hong Kong women take a break from their work. As the number of elderly people around the world increases, the UN has been active in promoting greater understanding of their needs.*

## Aging

With the life expectancy of the world's population increasing, care for the elderly is a growing concern for the UN. The General Assembly has been discussing the issue of aging since 1948, but it was not until 1982 that the UN captured international attention by convening the World Assembly on Aging in Vienna. The assembly, which was attended by delegates from 124 countries, launched the International Plan of Action on Aging to help countries deal more effectively with their aging populations. The purpose of the plan was to promote a better understanding of the aging process and to further education and training that encourages an international exchange of skills and knowledge. Other initiatives set in motion by the world assembly included a global information campaign, the creation of the Trust Fund for Aging, and the establishment of the African Society of Gerontology and the International Institute of Aging in Malta.

The General Assembly marked the 10th anniversary of the 1982 International Plan of Action on Aging with a special international conference during its plenary sessions on October 15 and 16. Later it issued a Procla-mation on Aging, which called for the promotion of life-long health, income security, and ways to make older people more productive. The assembly also designated 1999 as the International Year of Older Persons, which the Commission for Social Development has since requested be renamed the International Year of the Elderly.

## The Disabled

The United Nations has been concerned about disabled people since 1971, when the General Assembly adopted the Declaration on the Rights of the Mentally Retarded. The declaration stated that mentally retarded people have the same basic human rights as all other people, including the rights to medical care and economic security, and the right to live with their family or foster parents. Four years later, the General Assembly adopted the Declaration on the Rights of Disabled Persons. This declaration stated that disabled people have the same civil and political rights as other human beings, as well as the right to treatment and services that will allow them to live and work more successfully in their societies.

# MAINSTREAMING
# THE DISABLED

*A hearing-impaired Palestinian boy works on his speech at a UNRWA center for the disabled.*

Outside the school in the Baqa'a camp for Palestinian refugees in Jordan, the children walked in a line toward the classroom. Two of the children, Abdel and Yousef, were walking more slowly than the others. When they tried to speed up, Abdel fell down. He was about to cry when the other boys quickly helped him get back on his feet. Together, they all walked into the classroom as if nothing had happened. Abdel and Yousef have cerebral palsy.

Their teacher, whom the students respectfully call "Mr. Darwish," agreed to be the first to have children with cerebral palsy in his class at UNRWA's third Elementary School for Boys in the Baqa'a camp. "I always thought these children should be with their peers—for their emotional and psychological well-being," said Darwish, whose own son has cerebral palsy. "Now these children with special needs are in my class. They are seated among the other 44 pupils."

Darwish admitted there had been problems in the beginning because "some pupils were not very accepting about the presence of the disabled children and tried to point out their disabilities."

In the playground where a large crowd of children gathered around them, Abdel was asked to point out his friends. He waved his hand. "All of them!" When his classmates were asked why they enjoyed having him in class, one answered, "He is a boy like the rest of us," and another said, "He studies and plays with us."

Almost every day for three years, Abdel had gone to the UNRWA rehabilitation center in Baqa'a, where he learned to speak and walk before being transferred to the school. Now, both he and Yousef visit the rehabilitation center twice a week to keep up with their rehabilitation program. There they do physical therapy exercises and work on their spelling and pronunciation.

Abdel and Yousef are part of the UNRWA effort that began in 1991 to integrate the camp's disabled children into regular classes. As the program has expanded and spread through other Palestinian camps and schools run by UNRWA, an increasing number of children and teenagers are being "mainstreamed."

Abdel admitted he likes to visit the rehabilitation center to do his exercises, but he said he would not want to stay there all day. "I want to be in school with Yousef and the others."

*This factory in Japan employs physically handicapped people to assemble parts. To promote and encourage full participation and equality for the disabled, the General Assembly proclaimed 1981 as the International Year of Disabled Persons.*

One year after the General Assembly proclaimed 1981 as the International Year of Disabled Persons and called for a plan of action to promote equality for disabled people, it adopted the World Program of Action Concerning Disabled Persons. The goal of the program was to strengthen long-range national, regional, and international programs that promoted the rehabilitation of disabled persons and their full participation in their societies. The years 1983–92 were designated as the United Nations Decade of Disabled Persons.

**Refugees**

Zoltan Slavnic remembers the exact moment he decided to become a refugee. "It was when one of the 'gang of four' [Bosnian Serb leaders] said children of mixed marriages should be turned into soap. I knew we had no future." Slavnic, a former lecturer in sociology, is half Serb and half Croat, while his Muslim wife is part Serb and part Russian. His wife and two young children made it to Sweden, where he hopes to join them.

Slavnic is but one of the 3.5 million refugees and displaced persons created by the conflict in the former Yugoslavia. In 1993 there were more than 625,000 refugees or displaced persons officially registered in Croatia, 430,000 in Serbia, and more than 1.5 million in Bosnia. More than half a million others were able to find refuge abroad, 80 percent of them in Germany, Austria, Hungary, Switzerland, and Sweden.

According to Jean Noel Wetterwald of the Office of the United Nations High Commissioner for Refugees (UNHCR), the flood of refugees within and out of what was once Yugoslavia is the direct result of the special kind of war that is being fought there. "The displacement of the population is not a by-product of this war, but the objective."

These refugees in the former Yugoslavia are part of the world's 19 million refugees that the UNHCR is trying to help. Long recognized internationally for its outstanding work, the UNHCR has helped more than 30 million refugees since it was founded, earning two Nobel Peace Prizes (1954 and 1981) in the process.

The General Assembly established the UNHCR in 1951 to replace the International Refugee Organization, which it had set up to protect and resettle refugees and people displaced by World War II. Since its creation, the UNHCR has grown from a tiny unit into an organization with a 1,500-member staff and an annual budget of $550 million.

The UNHCR helps refugees who are unable to return home resettle in other countries. The UNHCR tries to help them obtain a favorable legal status in the country in which they have sought asylum so that they will not be expelled or forcibly returned to their home country, where they could face persecution. In Africa, where about half the world's 10 million refugees live and

*The International Refugee Organization, the forerunner to the Office of the UN High Commissioner for Refugees, was responsible for assisting the huge number of refugees created by World War II. Here, a boy and his father prepare to leave Germany to find a new home in the United States.*

"It's pretty," she said, "and I think my children will live happily in the house. Where I live there is much discomfort. We all get wet, and there is nowhere to sleep."

The project will give a fresh start to 63 families, with priority given to widows and single mothers who head households. It will also create jobs that will help the local economy, and the improved sanitation will help combat health threats like cholera.

The legal status of refugees like Maria Zambrano was defined in UN agreements in 1951 and 1967, which set forth the rights and duties of refugees, including their right to employment, education, property, public assistance, and travel documents. More than 100 countries have agreed to be bound by these UN agreements.

The UNHCR has also undertaken major refugee relief efforts in Afghanistan and Southeast Asia. The UNHCR works closely with other UN bodies and specialized agencies, such as the Food and Agriculture Organization, the World Health Organization, the United Nations Children's Fund, and the International Labour Organization.

The UNHCR does not care for Palestinian refugees, who are the responsibility of

where half of the UNHCR's work takes place, the organization helps refugees resettle by establishing new rural communities and finding communities where the refugees will feel at home with the local population.

In Nicaragua, the UN provided relief to the refugees who returned to their homes after the end of the civil war. It is estimated that during the 1980s, 600,000 Nicaraguan refugees—15 percent of the country's population—were forced to flee the fighting.

Maria Zambrano is a typical refugee. In 1981 she left Jalapa, a town near the Honduran border, and went to live in Honduras for 10 years. When Zambrano's husband was killed, she was left with six children to support.

After the fighting ceased, Zambrano returned to Nicaragua, which years of fighting had made one of the poorest countries in Latin America. In Jalapa, Zambrano works as a cook in a private household, earning $20 a month. She lives with her children in a shack that has no running water or sanitation.

With the help of the Finnish government, the UNHCR is building houses in the Jalapa region to help women like Maria Zambrano who have lost their husbands. One of the houses has been assigned to Zambrano and her family.

*UNHCR provides relief to refugees who are victims of disasters—natural and man-made. Here, grain is being distributed to Ethiopian refugees, victims of famine.*

the United Nations Relief and Works Agency for Palestine Refugees in the Near East.

## Disaster Relief

After a series of major natural disasters—floods, earthquakes, fires, and volcanic eruptions—in East Pakistan (now Bangladesh), Afghanistan, Jordan, Peru, and elsewhere in the late 1960s and early 1970s, the General Assembly created the United Nations Disaster Relief Organization. This agency began operations in 1972 to mobilize and coordinate relief efforts to afflicted countries, set up planning and emergency preparedness programs, and promote and encourage disaster prevention. Since then, the organization has coordinated international relief efforts for hundreds of disasters throughout the world.

In 1992 the General Assembly established the Department of Humanitarian Affairs (DHA) to coordinate all aspects of UN emergency assistance. The DHA assumed the responsibilities previously performed by the UN Disaster Relief Organization and other specialized UN emergency relief bodies. The main functions of the DHA are to coordinate UN and other international disaster relief efforts and to formulate UN relief policy.

Today emergencies occur in the world almost every day. These include not only natural disasters, but also, increasingly, manmade disasters. One of the worst man-made disasters of modern times was the 1986 accident at the Chernobyl nuclear power station near the settlement of Pripyat, north of Kiev in what was then the Ukrainian Soviet Socialist Republic.

Early on the morning of Saturday, April 26, a series of safety procedure violations and mistakes led to a chain reaction in the core of the Number 4 reactor. Two explosions and the large fireball that followed blew the heavy steel and concrete lid off the reactor, releasing large amounts of radioactive material. Although the fire in the reactor building was brought under control several hours later, radioactive material kept escaping into the atmosphere, where it was carried great distances by air currents.

On April 28, when monitoring stations in Sweden reported abnormally high levels of radioactivity in the air, the Swedish government pressed the Soviet Union for an explanation. Finally, when the Soviets admitted to the world there had been a nuclear accident at its Chernobyl station, there was

*After famine set in among the drought-stricken countries of West Africa in 1974, the UN responded with massive shipments of food and supplies. Here, at the port of Dakar, shipments of sorghum are being prepared for transportation to the inland areas of Senegal.*

an international outcry. While the Soviet government started evacuating the 30,000 inhabitants of Pripyat almost immediately, it took another week for it to contain the heat and radioactivity leaking from the reactor core.

In all, eight tons of radioactive material escaped into the atmosphere, more radioactivity than was created by the atomic bombs the United States dropped on Hiroshima and Nagasaki, Japan, in 1945. Winds spread the radioactivity widely over Byelorussia (now Belarus) and the Ukraine, with traces of it reaching as far west as France and Italy.

The blast killed two people, 29 more died from exposure to radiation, and 200 people contracted serious radiation sickness. However, the true scope of the tragedy only showed up later in the form of the thousands of extra cancer deaths in the area, a catastrophic drop in the birthrate in Belarus, and the severe contamination of all the soil and ground water within a 32-kilometer radius of the plant. In all, more than 135,000 people had to be evacuated from a 780-square-kilometer area around the accident.

In 1990 the United Nations heeded the call of three Soviet republics when they asked for its assistance in dealing with the long-term effects of the disaster. Working together under the leadership of the director-general of the UN office in Vienna, 15 UN organizations and agencies established a special interagency Chernobyl task force to develop funding and programs to help reduce the effects of the accident and assist the people who suffered the most. Despite the breakup of the Soviet Union, the three former Soviet republics, now the countries of Ukraine, Belarus, and Russia, remain committed to working together with the UN.

In May 1993 Secretary-General Boutros Boutros-Ghali appointed Jan Eliasson, undersecretary-general for Humanitarian Affairs, as UN coordinator of international cooperation on Chernobyl. At the time of the accident, Eliasson had been working in the foreign ministry of Sweden, where he had been among the first to be alerted about the high levels of radioactivity in the atmosphere. Deep down he and his

An aerial view of the Chernobyl nuclear power plant after a series of explosions triggered one of the worst man-made disasters of modern times. The arrow marks the spot where the explosions occurred.

colleagues had hoped they were wrong about the scope of the tragedy, but they also knew they had a responsibility to make sure the rest of the world learned the truth.

At the time, the prevailing winds had been northwesterly, bringing contaminated clouds over Sweden, where they later turned into rain clouds over Lapland province. Eliasson said that when a heavy rainfall fell on the nomadic Laps and the grazing lands of their reindeer, "their land was doomed, the reindeer meat was contaminated, and the Lap culture was dealt an almost fatal blow."

Shortly after his appointment, Eliasson visited the area around Chernobyl to get a firsthand look at the damage. He saw vast stretches of burned-out forests, burial grounds for contaminated trucks and helicopters, and the "ghost town" of Pripyat—devoid of its 30,000 people—where time seemed to stand still after April 1986. What disturbed him most was the children, some with bulging necks, others with huge scars across their throats, all victims of thyroid cancer.

Today, Eliasson hopes the UN, working with the governments of the three countries most affected and with other interested parties, will be able to make a real difference in the lives of the people still suffering from the Chernobyl disaster.

Although the initial pledges by UN member states for the UN Trust Fund for Chernobyl fell far short of the $125 million goal, later commitments brought the fund closer to that figure. Research and treatment of children with thyroid cancer, establishment of nine psychological rehabilitation centers, and registration, diagnosis, and treatment of thousands of Chernobyl cleanup workers are some of the projects the UN is currently supporting.

In addition to aiding disaster victims, the United Nations also helps countries pre- pare for possible future disasters. UN Disaster Relief Organization missions have helped Chad and the Sudan to set up emergency information centers; Tanzania, Mozambique, Samoa, and Papua New Guinea to create their own national disaster relief organizations; and Egypt, Madagascar, Mali, and the Congo to upgrade their disaster prevention programs. The Disaster Relief Organization also promotes the study of natural disasters, publishes information on emergency preparedness, and develops relief programs with other UN agencies.

## Crime and Drugs

Every five years, the United Nations holds a congress on the issue of crime. The first United Nations Congress on the Prevention of Crime and the Treatment of Offenders, which was held in Geneva in 1955, established a set of standards for the treatment of prisoners. The second congress, held in London in 1960, dealt primarily with juvenile delinquency. Congresses include criminologists (experts on the study of crime and the treatment of criminals), senior police officers, penologists (those who study prisons and prison reform), and experts in criminal law and human rights.

The fifth congress in Geneva (1975) adopted a declaration urging the protection of all persons from torture and other cruel, inhuman, and degrading treatment, which the General Assembly adopted the same year. The congress also laid the foundation for a code of conduct for law enforcement officials, which the General Assembly approved in 1979.

The sixth congress, held in Caracas in 1980, produced a survey of crime trends and criminal justice systems and suggested crime prevention strategies. The updated version of this UN survey serves as the world's main source of crime statistics. Later UN congresses on crime adopted plans to

*A UN technician advises farmers in Colombia on how to grow coffee. The farmers had previously been growing coca, which was used to make cocaine.*

*The official emblem for the UN conference on drug abuse, held in Vienna, Austria, in 1987.*

strengthen international cooperation in crime prevention and criminal prosecution and called for a more effective UN crime prevention program.

Despite international treaties designed to stem the flow of illegal drugs, this problem continues to plague the world. Since the first international conference on the control of drugs in Shanghai in 1909 and subsequent discussions about the problem by the League of Nations and the United Nations, a series of treaties has provided a legal foundation for an international drug control system. The treaties—the Single Convention on Narcotic Drugs (1961), the Convention on Psychotropic Substances (1971), and the Convention against Illicit Traffic in Narcotic Drugs and Psychotropic Substances (1988)—require governments to control the production and distribution of narcotic drugs and psychotropic substances (hallucinogens, amphetamines, barbiturates, and tranquilizers), combat illegal traffic and drug abuse, and report their actions to the international community.

In 1987 the International Conference on Drug Abuse and Illicit Trafficking in Vienna recommended measures to eradicate drug abuse at the national, regional, and international levels. These recommendations led to the 1988 UN treaty. Monitoring of these agreements is the responsibility of the Commission on Narcotic Drugs. The commission, which reports to the UN Economic and Social Council, is the main UN policy-making body for international drug control. The 1990 General Assembly Special Session on Drugs produced a global program of action that included further measures to prevent and reduce demand for drugs, control supply, suppress illicit trafficking, and support effective treatment and rehabilitation programs.

### United Nations University

The United Nations University is not a traditional university, in that it has no undergraduate students and offers no degrees. Rather, it is more of an international think tank of scholars, teachers, and postgraduate students from different parts of the world working together. "They come for a discussion initially to plan their research, then they go back to their home base and they continue the work there," explains Professor Heitor Gurgulino de Souza, the university's rector. "In the end we publish the results of the research."

The headquarters of the university is in Tokyo, but it also has training and research centers in other parts of the world—the World Institute for Development Economics Research in Helsinki, Finland, the Institute for Natural Resources in the Ivory Coast, and the International Institute for Biotechnology in the Netherlands, whose focus is the emerging conflict between the development of natural resources and the need to respect the environment.

The idea originated in 1969 when Secretary-General U Thant proposed the creation of "a United Nations University, truly international in character and devoted to the charter objectives of peace and progress." After the Japanese government pledged $100 million to the endowment fund of the proposed university, the General Assembly decided to locate it in Tokyo.

The university was chartered as an independent academic institution within the framework of the United Nations to promote approaches to academic and scientific research that would cross national borders and

offer wide access to knowledge and information, especially in developing countries.

Within the framework of its three program divisions—Development Studies, Regional and Global Studies, and Global Learning—the university investigates such subjects as population growth, the roots of violence and poverty, the dynamics of rapid social change, universal human values, new directions for the world economy, and advances in science and technology. It sends annual reports on its scholarship to the General Assembly, the Economic and Social Council, and UNESCO. Governments, international organizations, other scholars, and the general public also have access to its research through five university journals and more than 330 books published by the United Nations University Press.

*The Japanese ambassador to the UN (left) and a representative from the UN sign an agreement that establishes Tokyo as the site of the United Nations University.*

# CHAPTER 8

# Human Rights: Justice for All

Eleanor Roosevelt was already one of the most admired women in the world when, in January 1946, President Harry Truman appointed her to the American delegation to the opening of the United Nations in London. During her years in the White House as First Lady, Mrs. Roosevelt had established herself as a humanitarian, civil rights advocate, and champion of the poor and disadvantaged. On her trips around the country she acted as the "eyes and ears" of her husband, President Franklin Roosevelt, and as a voice for reform and justice. After the death of the President in April 1945, she devoted the major portion of her time and energy to the UN.

Her UN appointment provided her for the first time with an official position from which to work for the things she believed in. Eleanor Roosevelt, who was the only woman in the American delegation, quickly made her presence felt—especially on the UN Commission on Human Rights, on which she served from 1946 to 1953 and which she headed from 1946 to 1951.

The human rights lessons of World War II, which made clear the connection between the ruthless way nations treated their own citizens and the way they treated other countries, was not lost on the UN founders. The preamble of the UN Charter declared that the United Nations was determined not only to end the "scourge of war" but also to "reaffirm faith in fundamental human rights, in the dignity and worth of the human person, in the equal rights of men and women and of nations large and small."

The Economic and Social Council, charged by the UN Charter with making "recommendations for the purpose of promoting respect for, and observance of, human rights and fundamental freedoms for all," established the Commission on Human Rights in 1946. The 43-member commis-

*Eleanor Roosevelt headed the UN Commission on Human Rights from 1946 to 1951. Here, at the first session of the UN General Assembly in 1946, she greets V. M. Molotov, the Soviet foreign minister.*

sion, which meets for six weeks each year in Geneva, directs the UN campaign for human rights by making recommendations, drafting international treaties, and keeping an eye on human rights violations around the world.

Not only was Eleanor Roosevelt a tireless worker for international human rights in her capacity as head of the Commission on Human Rights, but she also served as a member of the U.S. delegation to the UN General Assembly, chief U.S. representative to the Third Committee (social, humanitarian, and cultural matters), and U.S. representative to the Economic and Social Council.

Even after she left the UN in 1953 at the request of the new Republican President, Dwight Eisenhower, Eleanor Roosevelt continued to support international human rights and the United Nations through her writings, speeches, worldwide travel, and work with the United Nations Association, a private group active in building popular support for the UN in the United States.

Her greatest contribution to the UN during her years on the Commission on Human Rights was the leadership she brought to the drafting of human rights documents. Today these documents—the Universal Declaration of Human Rights, the Covenant on Civil and Political Rights, and the Covenant on Economic, Social, and Cultural Rights—play a major role in efforts to protect human rights worldwide.

Eleanor Roosevelt hoped that by spreading the word about these documents, "we may awaken in the people of every nation a more vivid realization of the importance of the individual and of the need for recognizing his rights and freedoms, and in doing so we may build a bulwark against the greatest menace to these rights and freedoms, namely, war among nations."

## Universal Declaration of Human Rights

The Universal Declaration of Human Rights, which the General Assembly adopted on December 10, 1948, is one of the UN's greatest achievements. The declaration, which consists of a preamble and 30 articles (see Appendix 3), calls on "every individual and every [group] of society" to strive to "promote respect for these rights and freedoms and . . . to secure their universal and effective recognition and observance." Eleanor Roosevelt called the Universal Declaration a bill of rights for all the people of the world.

The first article of the declaration states that "all human beings are born free and equal in dignity and rights" and "are endowed with reason and conscience and should act towards one another in a spirit of brotherhood." Reinforcing this call for tolerance and equality, the second article proclaims that everyone is entitled to all the rights and freedoms set forth in the declaration "without distinction of any kind, such as race, color, sex, language, religion, political or other opinion, national or social origin, property, birth or other status."

Other articles set forth the civil, political, economic, social, and cultural rights to which all people are entitled. The document affirms the right of people to freedom from slavery, torture, and cruel treatment; the right to recognition as a person and equal protection before the law; freedom from arbitrary arrest, detention, or exile; the right to a fair and public hearing by an independent court to determine rights and charges; and the right to be presumed innocent until proven guilty.

Other rights include freedom from arbitrary interference with privacy, family, home, or correspondence; freedom of movement; and the rights of asylum (to seek shelter from political or religious persecution in another country), to have a nationality, to marry and raise a family, and to own property. Freedom of thought, conscience, religion, opinion, expression, association, assembly, and the right to participate in government and to have equal access to public service are also cited.

Articles 22 to 27 of the declaration describe the economic, social, and cultural rights to which people are entitled. These include the right to work, rest and leisure, an adequate standard of living, education, essential social services, and the right to take part in the cultural life of the community.

## Human Rights Covenants

After the adoption of the Universal Declaration of Human Rights, Eleanor Roosevelt and her Commission on Human Rights immediately began drafting a covenant, or treaty, that would translate the rights proclaimed in the declaration into laws that nations would be expected to implement. The basic work on what came to be *two* covenants took place during Eleanor Roosevelt's time as head of the Commission on Human Rights, although

The Universal Declaration of Human Rights was adopted on December 10, 1948. Eleanor Roosevelt called it a bill of rights for all the people of the world.

# UN SPEAKS UP FOR CONDEMNED WRITER

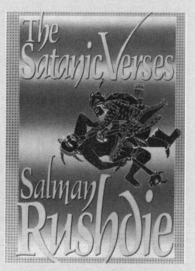

On March 10, 1993, the UN Commission on Human Rights condemned Iran for its abuse of human rights and its continued violations of the International Covenant on Civil and Political Rights. The commission's strongly worded resolution held governments "accountable for assassinations and attacks by their agents against persons on the territory of another State, as well as for the incitement, approval or wilful condoning of such acts."

The commission also reaffirmed the principle of freedom of expression defined in Article 19 of the Universal Declaration of Human Rights. Article 19 states, "Everyone has the right to freedom of opinion and expression; this right includes freedom to hold opinions without interference and to seek, receive and impart information and ideas through any media and regardless of frontiers."

The commission's resolution for the first time made reference to the case of British writer Salman Rushdie when it expressed the "grave concern that there are continuing threats to the life of a citizen of another State which appear to have the support of the Government of the Islamic Republic of Iran."

Rushdie, who is living in hiding in England, is author of *The Satanic Verses,* a novel that Iran claims is an insult to Islam. Iran has called for Rushdie's death and is offering a large reward to anybody who kills him.

The commission's vote (23 to 11, with 14 abstentions) shows there is a growing international willingness to openly condemn the government of Iran for its human rights abuses and its censorship campaign, which it conducts through fear, imprisonment, torture, and murder.

*President Jimmy Carter (left) and Andrew Young (right), the U.S. ambassador to the UN, sign the International Covenants on Human Rights at the UN in October 1977. UN Secretary-General Kurt Waldheim is at center. These covenants translated the rights proclaimed in the Universal Declaration of Human Rights into laws that nations are expected to implement.*

the Covenant on Economic, Social, and Cultural Rights and the Covenant on Civil and Political Rights were not finally approved by the General Assembly until December 1966.

The two covenants express in clear language the rights contained in the Universal Declaration. The Covenant on Civil and Political Rights deals with freedom of conscience, religion, speech, association, assembly, and many of the other rights mentioned in the declaration. The Covenant on Economic, Social and Cultural Rights covers rights associated with work, social services, health, education, trade unions, living standards, protection of the family, and freedom from discrimination. Together with the Universal Declaration of Human Rights, these treaties constitute what has been called "the International Bill of Human Rights."

In 1975 the General Assembly adopted the UN Declaration against Torture in the spirit of both the Universal Declaration of Human Rights and the Covenant on Civil and Political Rights, which declare that nobody should be subjected "to torture or to cruel, inhuman or degrading treatment or punishment." The declaration recommends that all acts of torture be made crimes and that all nations conduct a complete re-

view of the way their police forces question prisoners in order to eliminate torture. In 1984 the General Assembly adopted the Convention against Torture, which nations are in the process of approving. The convention obliges countries which approve it to make torture a crime and prosecute and punish those guilty of it.

In 1971, 30-year-old Norma Merello was teaching school in an isolated rural area in the northern Argentine province of Corrientes when an army lieutenant walked into her classroom. Thus began five months of torment and torture for her. She was never charged with a crime or brought before a judge. She was a Roman Catholic activist suspected of having ties with left-wing guerrilla fighters. That apparently was enough of a crime to persuade Argentina's right-wing military government to arrest the teacher and subject her to what she later described as "a world of terror."

After the soldiers blindfolded and handcuffed her, they took her to a country house where a radio was blaring classical music. A loud voice said, "Opera music—for an operation. Now take off your clothes." Still blindfolded—as she would remain for the next eight days—Morello was interrogated about her involvement in guerrilla activities and threatened with rape.

"Then," she recalled, "the torture began. With an electric prod they touched me. . . . I tried to think of other things. I asked them to kill me. They told me, 'When you get out of here, you won't be a woman for any man. We'll ruin you.'"

They interrogated and tortured her around the clock in shifts. "They wanted me to say things that would link the Catholic movement with the armed struggle against the military dictatorship," Merello said. "But they didn't get anything from me."

After almost a month in the hands of the Argentine army's security police, Morello was sent to a federal prison 170 miles north of Buenos Aires. Despite repeated inquiries by her family, by the Catholic bishop of her home town of Goya, and by lawyers, the Argentine government refused to release her or charge her with a crime. After more than five months of imprisonment, she finally was released.

Jacobo Timerman, a Jewish newspaperman, was also a victim. After he left Argentina, he described his experiences in the book *Prisoner Without a Name, Cell Without a Number.* Timerman was editor and publisher of a leading Buenos Aires newspaper when the right-wing military government arrested him. He was tortured and held without charge for 29 months.

In his book he described the time he was blindfolded and seated in a chair with his hands tied behind his back. As electric shocks were administered, his unseen torturer shouted a single word, and the others

Jacobo Timerman, an Argentine newspaper editor, was arrested and tortured by the military regime that ruled Argentina in the 1970s.

joined in: "Jew! . . . Jew! . . . Jew! . . . Jew!" As they chanted, they clapped their hands and laughed.

Because Timerman was well known, his case attracted attention. The administration of U.S. President Jimmy Carter, in keeping with its human rights campaign, tried to get him released. The Supreme Court of Argentina ordered his release twice, but the military government refused to comply. Finally the generals gave in, but not before they revoked his citizenship, confiscated his newspaper and all his other property, and expelled him from the country by taking him under guard to a plane bound for Israel. Unlike the many other citizens the military seized over the years, however, Timerman lived to tell his story.

Morello and Timerman were just two of the thousands of Argentine torture victims during the 1970s when the struggle between the government and leftist guerrillas gave the government an excuse to torture, maim, and murder anybody they suspected of having links to, or even sympathy for, the guerrillas. Torture cases like these around the world prompted the United Nations to take up the issue.

To end what Undersecretary-General for Human Rights Jan Martenson described in 1990 as "one of the most deplorable of all human rights violations" the Commission on Human Rights established the Committee against Torture and appointed a Special Reporter (called by the French word *rapporteur*) on Torture to monitor abuses. The United Nations also established working groups and special *rapporteurs* on summary or arbitrary executions, arbitrary detention, religious intolerance, and disappearances. (A disappearance occurs when an individual is seized, usually by persons in plainclothes in government service or protected by the government, and is not seen or heard from again.)

## Promoting Respect for Human Rights

The UN seeks to promote respect for human rights through publicity, education, special observances, and declarations and conventions that target specific violations. At times it can seem like a losing battle, since human rights violations are widespread and often governments themselves are the worst offenders.

While Amnesty International and other human rights groups around the world that keep track of violations report them to the United Nations, as well as to governments, media, and other interested parties, the UN also receives complaints directly.

Any person or group can now protest to the UN under the so-called 1503 procedure, named after the Economic and Social Council resolution 1503, adopted on May 27, 1970. The 1503 procedure allows people to submit letters to the UN Commission on Human Rights. The letters are summarized in copies that keep the identity of the sender or senders confidential and then are sent to commission members. Member states cited in a complaint are asked to respond to the accusation. The commission discusses the complaint privately until it re-

ports its findings to the Economic and Social Council. The 1503 procedure is limited, however, because an investigation can be undertaken "only with the express consent of the state concerned and conducted in constant cooperation with that state and under conditions determined by agreement with it."

The tradition of lodging human rights complaints with the UN goes back to its earliest years, and many groups have drawn attention to their cause by doing so. In 1947, for example, a group of American blacks under the auspices of the National Association for the Advancement of Colored People (NAACP), led by W. E. B. Du Bois, presented a well-publicized 155-page petition to the UN. The petition—"A Statement on the Denial of Human Rights to Minorities in the Case of Citizens of Negro Descent in the United States of America and an Appeal to the United Nations for Redress"—said American blacks were denied their human rights. American Black Muslim leader Malcolm X submitted a similar petition in the 1960s.

The body within the Secretariat that coordinates all UN human rights activities is the UN Center for Human Rights, which is located in Geneva. The center provides staff for the Commission on Human Rights and also oversees the human rights programs of action that the General Assembly adopts. In late 1993 the center announced that it would begin a training program on human rights and humanitarian law in Russia for the police, the military, the civil service, and the judiciary.

Every year the Commission on Human Rights and its Subcommission on Prevention of Discrimination and Protection of Minorities hold meetings that are open to the public. These meetings can lead to the creation of fact-finding groups, inspection visits, discussions with govern-

*A poster commemorating the International Year for Human Rights.*

INTERNATIONAL YEAR FOR
**HUMAN RIGHTS**

# NOBEL LAUREATE UNDER HOUSE ARREST

When Daw Aung San Suu Kyi, the daughter of the assassinated founder of modern Burma, was awarded the Nobel Peace Prize in 1991 "for her nonviolent struggle for democracy and human rights," she was under house arrest in the Burmese capital of Yangon (Rangoon). Years later, she continues under house arrest, cut off from her husband and two teenage sons.

Aung San Suu Kyi grew up feeling she had a special duty to her father, U Aung San, who was killed by an assassin's bullet in 1947 when she was only two years old. But it would take many years before she understood the nature of her responsibility.

Aung San Suu Kyi was born in Rangoon in British-ruled Burma on June 19, 1945. She left Burma at the age of 15 when her mother was named ambassador to India. After studying in India, she went to Oxford University in England, where she took a degree in politics, philosophy, and economics. There she met Michael Aris, a scholar of Tibetan anthropology.

After they married in 1972, they lived in Bhutan, where he was a tutor to the royal family, and in Japan, where she was a visiting scholar at Kyoto University. In 1974 they moved to Oxford after her husband accepted a teaching position at the university, and had two sons.

It was the severe illness of her mother that made Aung San Suu Kyi return to Burma, now called Myanmar, in 1988. For the four months she nursed her mother, opposition to the 30-year dictatorship of U Ne Win was gathering momentum. After a brutal crackdown by the army that killed 3,000 protestors, the military regime promised elections and a gradual return to democracy, which had been suspended since Ne Win's coup in 1962.

Aung San Suu Kyi's political involvement was gradual. "I obviously had to think about it," she said. "But my instinct was, 'This is not a time when anyone who cares can stay out.' As my father's daughter, I felt I had a duty to get involved."

As secretary-general of the newly formed National League for Democracy, she became a powerful voice for the aspirations of Burmese people. Elegantly dressed in her sarong and short jacket and well-spoken in Burmese and English, she symbolized her father's hope for a democratic, progressive Burma at peace with its minorities and history. During the election campaign she often displayed courage by facing down armed soldiers who threatened to disrupt her rallies.

When she criticized Ne Win in her campaign speeches, the governing military council cracked down. They put her under house arrest, disqualified her from running for office, and cut off her contacts with other people.

The military government carried out its pledge to hold parliamentary elections in May 1990, but then it simply ignored the results. Despite the arrest and disqualification of most of the leadership of the National League for Democracy, Aung San Suu Kyi's party won 392 of the 485 contested seats.

Not only did the generals refuse to accept the results of the election, they launched a slander campaign against Aung San Suu Kyi, attacking her and the

*In July 1989, before she was placed under house arrest, Aung San Suu Kyi addressed a crowd of supporters in Rangoon, the capital of Myanmar.*

"tainted race" of her children who were in boarding schools in England. "Fearlessness may be a gift," she wrote in an essay included in a volume published to honor her father, "but perhaps more precious is the courage acquired through endeavor, courage that comes from cultivating the habit of refusing to let fear dictate one's actions, courage that could be described as 'grace under pressure'—grace renewed repeatedly in the face of harsh, unremitting pressure."

Aung San Suu Kyi was under house arrest and cut off from the rest of the world at the time of the Nobel Peace Prize announcement. The chairman of the Nobel Committee had sent a telegram to the head of the governing council, asking his government to inform Aung San Suu Kyi of the award and its citation.

The citation described her as "the leader of a democratic opposition which employs nonviolent means to resist a regime characterized by brutality." In making the award, said the committee, it wanted "to show its support for the many people throughout the world who are striving to attain democracy, human rights and ethnic conciliation by peaceful means."

In 1992, after Aung San Suu Kyi's receipt of the Nobel Peace Prize, the UN General Assembly adopted its first resolution criticizing Burma's "grave human rights situation" and calling for "early improvement." After passage of the assembly resolution, the Commission on Human Rights appointed a special *rapporteur* to visit Burma in order to make contact with the Burmese government and people, including the political opposition, and to report back to the commission on progress toward democracy and restoration of human rights.

The UN action did prompt the Burmese government to release some political prisoners and grant permission to the family of Aung San Suu Kyi to pay her a visit, but the special *rapporteur,* Professor Yozo Yokota of Japan, was not allowed to meet with her or any other political prisoners.

"Suu Kyi's struggle is one of the most extraordinary examples of civil courage in Asia in recent decades," said the Nobel Peace Prize citation. As the imprisoned leader of the Burmese democracy movement, she remains a powerful symbol of hope for the future of her country.

ments, new declarations, and censure of violators.

At its 1992 meeting, for example, the Commission on Human Rights approved two new draft declarations—on the rights of ethnic and religious minorities and on protection of all persons from enforced disappearances. It also adopted a program of action for the prevention of the sale of children, child prostitution, and child pornography, which it described as modern forms of slavery incompatible with human dignity and human rights.

The 1993 meeting adopted a program of action that called for the elimination of child labor. It drew attention to children and youth it thought especially vulnerable—street children, children of immigrants, refugees, minorities, and indigenous peoples.

The UN has also tried to spread the human rights message by observing special days. Each year Human Rights Day is observed on December 10—the anniversary of the adoption of the Universal Declaration of Human Rights. The International Day for the Elimination of Racial Discrimination is March 21—the anniversary of the Sharpeville massacre in South Africa when white police killed 70 blacks who were demonstrating peacefully against the so-called "pass laws," which limited where blacks could work and visit within the country. The UN observes International Women's Day on March 8.

The United Nations has also campaigned against the deliberate destruction of an entire ethnic, racial, or religious group (called *genocide*). The prevention and punishment of genocide was one of the first issues the General Assembly took up after World War II. In 1948 the assembly adopted an agreement against genocide. Nations that sign the agreement promise to prosecute and punish anyone guilty of geno-

cide or of inciting or conspiring to commit genocide.

In this connection the General Assembly has regularly expressed its concern over the possible revival of Nazism and other totalitarian ideologies that promote racial hatred. The assembly has called on nations to curb organizations that advocate such views and to cooperate with other countries in identifying, catching, and trying those suspected of crimes against humanity.

For many Europeans the racial hatred among Serbs, Croats, and Muslims in Bosnia in the 1990s was an echo of the Nazi past. The atrocities brought back memories of the horrors of an earlier era: skeletal figures behind barbed wire; murdered babies in a bus; three million people driven from their homes in an orgy of "ethnic cleansing"; mass graves; detention centers reminiscent of the concentration camps of World War II.

In 1992 new charges surfaced that each faction in Bosnia was running a network of internment camps where beatings, interrogation, torture, miserable sanitation, starvation, and even murder were common.

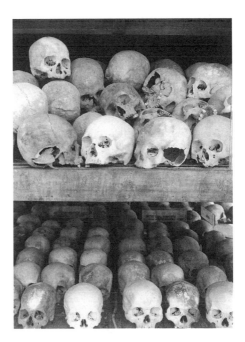

At a memorial near Phnom Penh, the capital of Cambodia, shelves filled with skulls testify to the genocide carried out under the brutal regime of Pol Pot.

*At the UN World Conference on Human Rights in 1993, delegates were presented with this display, a testament to the atrocities being committed in Bosnia.*

Because investigators and reporters were kept out of the camps they most wanted to see, there were fears that the camps could be much worse than the detention centers they already knew about. Detention centers were where each side confined their enemies, civilian and military, in harsh and inhuman conditions before their expulsion or exchange.

Bosnian officials charged Serbs with committing atrocities at their more than 100 makeshift camps. They said that at the Vuk Karadzic primary school in Bratunac, Serbs bled 500 Muslims to death so that wounded Serbs could get blood transfusions.

Although Red Cross or UN inspections that some have proposed might check some of the abuses in the camps, there are "impromptu killing grounds," said a Western diplomat, "where massacres take place, then the killers move on. This is not the kind of murder the UN or Red Cross can monitor."

## Discrimination

Racial and religious intolerance and discrimination is at the heart of many human rights violations. In 1963 the General Assembly adopted the Declaration on the Elimination of All Forms of Racial Discrimination. It condemns discrimination against people on grounds of race, color, or ethnic origin and declares such discrimination an offense against human dignity and the prin-

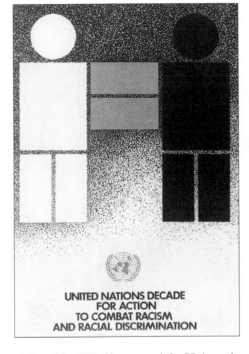

*The 10-year period that began on December 10, 1973, was designated as the Decade for Action to Combat Racism and Racial Discrimination.*

**UNITED NATIONS DECADE FOR ACTION TO COMBAT RACISM AND RACIAL DISCRIMINATION**

ciples of the UN Charter and the Universal Declaration of Human Rights. The declaration also states that any policy or political thought based on differences of race or racial superiority is false, unjust, and reprehensible.

Racial discrimination, especially when sanctioned by law or approved by a government, said the declaration, not only violates human rights but also gets in the way of friendly and peaceful relations between peoples and states. The declaration urges all countries to end laws and policies that discriminate on the basis of race, enact legislation against discrimination, and take steps to end prejudice. In 1965 the General Assembly put the words of the declaration into a convention, a form of international treaty, which requires nations to eliminate racial discrimination.

The General Assembly designated the 10-year period that began on December 10, 1973 (the 25th anniversary of the Universal Declaration of Human Rights) as the Decade for Action to Combat Racism and Racial Discrimination. The decade program called on member states to advance human rights and basic freedoms for all without regard to distinctions of race, color, and national or ethnic origin. The program asked the UN and its member states to launch a worldwide education and media campaign against racism and racial discrimination, denounce racist policies and beliefs that encourage racism, and isolate and condemn racist regimes.

Two years later, in 1975, the growing consensus the General Assembly was reaching on this issue was shattered when a coalition of Arab, Eastern European, and other nations opposed to Israel prevailed on the assembly to pass a resolution that declared Zionism (the movement to establish a Jewish state in Palestine) a form of racism. The resolution remained a great source of bitterness and controversy at the UN until the General Assembly repealed the resolution in December 1991. This was the first and only time the General Assembly ever repealed one of its own resolutions.

## Apartheid

In December 1993 two events, which took place thousands of miles apart, symbolized the dramatic transformation of South Africa after 40 years of condemnation by the world community. On December 10 in Oslo, Norway, two South Africans—one black, one white—accepted the Nobel Peace Prize. Nelson Mandela, the freedom fighter who had spent nearly three decades in prison, and President F. W. de Klerk, head of the white government, were recognized for their work in setting South Africa on the road to democracy and racial harmony.

On December 22 in South Africa the country's

*A triumphant Nelson Mandela acknowledges the tumultuous applause following his speech to the General Assembly on June 22, 1990.*

*UN Secretary-General Boutros Boutros-Ghali greets Nelson Mandela at UN headquarters in 1993. Since its earliest days, the UN fought against and condemned apartheid, South Africa's policy of racial discrimination and segregation.*

white parliament took an historic step toward giving the long-oppressed South African blacks equal rights for the first time. In the chambers where the ruling National Party had established the policy of racial separation two generations earlier, the parliament voted overwhelmingly (237 to 45) for a transitional constitution that would guide South Africa to black majority rule (blacks outnumber whites 5 to 1). As a result of the national election that began on April 27, 1994—the first South African election open to people of all races—a multiracial government headed by the black leader, Nelson Mandela, took power.

The policy of racial discrimination and segregation against black South Africans called *apartheid* (an Afrikaans word meaning "separateness") had been the official policy of the white South African government since 1948. Under this policy the government denied black South Africans—the vast majority of the country's population—and South Africans of mixed race their basic human rights, such as free-

dom of movement and the right to vote and hold office.

Apartheid was maintained by the division of the country into a European area reserved for whites and African reserves called "homelands" scattered around the country. Although black South Africans greatly outnumbered whites, these homelands constituted only 13 percent of the land and were located in the most remote and barren parts of the country.

As early as 1946—two years before apartheid became the official policy of South Africa—the United Nations got involved in the issue in response to a complaint that the South African government was discriminating against citizens of Indian descent. Shortly after South Africa began apartheid, the General Assembly condemned it as a crime against humanity and a violation of the United Nations Charter.

Since then the General Assembly, the Security Council, and all UN bodies concerned with human rights and racial discrimination consistently condemned apartheid and urged South Africa to abandon it. However, just as consistently South Africa rejected their appeals with the argument that the UN does not have the authority to interfere in its internal affairs. In 1973 the General Assembly adopted a convention against apartheid. Any country that signed the convention was obliged to try any individuals, members of organizations, or government representatives charged with the crime of apartheid.

In 1982 the General Assembly anticipated what South Africa would become when it advocated "the total eradication of apartheid and the establishment of a democratic society in which all the people of South Africa as a whole, irrespective of race, color, sex or creed, will enjoy equal and full human rights and fundamental freedoms and participate freely in the determination of their destiny."

For four decades the UN led an international campaign against the South African government to try to get it to change its ways. The chief weapons of the campaign were economic, athletic, and cultural boycotts that kept businesses, athletes, and entertainers away from South Africa; an arms embargo; diplomatic isolation; assistance to refugees; support for political prisoners; antiapartheid conferences; UN resolutions in support of human rights and political freedom; and support for national liberation movements directed against South African rule.

The United Nations also denounced specific policies of the South African government—separate homelands for the black majority, raids into Angola and Zambia, the occupation of Namibia and its use as a military staging area, and mass killings of blacks by government security forces in the black townships of Sharpeville and Soweto.

The pressure put on South Africa by the international community finally paid off in 1994 when for the first time in South African history all races were allowed to vote for a new government that represented *all* South Africans, not just whites. The new just and democratic society that finally emerged in South Africa was the result in no small measure of the persistence of the United Nations.

The coffins of those killed by South African police during a protest held in 1985 on the anniversary of the 1960 Sharpeville massacre.

*Shimon Peres, foreign minister of Israel (second from left), speaks to reporters during the World Conference on Human Rights in 1993.*

### 1993 Human Rights Conference

The World Conference on Human Rights in Vienna in June 1993 was the first UN human rights conference in 25 years. However, even before the Vienna Conference began, differing views about human rights threatened to divide the conference and weaken the claim that the human rights defined in the 1948 Universal Declaration of Human Rights applied to all people equally.

The Universal Declaration of Human Rights is the foundation of all UN human rights work. The rights listed in the declaration have received virtually universal approval. Western nations, however, tend to emphasize the civil and political rights while other nations often downplay their importance in favor of economic, social, and cultural rights.

Developing countries (most of them non-Western) have argued that the Universal Declaration, which was written and adopted when they were still colonies and not members of the UN, reflects the interest of Western industrialized nations in individual rights and says little about collective rights such as "the right to development." Many developing countries think it unfair that developed countries and the International Monetary Fund tie money for development assistance to a country's respect for the individual human rights of its citizens. Some argue that in many places in the world the need for freedom from famine and disease is more urgent than many of the rights outlined in the Universal Declaration.

At preparatory meetings prior to the Vienna Conference, in Bangkok, Tunis, and the Costa Rican capital of San José, Asian and African delegates submitted statements suggesting that different cultures have different standards of human rights. The Asian statement maintained that human rights standards should be measured against "regional particularities and various historical, cultural and religious backgrounds." The African statement stressed the need to take into account "the historical and cultural realities of each nation" and the importance of "the right to development."

When the fourth and final preparatory meeting in Geneva produced a 50-page committee report mostly in brackets, meaning that delegates disagreed with what was said, many worried that the Vienna Conference would fail to come to any agreement and compromise already established human rights principles.

The World Conference on Human Rights in Vienna, attended by nearly 2,100 delegates from 171 countries as well as more than 3,700 representatives of 841 nongovernmental organizations (NGOs), attracted many notable supporters of human rights. These included former U.S. President Jimmy Carter, Russian human rights activist Elena Bonner, and former President Corazon Aquino of the Philippines. Also attending was Guatemalan activist Rigoberta Menchu, the Nobel Peace Prize–winning activist who spoke on behalf of indigenous people, repressed minorities, and women and children in her capacity as UN-designated Goodwill Ambassador for the International Year of the World's Indigenous People.

# RIGOBERTA MENCHU

In 1992 Rigoberta Menchu, a 33-year-old Guatemalan Indian-rights activist, was awarded the Nobel Peace Prize. Head of a group called the Committee of Peasant Unity, which her father had helped lead, she was a spokeswoman for victims of government repression in Guatemala and an advocate for indigenous peoples throughout the Americas.

A Mayan of the Quiche group from northwestern Guatemala, Menchu moved to Mexico in 1981 after government forces killed her father, mother, and brother. The Nobel committee said that amid the "large-scale repression of Indian peoples" in Guatemala, she plays a "prominent part as an advocate of native rights." The committee said it was awarding the prize "in recognition of her work for social justice and ethno-cultural reconciliation."

Born in poverty, Menchu was forced to become a farm worker while still a small child. She tended beans and corn on her parents' tiny plot and traveled with them to the south to work on coffee, cotton, and sugar plantations. She did not learn to speak Spanish until she was 20.

The world first learned her story with the 1983 publication of her autobiography *I, Rigoberta Menchu,* which was eventually translated into 11 languages. It tells of Quiche life in the mountains and how the descendants of European colonists who control the government dominate the Indians, who make up 60 percent of the population. Her book describes in horrifying detail the torture and death of family members.

Menchu's father was one of the early underground organizers of an agrarian trade union called the Committee of Peasant Unity. To punish him, government security forces seized his son and had him skinned and burned alive in public. Later when Menchu's father and some of his comrades occupied the Spanish embassy in Guatemala City to draw attention to their grievances, police arrived and the building caught fire, burning to death many of the demonstrators.

A few weeks later soldiers captured Menchu's mother. After they raped and tortured her, they left her under a tree to die of her wounds. Menchu tried to live in hiding but soon had to flee to Mexico. Two of her sisters joined the guerrilla forces in the mountains. In 30 years of struggle against Guatemala's repressive government, more than 120,000 people have been killed.

Menchu is using the prize money to set up a foundation in her father's name to defend the rights of indigenous peoples. She said, "The only thing I wish for is freedom for Indians wherever they are. As the end of the 20th century approaches, we hope that our continent will be pluralistic."

Rigoberta Menchu was a leading member of the campaign—which was ultimately successful—to have the UN designate 1993 as the International Year of the World's Indigenous People. To honor her work, the UN appointed her Goodwill Ambassador for the year and invited her to address the Vienna Human Rights Conference.

*José Ayala Lasso of Ecuador was appointed as the UN's first High Commissioner for Human Rights.*

While the conference provided a forum for divergent points of view, the conference's final document—the Vienna Declaration and Program of Action—did not compromise the principle of the universal nature of human rights. It stated that nations had a right to economic development and took note of the arguments of nations like China, Indonesia, Iran, and Syria that ideas about human rights were to some degree different in different countries (depending on a country's history, culture, and level of development). Nonetheless, the conference urged the nations of the world to promote and protect all human rights "regardless of their political, economic and cultural systems," adding that "the universal nature of these rights and freedoms is beyond question."

The conference broke new ground by extending the definition of human rights to embrace the special rights of children, women, minorities, and indigenous peoples. In recent years the United Nations has been paying more attention to the special problems of indigenous peoples—the descendants of the original inhabitants of a land who were subjugated by the people who came after them. According to Erica-Irene A. Daes, chairwoman of the Working Group on Indigenous Populations, they are "the poorest, most discriminated against and disadvantaged groups of society." As estimated by UN studies, there are 300 million indigenous people in more than 70 countries around the world.

The General Assembly proclaimed 1993 the International Year of the World's Indigenous People to focus attention on their plight. A UN working group, originally created by the Economic and Social Council in 1982, is presently drafting the Universal Declaration of the Rights of Indigenous Peoples. The declaration, which will eventually be presented to the General Assembly, will establish international standards for the protection of the rights of indigenous peoples to land, resources, culture, and self-determination.

The Vienna conference also supported the establishment of a High Commissioner for Human Rights to promote and protect human rights around the world. Since the conference had no legislative authority and could only make recommendations for later action, it urged the General Assembly to take up the proposal for a High Commissioner for Human Rights "as a matter of priority" at its next session.

In December 1993 the General Assembly agreed to the idea, and early in 1994 the secretary-general appointed José Ayala Lasso, Ecuador's ambassador to the UN, as the UN's first High Commissioner for Human Rights. Lasso, who has written extensively on the subject, began his four-year term on February 28. Though the new high commissioner does not have the power to force governments accused of abuses to change their ways, he can try to shame them into respecting human rights by publicizing the violations and reporting them to the General Assembly or the Commission on Human Rights in Geneva.

While Western nations were relieved that there was no erosion of fundamental human rights principles and women's groups were generally pleased with what the conference recommended, not everybody was satisfied. Some nongovernmental human rights organizations excluded from the drafting of the final declaration called it "a flawed document" that let governments shirk their human rights obligations. Pierre Sané, the secretary-general of Amnesty International, called the conference "a summit of missed opportunities" that "dealt with the past and not the future, reaffirming principles agreed to 45 years ago instead of addressing the challenges of the future."

The United Nations is now in a much stronger position to deal with human rights abuses because it has enforcement mechanisms that were not available earlier in its history. These include working groups and *rapporteurs* who work on special issues

## YOUNG PEOPLE ATTEND THEIR OWN CONFERENCE

In June 1993, 175 young people (ages 10 to 18) attended the NGO-sponsored Children's World Conference on Human Rights in Vienna while the "adult" UN Conference on Human Rights was taking place.

The young people came from many different places—refugee camps, the Arctic region of Siberia, the inner cities of New York and Los Angeles. Some came to the conference on the Earth Train for Peace from Zagreb, in the former Yugoslavia.

During the conference they talked about their lives and the importance of human rights, and they expanded their global perspective. They made new friends, learned about other people from cultures very different from their own, and sought ways to stay connected after the conference was over.

On the day the official UN conference designated "Child Rights Day," the young people attended and heard two of their members address the delegates. The two young speakers—Rosa from El Salvador, whose father was murdered before her eyes, and Sleepy Eye, a Native American from the Tonawanda Indian Reservation in upstate New York—called for an end to violence against children and asked that young people be given a voice at the UN. They asked the official delegates to join in a moment of silence for the children of the world who had died as a result of violence. The delegates were clearly moved by what they heard. At the end of the speeches, they gave the young people a standing ovation.

These young people knew that by addressing an official UN conference they had established an important precedent. Their hope is that the United Nations will continue to seek them out.

such as arbitrary executions, disappearances, and torture; special *rapporteurs* for individual countries; increased responsibility for committees that monitor compliance with human rights treaties; and more public information about human rights and the UN machinery that allows individuals to claim their rights.

Recent developments—the change of Soviet (now Russian) policy from opposition to cooperation with UN policies, the active participation of nongovernmental human rights organizations, publicity about human rights violations around the world, and growing international interest in the issue—have created new opportunities for UN human rights work. In his message to the final session of the conference Secretary-General Boutros Boutros-Ghali said the expectations raised in Vienna would mean for the United Nations "a more vigorous approach to human rights."

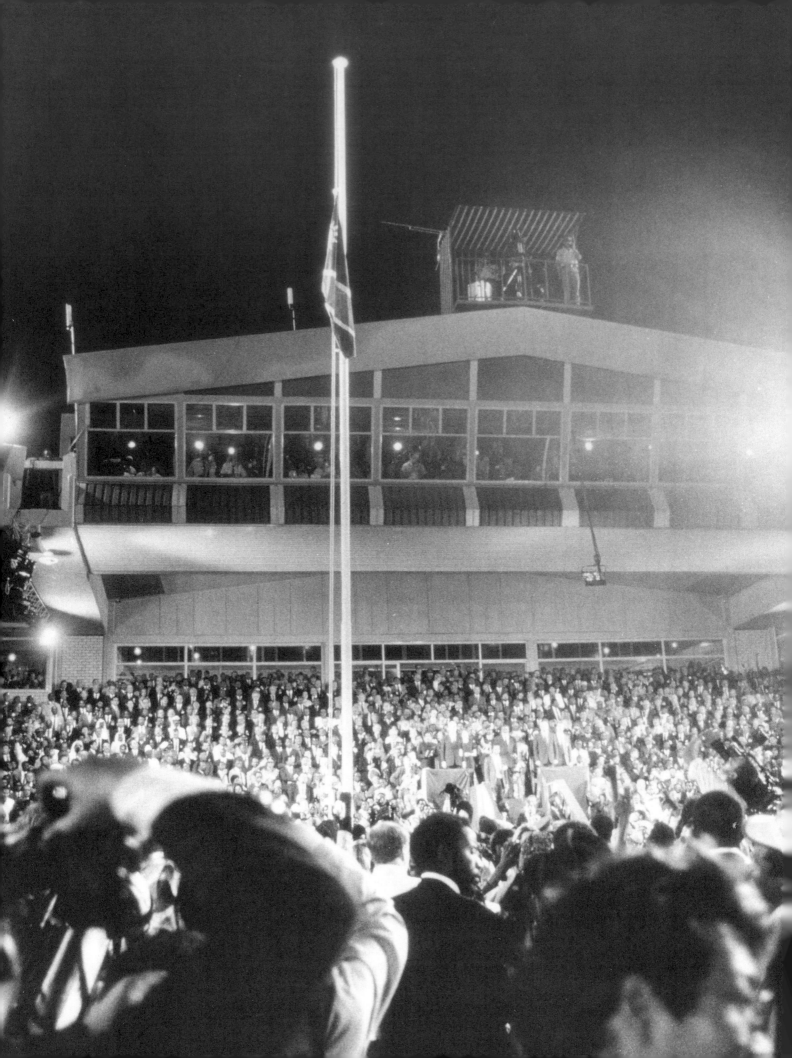

# CHAPTER 9

# Old Colonies, New Nations

On April 23, 1990, a standing ovation greeted Namibian prime minister Hage G. Geigob as the UN chief of protocol escorted him to his country's seat in the General Assembly hall. Just minutes before, the Republic of Namibia had been admitted to the United Nations.

General Assembly president Joseph Garba called the occasion "a truly historic moment," and Secretary-General Javier Pérez de Cuéllar said it was "with considerable emotion and pride" that he welcomed the UN's newest member. Prime Minister Geigob said that his country accepted as sacred its responsibilities as a member of the world body. "We are committed to building a democracy in which violent confrontation and the politics of hate will be a thing of the past," he declared.

Afterward the assembly president and secretary-general accompanied the Namibian prime minister outside, to the area just behind the First Avenue fence for the traditional flag-raising ceremony that marks the admission of all new UN members. With the Namibian flag fluttering overhead, Secretary-General Pérez de Cuéllar recalled "the many people, Namibians and others, who dedicated their lives' work, and sometimes their very lives, so that this day might dawn."

That day, which also was marked by the opening of a special photographic exhibit—"Namibia: New Nation, New Need"—in the public lobby, was a very emotional one for the UN. The admission of Namibia to membership had been a long time coming. Although Namibia was but one of the many former colonies that had gained its independence, no nation's journey from colony to nationhood had been longer or more difficult.

## One Nation's Struggle

South West Africa—as Namibia used to be called—was a German colony before World War I, but after Germany's defeat it was administered by South Africa under the authority (called a mandate) of the League of Nations. When the United Nations replaced the league after World War II, it called on South Africa to turn its mandate over to the UN trusteeship system. This same request had been made to and accepted by countries that had ruled six other African territories that had been part of the League of Nations mandate system. Unlike these other countries, however, South Africa refused to turn

*On March 21, 1990, Namibia was established as a free and independent nation. As thousands of supporters watch, the Namibian flag is raised in a ceremony in the capital of Windhoek.*

*In 1981, under the watchful eyes of Marx and Lenin, these SWAPO commanders receive political and military training at an Angolan base near the Namibian border.*

over its mandate. This refusal made South Africa and the United Nations bitter opponents—not just over Namibia, but also over South Africa's policy of apartheid, or racial separation.

From that point on the General Assembly and Security Council repeatedly called on South Africa to withdraw from South West Africa, the territory that would later become the nation of Namibia. In 1950, at the request of the General Assembly, the International Court of Justice issued an opinion that South Africa was obligated to promote social and economic progress in the territory. Moreover, the court ruled that, as the heir of the League of Nations, the United Nations, not South Africa, had the right to administer the territory. South Africa refused to accept the court's decision.

In 1966 the General Assembly placed the territory directly under the authority of the United Nations, declaring South Africa's occupation illegal and its authority void on the grounds that it had not lived up to its obligations. In 1967 the assembly established the UN Council for South West Africa to administer the territory until independence. The following year it declared that from then

on the territory would be known as Namibia in accordance with the wishes of the majority of its people. Still, South Africa continued its defiance of the United Nations.

From 1971 to 1973 the Security Council called on UN member states to take various actions to put pressure on South Africa to change its apartheid policy and its occupation of Namibia. In 1971 the Security Council established the Fund for Namibia to help refugees, and in 1973 it set up the Institute for Namibia to give young Namibians education and training to prepare them for self-rule.

Throughout the 1970s and 1980s the UN continued its campaign to promote Namibian independence and uphold the rights of the Namibian people. In 1973 the UN General Assembly recognized the South-West Africa People's Organization (SWAPO) as "the authentic representative of the Namibian people" and one year later appointed its first full-time commissioner for Namibia. The assembly also tried to curb the economic exploitation of the territory by multinational corporations by passing a decree stating that it was unlawful for companies to export and profit from Namibia's natural resources without the permission of the Council for Namibia.

An important step in the direction of Namibian independence was taken in 1977 when five Western members of the Security Council—England, France, West Germany, Canada, and the United States—presented a detailed plan to the Security Council. The Western plan called for territory-wide elections under UN supervision, a UN peacekeeping force to maintain order, and a special representative of the UN secretary-general to oversee the territory's transition to independence.

The secretary-general recommended that the plan be put into force in three stages: first a cease-fire and withdrawal of all armed forces, then UN-supervised elections, and finally the creation of a constitution for a free and independent Namibia.

When Cuban troops withdrew from the civil war in neighboring Angola, the movement for independence in Namibia picked up momentum.

Because South Africa no longer needed Namibia as a military staging area for the Angolan war, they agreed to let the United Nations begin the process of freeing Namibia from South African rule.

The Security Council plan to implement Namibian independence began on April 1, 1989, with 20 countries contributing troops, police, and civilian support staff to a UN transitional assistance group. The mission, which numbered almost 8,000 soldiers, police, and civilians from 109 countries and cost $375 million, turned out to be one of the most complex UN operations ever undertaken.

It was also one of the most successful. In November, 97 percent of the eligible voters went to the polls to elect a constituent assembly, which then went on to write a national constitution. The constitution made Namibia a multiparty, racially inclusive, democratic nation with three branches of government. About 43,000 Namibian exiles scattered throughout 40 countries

*Namibians line up to register to vote in the November 1989 election. Thousands of UN soldiers and civilians were sent to Namibia to guarantee a fair election.*

# THE WOMEN OF NAMIBIA

During the fight for Namibian independence, women marched and fought side by side with their husbands and brothers. But now that Namibia is an independent country, women are having to take up another struggle—for equality with men.

Although the Namibian constitution guarantees equality between men and women, women do not have access to the same jobs and pay as men and they cannot enter into a contract without their husband's consent.

Sixty percent of Namibian women are illiterate, and most raise their children by themselves. Under apartheid laws, men had to leave their families behind when they migrated for work.

To help women acquire the skills that will allow them to be self-supporting, the UN Population Fund is supporting a handicraft center in the Namibian capital of Windhoek. The center collects, finishes, and packages needlework done by rural women and then sells the finished work to Europe.

"I would like to sew for my children," said Hettie Alugodhi, mother of four, "and also sell my own handiwork." The center helps women gain self-confidence. "When they walk out of here they feel they've accomplished something," said the director. "They feel more positive about their households and what they can contribute to their community."

*A mural in Windhoek, the Namibian capital.*

were brought home with the help of the UN High Commissioner for Refugees.

The long struggle for Namibian self-determination, which the United Nations did so much to support, came to an end on March 21, 1990, when Namibia became an independent nation. It was only fitting that one month later—on April 23—the new country entered the United Nations, the organization that had done so much to make its existence possible.

## The Colonial Legacy

The decolonization of the world was one of the greatest revolutions of the 20th century. Like Namibia, almost three-quarters of all UN members are former colonies. When the United Nations was founded in 1945, about 750 million people—almost a third of the world's population—lived under the colonial rule of European nations that controlled much of Africa and Asia.

During the modern colonial period European nations competed with each other to establish overseas colonies in Africa, Asia, and other parts of the world. Although the Dutch and Portuguese had established trading posts on the coast of Africa in the 1600s, there had been little contact between Europe and Africa until the 1800s when Britain, France, Germany, Belgium, and Portugal carved up the African continent.

Asia was colonized for the most part by the Dutch (East Indies), British (India, Burma, Malaya), and French (Indochina). Europeans divided China into separate zones of influence, while islands in the Pacific Ocean became colonial prizes for the British, French, German, Dutch, and Americans. After World War I the Allied victors stripped the Ottoman Empire and Germany of their colonies, but most of these territories came under Allied control. It was not until after World War II that the transformation of colonies into countries took place in earnest.

From the outset the UN supported the hopes of dependent peoples. The basic principles of decolonization were written into the charter. Article I of the charter states that one of the purposes of the UN is "to develop friendly relations among nations based on respect for the principle of equal rights and self-determination of peoples." Other articles spell out the UN policy toward dependent peoples.

*This 1952 map shows the UN Trust Territories around the world.*

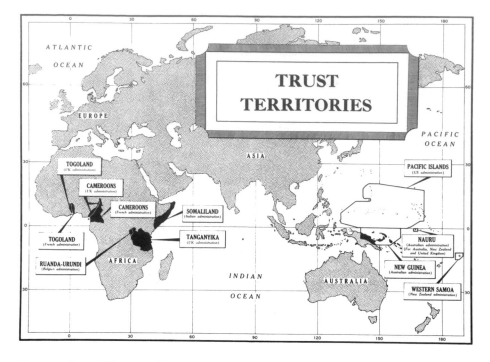

## International Trusteeship System

The United Nations trusteeship system which helped lead Namibia and other former colonies to independence was set up after World War II. That system and the Trusteeship Council of the United Nations were established to supervise the administration of these "trust territories." As spelled out in the UN Charter, the basic objective of the trusteeship system was "to promote the political, economic, social, and educational advancement of the inhabitants of the trust territories, and their progressive development towards self-government."

The Trusteeship Council was set up to send elaborate questionnaires to nations that administer trust territories and carefully review the reports upon their return to the council. The Trusteeship Council was also to examine petitions from individuals and groups residing in the trust territories and organize periodic missions to the territories to report on conditions and progress toward self-rule.

By 1950, 11 territories had been placed in the United Nations trusteeship system. Ten of them—located in Africa and the Pacific—were under the authority of the General Assembly; the "strategic" Trust Territory of the Pacific Islands was put under the authority of the Security Council. By 1975 the original 10 trust territories under the authority of the General Assembly had left the United Nations trusteeship system, either by becoming independent or by joining a neighboring country.

Somaliland, which was under Italian administration, was the first trust territory to leave the trusteeship system. In 1960, it united with the British Somaliland Protectorate to form the nation of Somalia. Two French trust territories—Togoland and Cameroons—also achieved independence in 1960 when they became the sovereign nations of Togo and Cameroon. Two years later, in 1962, the Belgian trust territory of Ruanda-Urundi became two separate nations—Rwanda and Burundi.

## UN BACK IN RWANDA

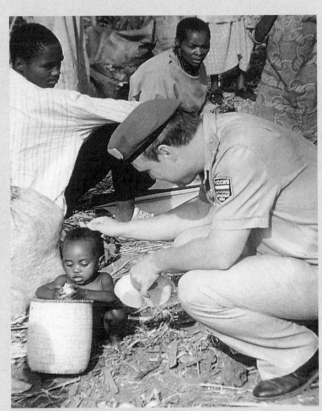

*A UN soldier from Russia with a Rwandan baby at a relief camp set up in the town of Ruhengeri.*

More than 30 years after the UN helped Rwanda change from trust territory to independent nation, the United Nations returned to try to help the country recover from three years of civil war.

Two months after the government and the Rwandese Patriotic Front signed a peace agreement in Tanzania in August 1993, the UN Security Council set up the United Nations Assistance Mission to Rwanda (UNAMIR).

The mandate of UNAMIR—designed to reach a peak strength of 2,548 military personnel—was to monitor the cease-fire, keep peace in the Rwandese capital city of Kigali, coordinate humanitarian assistance, resettle refugees, and supervise the local police.

The UN World Food Program also became involved in Rwanda. In 1993 it redeployed the bulk of its trucking fleet in Somalia to its emergency program in Rwanda where close to one million displaced people—about 15 percent of the population—were in desperate need.

In 1994 mass killings and intensified fighting between rebel and government forces drove hundreds of thousands of people across the border into Zaire. There tens of thousands of refugees died of cholera before relief efforts by the UN and other international organizations were finally able to contain the epidemic.

Britain administered three of the UN trust territories. In 1957, British Togoland united with the British territory of Gold Coast to become the nation of Ghana. In 1961, British-administered Cameroons divided into two parts. The northern part joined Nigeria and the southern part joined the newly independent Republic of Cameroon. British-administered Tanganyika gained its independence in 1961 and three years later joined newly independent Zanzibar to form the United Republic of Tanzania.

The U.S. delegate on the Trusteeship Council with special responsibility for the Cameroons and Togoland was Marian Anderson, a black concert singer whom President Eisenhower appointed a member of the American delegation in 1958. It was a brilliant choice, since Marian Anderson was one of the most admired women in the world. In 1955, after a distinguished career in Europe and the United States, she became the first black singer to perform at the Metropolitan Opera in New York.

In 1957—the year before her UN appointment—the U.S. State Department sent Anderson on a goodwill tour to Asia. The trip took her to Korea, Vietnam, Thailand, Burma, Malaysia, India, Pakistan, and six other countries and covered more than 40,000 miles. The insights she gained from

her tour were useful on the Trusteeship Council, where her dedication and hard work helped speed up the granting of independence to the Cameroons and Togoland.

Three of the trust territories under the authority of the General Assembly were in the Pacific Ocean. Western Samoa, administered by New Zealand, became independent Samoa in 1962. Nauru, administered by Australia, gained its independence in 1968. New Guinea, also administered by Australia, united with the Australian territory of Papua to become the independent nation of Papua New Guinea in 1975.

After 1975 the only UN trust territory left in the system was the Trust Territory of the Pacific Islands, a "strategic" territory formerly under Japanese control that the Security Council placed under the administration of the United States in 1947. (It was considered strategic because of its key position in the Pacific between Asia and the Americas.) The territory consisted of four island groups—Micronesia, the Marshall Islands, the Northern Marianas, and Palau. In 1990 the Security Council ended trusteeship over three of the four island groups. The Northern Marianas agreed to become an American commonwealth, while the Federated States of Micronesia and the Marshall Islands drew up compacts of free association with the United States and joined the UN as independent nations on September 17, 1991. The last remaining UN trust territory—Palau—drafted a compact of free association with the United States that would make it independent, like Micronesia and the Marshall Islands, which its people ratified in 1994. The termination of the UN trusteeship agreement with Palau in effect completes the work of the Trusteeship Council.

Even as the UN General Assembly became larger with the addition of each new member state (184 as of 1994) and the size

*Secretary-General Kurt Waldheim (right) greets singer Marian Anderson, the U.S. delegate on the Trusteeship Council, after her performance at a concert at UN headquarters. They are joined by Antal Dorati, the conductor of the National Symphony Orchestra of Washington, D.C.*

of the Economic and Social Council tripled from 18 to 54 as a result of two charter amendments, the Trusteeship Council became smaller as the number of trust territories and their administering countries who made up the membership of the Trusteeship Council decreased.

As the Trusteeship Council, which meets once a year, completed its original assignment of guiding the UN trust territories toward self-determination, other duties have been suggested for it. Some want the council to focus next on issues of self-determination generally, while others have suggested the council take over administration of the environment.

### Decolonizing "Non-Self-Governing Territories"

The UN Charter committed itself to decolonization much more firmly than the League of Nations Covenant, which only suggested conditions for colonial territories and said nothing about their eventual independence. The charter calls on UN member states with responsibilities for administering territories "whose people have not yet attained a full measure of self-government" to recognize "as a sacred trust" that they must act in the best interests of the inhabitants of those territories. The charter also says that those UN member states should promote the interests and well-being of colonial peoples by providing for their political, economic, social, and educational advancement, and by helping them develop free political institutions (such as a free press, political parties, and labor unions) that will lead them toward self-government.

In 1946, eight UN members—Australia, Belgium, Denmark, England, France, the Netherlands, New Zealand, and the United States—provided the United Nations with information about the more than 70 "non-self governing territories" under their administration. Spain and Portugal, which joined the UN in 1955, also provided information about the territories under their authority.

*When the Netherlands agreed to grant control of West New Guinea to Indonesia, the UN Temporary Executive Authority was created to serve as a transitional government. Here, the flag of Indonesia is raised alongside the UN flag to mark the occasion.*

Because decolonization was so important to the UN from its earliest days, the world body has played an important role in transforming many colonies into independent countries. During Indonesia's struggle for independence from the Netherlands in the late 1940s, for example, the Security Council arranged cease-fires, maintained a small unit to observe the truce, and helped with the negotiations. UN pressure on the Dutch to grant Indonesian independence resulted in the final agreement in December 1949. The UN also later resolved the controversy over West New Guinea, which the Dutch had refused to turn over to Indonesian rule in 1949.

The United Nations also set the former Italian colonies of Libya, Italian Somaliland, and Eritrea on the road to independence. The World War II peace treaty with defeated Italy had left the question of the future status of the Italian colonies to the UN General Assembly. The issue occupied several assembly sessions. In the end Libya was granted independence in 1951, Somaliland was placed under Italian trusteeship until it achieved independence in 1960, and Eritrea was integrated into Ethiopia until it achieved its full independence in 1993.

The tone of the United Nations in its early years became increasingly anticolonial as former colonies joined it in growing numbers. Twelve former colonies were admitted to the UN between 1955 and 1958, and 17 more joined in 1960. That year the General Assembly demanded "self-determination" for the people of Algeria, which achieved its independence from France two years later.

## Declaration on Decolonization

In 1960 the General Assembly adopted the Declaration on the Granting of Independence to Colonial Countries and Peoples. By then former colonies were numerous enough in the United Nations for the assembly to respond to the urgent demands that dependent peoples be free of colonial rule, and to the widespread perception that decolonization was not proceeding fast enough.

The declaration—known as the Declaration on Decolonization—proclaimed that subjecting people to foreign domination was a violation of basic human rights, a hindrance to world peace, and a denial of the UN Charter principle that colonial peoples had a right to full and immediate independence. Not a single UN member state voted against the declaration, although nine countries (eight of them colonial powers) abstained. The passage of the declaration put even more pressure on the colonial powers to speed up the decolonization process.

In 1961 the General Assembly established a 17-member special committee—enlarged to 24 members the following year—to study how the Declaration of Decolonization could best be carried out. The General Assembly also requested that the Committee of 24, as it came to be called, inform the Security Council of any developments in any of the non-self-governing territories that could threaten international peace and security. During the cold war the smallest conflict in a remote part of the world had the potential of being the spark that might set off a wider war.

Much of the decolonization effort of the General Assembly focused on Africa, especially southern Africa. The assembly urged UN agencies and other organizations to assist the colonial peoples of Africa and their national liberation movements and encouraged member states to provide technical and vocational training and secondary and university education to the peoples of dependent territories. In 1967 the General Assembly integrated three existing UN programs for educating and training people from South West Africa (Namibia), Portu-

guese colonial territories (Angola and Mozambique), and South Africa into the United Nations Educational and Training Program for Southern Africa, which offered more than 1,000 scholarships every year to people from southern Africa.

In new countries where independence has not brought hoped-for economic progress, people have complained that the old colonial system has merely been replaced by "neocolonialism." This is a less obvious form of control, economic rather than political, by which rich countries rule over poor ones. Since 1974 the Committee of 24 has been studying the effect of foreign economic involvement in the non-self-governing territories. It has determined that

foreign economic interests have been a major obstacle to the self-determination of native peoples and their right to cultivate and enjoy their natural resources.

The Committee of 24 has also paid special attention to the smallest dependent territories—islands and groups of islands. The General Assembly has repeatedly affirmed the right of the peoples of these islands to self-determination and called on the administering powers to heed the 1960 Declaration on Decolonization. In some cases the UN has sent missions to these island colonies to gain firsthand information and find out the wishes of the inhabitants about their political future. As a result of UN pressure, a number of these island ter-

*Schoolchildren in Cape Verde, a group of islands off the west coast of Africa, wave flags to greet members of the Committee of 24. Cape Verde achieved independence from Portugal in 1975. The Committee of 24 was created in 1961 by the General Assembly to study how decolonization could best be carried out.*

ritories have gained their independence and joined the United Nations (for example, Brunei, Dominica, Solomon Islands, Saint Kitts and Nevis, Saint Lucia, and Saint Vincent and the Grenadines).

Of the more than 70 dependent territories that existed prior to 1960, there are 17 left that the Committee of 24 still watches over. These are American Samoa, Anguilla, Bermuda, British Virgin Islands, Cayman Islands, Guam, Montserrat, Tokelau, Turks and Caicos Islands, U.S. Virgin Islands, New Caledonia, Gibraltar, Pitcairn, East Timor, Falkland Islands (Malvinas), St. Helena, and Western Sahara. Palau was removed from the list in 1994.

Although much progress has been made, the work of decolonization is not over. In 1988 the General Assembly declared 1990–2000 to be the International Decade for the Eradication of Colonialism and promised to help the world's remaining dependent populations—mainly in the Caribbean and the Pacific—achieve their goal of self-determination and independence. Recently

Renagi R. Lohia of Papua New Guinea, who was chairman of the Special Committee on Decolonization, said that the era of colonialism is not over "as long as there are countries and peoples, whatever their size and location, who do not exercise their inalienable right to self-determination."

## Zimbabwe

The modern African nation of Zimbabwe used to be the British colony of Southern Rhodesia. Like many African and Asian countries, it had to struggle long and hard to win its independence.

British claims to the south-central part of Africa began in 1889, when the British South Africa Company, organized by Cecil Rhodes, obtained a charter to promote commerce and colonization in the area. By 1923, Southern Rhodesia had become a self-governing British colony ruled by its European settlers.

In 1961, when the white government of Southern Rhodesia drafted a new consti-

*In September 1979, England convened a conference in London to work out a transitional government that would lead to eventual black majority rule in Southern Rhodesia.*

*In the 1970s the white minority government of Southern Rhodesia came under increasing attack from guerrillas wanting to establish black majority rule. This border patrol keeps an eye out for guerrilla activity.*

tution that gave Europeans complete control over the African majority, the United Nations reacted strongly. The General Assembly called on Britain to suspend the 1961 constitution and not grant Southern Rhodesia independence until the African majority was guaranteed the right to vote and other basic human rights.

When the white minority regime of Ian Smith proclaimed a unilateral declaration of independence from Britain in late 1965, the UN joined Britain in condemning the action. One year later the Security Council voted to impose sanctions on Southern Rhodesia. Though the UN Charter grants the Security Council the right to impose sanctions against any country whose actions endanger international peace and security, this was the first time the United Nations ever employed such sanctions.

As the African inhabitants of Southern Rhodesia stepped up their campaign of guerrilla warfare against the white government,

the General Assembly called on all UN member states and agencies to support the struggle of the people of Zimbabwe (the African name for Southern Rhodesia). When Southern Rhodesia proclaimed itself a republic in 1970, the Security Council condemned "the illegal proclamation of republican status of the Territory by the illegal regime" and called for tougher measures against those who directly or indirectly supported the Southern Rhodesian government.

In September 1979, with UN encouragement, Britain convened a London conference on the future of Southern Rhodesia designed to find a way to establish majority rule. Shortly after the conference reached an agreement on a cease-fire and on a constitution that implemented majority rule, the Security Council called on UN member states to end their sanctions against Southern Rhodesia. After the UN-supervised elections, Zimbabwe became an independent nation on April 18, 1980. Four months later—on August 25—it joined the United Nations.

### East Timor

The island of Timor is at the southeastern end of the Indonesian archipelago north of Australia. The western part of Timor, which was part of the Dutch East Indies, became part of Indonesia when that country gained its independence in 1949. The eastern part of Timor was a Portuguese colony, which in 1951 Portugal proclaimed an integral part of itself as an "overseas province." The General Assembly placed East Timor on the UN list of non-self-governing territories in 1960, and later the Committee of 24 took a special interest in it.

In 1974, when a new government in Portugal recognized the right of all its colonial possessions to self-determination, the Portuguese began negotiations on de-

*Activists outside the Indonesian embassy in Manila protest what they say is genocide in East Timor.*

colonization with the main political parties in East Timor. Some people wanted to integrate East Timor with Indonesia, but the Frente Revolucionaria de Timor Leste Independente (FRETILIN) wanted immediate independence.

The civil war that broke out in late 1975 forced Portugal to withdraw its military and civilians. FRETILIN proclaimed the "Democratic Republic of East Timor," while others continued to call for the territory's integration with Indonesia. After Indonesia sent troops to the East Timor capital of Dili on December 7, 1975, Portugal broke off diplomatic relations with Indonesia and submitted the problem to the Security Council.

The Security Council and the General Assembly urged all nations to respect East

Timor's territorial integrity and the right of its people to self-determination, and they called for the immediate withdrawal of Indonesian troops. In 1976, the Security Council again called on Indonesia to withdraw from East Timor. In the meantime, the pro-Indonesian "provisional government" held elections for an assembly in the areas it controlled. The assembly then proceeded to call for the merger of East Timor with Indonesia. FRETILIN denounced the decision and continued its armed struggle against Indonesian rule.

Since 1975 East Timor has been the scene of savage fighting between the Indonesian army and FRETILIN guerrillas. International human rights groups have accused the Indonesian military of using torture, murder, and other repressive measures

*In 1981 the Special Committee on Decolonization took up the question of Indonesian rule in East Timor. José Ramos-Horta, a representative of FRETILIN, presented his group's case to the committee.*

to enforce its annexation of East Timor. They claim Indonesian forces have killed or allowed to die, as the result of torture, disease, malnutrition, and forced deportation, between 100,000 and 200,000 people.

In 1984 the secretary-general persuaded Indonesia and Portugal to begin talks aimed at achieving a comprehensive settlement, but the talks broke off. With persuasion by the UN, the talks resumed five years later. However, the human rights abuses in East Timor continued.

In November 1991 Indonesian troops opened fire on a crowd of mourners at the funeral of a supporter of East Timorese in-

dependence in the Santa Cruz cemetery in Dili, killing at least 180 people. There was immediate international condemnation of Indonesia. As a result of the massacre the United States and several other countries cut off millions of dollars of aid to Indonesia.

In 1993 the UN Commission on Human Rights adopted a resolution expressing "deep concern" at human rights violations in East Timor. In May of that same year in the Indonesian capital of Jakarta the leader of the separatist FRETILIN guerrillas in East Timor, José Alexandre Gusmao, was sentenced to life imprisonment. The Indonesian occupation force in East Timor, which numbers about 12,000 troops, has apparently succeeded in crippling the rebel movement. It is estimated there are only about 200 guerrillas left.

The General Assembly, which has repeatedly reaffirmed the right of the people of East Timor to freedom and self-determination, has called on UN specialized agencies and other organizations to provide the people of East Timor with humanitarian assistance. The UN does not recognize Indonesian sovereignty over East Timor and still regards Portugal as the administering power. However, Indonesia regards the decolonization process as complete. It has made East Timor its 28th province.

CHAPTER 10

# Laws and Nations: The UN and International Law

W ho owns the oceans? What laws govern the waters that cover more than two-thirds of the earth's surface? One of the greatest achievements of the United Nations is its Convention on the Law of the Sea, which was many years in the making. The convention, finished in 1982 and now in force, covers almost everything having to do with the use of the oceans, including navigation, conservation, pollution, air flight over oceans, shipping, fishing, and the exploration and use of ocean resources by drilling and undersea mining enterprises. The convention serves as a comprehensive guide to the nations of the world about behavior at sea. It defines ocean zones, lays down rules for drawing maritime boundaries and settling disputes, and defines the legal rights, duties, and responsibilities of nations.

At its meeting on December 10, 1992, the General Assembly marked the 10th anniversary of the convention. At the commemoration Secretary-General Boutros Boutros-Ghali hailed the Law of the Sea as "a milestone in our organization's almost 50-year history, a milestone in the building of a true community of nations."

Even before the convention went into force, José Luis Jesus of Cape Verde, chairman of the Preparatory Commission for the International Seabed Authority and for the International Tribunal for the Law of the Sea, said that the convention already had had "a major impact on state practice in maritime matters." Most of the countries of the world, he pointed out, had "adjusted their policies and national legislation to the new legal order for the oceans."

At the December 10 meeting, Secretary-General Boutros-Ghali paid tribute to the man whose dream of preserving the resources of the sea inspired the convention.

*This Danish fishing fleet, like the fleets of other UN member nations, is bound by international rules outlined in the Convention on the Law of the Sea.*

*A deep-sea diver conducts research on the seabed in the Gulf of Honduras.*

Twenty-five years earlier Ambassador Arvid Pardo of Malta, who supported the philosophy that the earth is humanity's common heritage, had urged the General Assembly to place the question of the law of the sea on its agenda. He believed that the earth's resources—especially its waters—belonged to all people and "could serve as sort of a bridge to the future and unite the world community in its quest to preserve our planet for generations to come."

The Law of the Sea puts the ocean floor off-limits to nations wishing to claim and exploit its resources on the assumption that the ocean floor belongs to all nations, rich and poor. "No doubt the declaration of the seabed and its resources as the common heritage of mankind was bound to change the relationship between rich and poor countries," said Pardo in an interview. "And that change amounted to a revolution not merely in the law of the sea but also in international relations."

## International Law on the High Seas

For centuries the oceans have been used primarily for navigation and fishing. Despite occasional disputes over navigation and fishing rights, use of the oceans was not a major source of conflict. For that reason few attempts were made to regulate maritime traffic. However, with the advent of sophisticated technology humans looked for new ways to benefit from the ocean's resources.

The United Nations and other international bodies have attempted to regulate certain aspects of ocean use. The International Maritime Organization, founded as a UN specialized agency in 1948, produced several treaties dealing with maritime safety and pollution, and the UN Environment Programme has come up with agreements to preserve the maritime environment. The Food and Agriculture Organization provides research and advice about fish as a food

*The official emblem for the UN Law of the Sea Conference.*

resource, the International Labour Organization deals with maritime labor issues, and the International Whaling Commission is trying to save the existing stocks of whales from extinction. Also, the Intergovernmental Oceanographic Commission, sponsored by the United Nations Educational, Scientific and Cultural Organization, monitors the oceans, conducts scientific research, and promotes the international exchange of oceanographic information.

As early as 1930 an international conference at The Hague in the Netherlands tried to put together various separate elements of maritime law into treaty form, but it was unsuccessful. However, later United Nations efforts to establish rules for ocean use were more productive.

The first UN Conference on the Law of the Sea, held in Geneva in 1958, produced four treaties—the Convention on the Territorial Sea and the Contiguous Zone,

The UN has long sought to preserve the sea and its resources for use by all the nations of the world. Here, a barrier is installed in the ocean to prevent beach erosion and encourage the return of marine life.

the Convention on the High Seas, the Convention on the Continental Shelf, and the Convention on Fishing and Conservation of the Living Resources of the High Seas, all of which came into force in the 1960s among the states that ratified them. The conventions not only organized and updated long-standing international maritime practices and customs; they also broke new ground by dealing with the issue of who has rights to the continental shelf (the shallow floor of the sea that extends out from continents, often as far as a hundred or so miles). This has only recently become an issue because of modern technology that makes possible the exploitation of oil and mineral resources on the ocean floor.

The second UN conference on the Law of the Sea, held in 1960, was not able to reach agreement about territorial sea and fishing zones, so the claims of individual countries continued unchecked. Some countries claimed jurisdiction as far as 200 miles out into the ocean, not just over seabed resources but also over navigation.

Faced with such a variety of national claims, the United Nations convened a new conference to create a single, comprehensive treaty. In preparation for the conference the General Assembly established the Sea-Bed Committee to study all aspects of the peaceful uses of the ocean floor and its resources beyond the limits of national jurisdiction.

Strongly influenced by Ambassador Pardo of Malta, the General Assembly in 1970 unanimously adopted the Sea-Bed Committee's declaration of principles, which stated that "the sea-bed and ocean floor, and the subsoil thereof, beyond the limits of national jurisdiction . . . as well as the resources of the area are the common heritage of mankind." The committee made it clear that the ocean floor was not subject to national claims and was not to be ex-

*The path to any UN treaty is a long and arduous one, filled with many meetings and conferences. Here, delegates gather for the Fourth Session of the Third United Nations Conference on the Law of the Sea.*

plored or exploited except under the authority of an appropriate international body.

Preparations for the third United Nations Conference on the Law of the Sea lasted six years. The business of the conference itself, which was the writing of the Convention on the Law of the Sea, took another nine years—from the brief opening organizational session in 1973 to the closing session in 1982.

The first version of the Convention on the Law of the Sea, which was completed in 1975, underwent several major revisions during the next seven years. The conference approved the final text of the convention at the UN headquarters in New York on April 30, 1982. At the signing ceremony later in the year at Montego Bay, Jamaica, on December 10, 117 countries signed the new Convention on the Law of the Sea—the largest number of signatures ever put on an international treaty on the first day of its signing. By the end of the two-year signing period, 159 countries had signed the convention, more countries than had signed any other international treaty.

Besides approving, slightly changing, and increasing the authority of the four treaties drafted in 1958 at the first UN Law of the Sea Conference, the Convention on the Law of the Sea added important new provisions about an exclusive economic zone, the rights of landlocked countries, an authority for the common area beyond national jurisdiction, the protection of the marine environment, and ocean research.

The extent of the offshore sea, previously claimed by different countries at 3, 4, 6, 12, and up to 200 miles and left unspecified in the 1958 treaty, was fixed at 12 miles with an additional 12-mile zone for enforcing regulations against smuggling. The 1982 convention also provided an exclusive economic zone that extends to at least 200 miles from shore and to 350 miles or even more under certain circumstances.

Coastal states retain control over the natural resources of the sea and the seabed below in these zones, but not jurisdiction over navigation. Any minerals mined from the continental shelf beyond 200 miles are subject to a royalty to be paid to an International Seabed Authority, which will benefit primarily developing countries.

Under the convention, countries must settle disputes over the interpretation and application of the Law of the Sea peacefully. They must submit disputes either to arbitration (judgment), to the International Court of Justice, or to the International Tribunal on the Law of the Sea, which the convention established, and accept the decision as binding.

The most controversial parts of the 1982 convention are those that set aside the ocean floor beyond national jurisdiction (called the "Area") as the common heritage of mankind and create an International Seabed Authority charged with regulating deep-seabed mining in the Area. The initial opposition of the United States and other industrialized countries to the convention involved their dissatisfaction with seabed mining provisions.

# HIGH SEAS FISHING

"No region of the world is immune to the impact of uncontrolled fishing and its inevitable results," said Satya Nandan of Fiji, chairman of the first UN Conference on Straddling Fish Stocks and Highly Migratory Fish Stocks.

The conference, which grew out of the Rio Earth Summit, met in July 1993 and again in March and August 1994. Using the 1982 UN Convention on the Law of the Sea as the basis for its work, the conference addressed the problem of the world's dwindling supply of fish.

Because the high seas have been freely exploited for years and because more fishing is now being done beyond the 200-mile exclusive economic zones established by the Law of the Sea, many species of fish are now either depleted or overfished.

Overfishing not only affects many tuna species, which prefer the open ocean, but also "straddling stocks." Even though straddling stocks, such as Atlantic cod and Alaskan pollack, spend much of their time in coastal waters, they often swim out past the 200-mile limit where other nations are allowed to catch them.

Today in Canada more than 30,000 people are losing their livelihood because of overfishing in the ocean. Species such as cod, flounder, and redfish straddle the 200-mile limit of Canada's exclusive economic zone off Newfoundland. Overfishing by other nations outside that limit has contributed to the depletion of straddling stocks in Canadian waters over the past five years.

Uncontrolled ocean fishing not only affects maritime countries such as Canada but also diminishes the ocean's resources for future generations.

*Fishermen in India haul in their catch.*

*In 1955, the International Court of Justice prepares to hear a dispute between the governments of India and Portugal concerning the right of passage over Indian territory.*

Under the terms of the convention, governments and private companies may obtain licenses to conduct mining operations in the Area, but they must follow the International Seabed Authority's rule about royalties, fees, and production regulations. However, to receive a permit each company must submit two different mining claims (with maps) to the authority. The authority will then choose one of them to be developed by its own operating agency, called the "Enterprise." Government and private companies that receive a permit to mine the ocean floor are required to share their technology with the Enterprise. So far the International Seabed Authority has received registration applications from pioneer investors in deep-seabed mining from France, India, Japan, China, and a group of several Eastern European countries, including Russia.

Although more than 60 nations went on to ratify the Law of the Sea, the United States and other industrialized nations refused. They opposed the deep-seabed min-ing provisions of the treaty, especially the power of the International Seabed Authority to regulate and intervene in matters related to mining the ocean floor. They viewed the regulations on private corporations as too restrictive and worried that the treaty could be amended to exclude private enterprise altogether. However, the new U.S. administration that took office in 1992 negotiated changes in the treaty that made it friendlier to business and more acceptable to the United States and other industrial countries. On June 30, 1994, American Secretary of State Warren Christopher announced that the U.S. Administration would sign the Law of the Sea treaty.

The Convention on the Law of the Sea, which took effect in November 1994, puts more than half the area of the world under international control and grants an international body the authority to govern and develop it. The Law of the Sea is a very large and important step in the direction of world government, on the high seas at least.

## UN Legal Responsibilities

The main legal responsibilities of the United Nations are to use law to settle international conflicts and to write international law, such as the Law of the Sea. The UN Charter states specifically that one of the purposes of the UN is to maintain international peace and security by resolving international disputes "in conformity with the principles of justice and international law."

One of the General Assembly's responsibilities is to initiate "studies and make recommendations for the purpose of . . . encouraging the progressive development of international law." Within the General Assembly, legal matters are the responsibility of the assembly's Sixth Committee. The assembly has also created legal bodies that report to it, such as the International Law Commission. The commission's reports go to the Sixth Committee, where they are debated before the General Assembly takes them up in full session.

## The International Court of Justice

The purpose of the International Court of Justice (ICJ), also called the World Court, which the UN Charter defines as "the principal judicial [body] of the United Nations," is to settle disputes that states bring to it. The General Assembly and the Security Council, voting separately, elect 15 judges (5 judges every three years for nine-year terms) to the World Court from a slate of candidates nominated by legal experts from different countries. Both the General Assembly and the Security Council must be satisfied that the candidates are international legal scholars of the highest order.

The Statute of the International Court of Justice calls for judges to be selected on the basis of their individual qualifications and that "the body as a whole [should be represented by] the main forms of civiliza-tion and the principal legal systems of the world." A candidate must win a majority of votes in both the General Assembly and the Security Council to be elected to the court. No two judges may be of the same nationality. Countries that are parties to the ICJ statute without being UN members are permitted to nominate candidates and take part in the General Assembly vote. The World Court elects its own president and vice president for three-year terms.

Although some of the powers of the International Court of Justice are set forth in the United Nations Charter itself, a much fuller description of the scope and purpose of the World Court is contained in the Statute of the International Court of Justice, which is a part of the UN Charter and serves as the court's constitution.

Although all UN members are automatically members of the court and bound by its statute, nonmembers can join the court "on conditions to be determined in each case by the General Assembly upon the recommendation of the Security Council." For example, Switzerland, which is not a member of the UN because of its centuries-old tradition of neutrality, is a member of the International Court of Justice. Likewise, Liechtenstein and San Marino were members of the ICJ long before they joined the United Nations in 1990 and 1992, respectively.

*A group of visitors tours the Peace Palace in The Hague, the headquarters of the International Court of Justice.*

A quorum of nine judges is needed to decide a case, and a majority vote determines the outcome. Decisions cannot be appealed. If there is a tie, the president of the court is authorized to cast the tie-breaking vote. If there is no judge of the same nationality as the party or parties to a case before the court, the party or parties may choose their own judge to join the other judges in hearing the case with full voting rights. The court's jurisdiction also extends to giving opinions on legal questions that the principal bodies of the United Nations and its specialized agencies ask for.

The court reaches its decisions by interpreting and applying treaties, international law and custom, and general legal principles recognized by most countries. Decisions handed down by national courts and the teachings of respected international judicial authorities may also be used.

Cases submitted to the ICJ cover a wide range of issues. A large number of them have to do with territorial and maritime disputes about the placement of boundaries and claims to land and water. For example, in a 1953 case involving France

and the United Kingdom the court declared that certain small islands in the English Channel belonged to the British. In 1959 the court supported the claims of Belgium to a parcel of land near its frontier with the Netherlands.

In 1986 the ICJ was asked to settle a frontier dispute between the African nations of Burkina Faso and Mali. The court selected a special five-judge chamber to hear the case, and the decision it rendered resolved the conflict.

A special ICJ court considered a maritime boundary dispute between Canada and the United States in the Gulf of Maine that began in the 1960s. The two countries had asked the ICJ to convene a special court (sometimes called a "chamber") to establish the boundary between their respective continental shelves and fishing zones. On October 12, 1984, the ruling of the special five-judge chamber established the maritime boundary between Canada and the United States in the Gulf of Maine.

Other ICJ cases have involved maritime disputes. In 1949 the court found Albania responsible for damage that mines in

Representatives of Denmark and the Netherlands prepare to present their maritime dispute with Germany to the World Court.

its territorial waters caused to passing British warships. In a 1951 dispute over fishing rights between Britain and Norway, the court ruled in favor of Norway by declaring that Norway's claim to waters off its shores was in line with international law. In 1969 the court resolved competing claims to the North Sea continental shelf by West Germany, Denmark, and the Netherlands.

The United Kingdom and West Germany brought suit against Iceland in 1972 as a way of impressing Iceland with their determination to resolve the longstanding dispute over Iceland's decision to extend its fishing boundaries. The World Court's ruling in favor of the British and Germans helped all three countries narrow their differences in later negotiations.

*The title page of the International Court of Justice's verdict in a case between the United Kingdom and Albania.*

Disputes about the Mediterranean continental shelf were submitted to the ICJ by Libya and Tunisia in 1982 and Libya and Malta in 1985. The parties asked the World Court to decide which principles and rules of international law could be used to decide their disputes. The court's judgment helped the countries settle their competing claims peacefully.

More recent territorial and maritime boundary cases brought before the ICJ have involved disputes between El Salvador and Honduras, Guinea-Bissau and Senegal, Libya and Chad, Qatar and Bahrain, Finland and Denmark, and Greenland (a possession of Denmark) and Jan Mayen (an island in the Arctic Ocean claimed by Norway).

In 1973 the court was helpful in breaking Pakistan's stalled negotiations with India over the release of Pakistani prisoners of war captured in East Pakistan (now Bangladesh) two years earlier. After Pakistan put the case before the court, then withdrew it, a final agreement for the release of the prisoners was signed in April 1974.

The United States has been party to cases before the ICJ as a result of conflicts with Iran and Nicaragua. On November 29, 1979, the United States began proceedings against Iran for its seizure of the American embassy and embassy workers in Teheran. On December 15, the World Court, by unanimous vote, ordered the Iranian government to return the embassy and its hostages to the control of the United States. Iran, which did not take part in the proceedings, ignored the order of the court. The court based its decision against Iran on the 1961 and 1963 Vienna Conventions about diplomatic relations between countries and on long-established and widely recognized principles of international law.

The ICJ also declared that Iran had to pay the United States for damages caused by its actions and that the court would settle the amount of the reparation (payment) if agreement between the parties could not be reached. However, before the World Court could decide on the amount, the two countries reached an agreement in Algiers on January 19, 1981. At the request of the United States the court removed the reparation claim from the list of the upcoming cases the court was scheduled to hear.

The dispute between the United States and Nicaragua was submitted to the court in 1984. The Nicaraguan government, ruled by pro-Cuban Sandinistas who came to power

by overthrowing an American-backed government, accused the United States of violating international law by bringing military force to bear against it and by interfering in its internal affairs. The United States claimed the court did not have jurisdiction to judge this case, but the court disagreed and declared that Nicaragua had the right to present the case. In 1986, the court declared the United States acted improperly and must cease its hostile activities. While the United States did not publicly recognize the validity of the court's decision, its ruling may have contributed to making American policy toward Nicaragua less hostile.

Other ICJ cases have involved questions of diplomatic protection, such as rights of asylum in Latin America (*Colombia* v. *Peru*) in 1950 and the rights of American citizens in Morocco (*France* v. *United States*) in 1951. In a 1970 case the World Court ruled against the right of Belgium to protect the money Belgian shareholders had invested in a Canadian company in Spain. In 1989 an ICJ chamber rejected a U.S.

claim for compensation against Italy in a case that involved the seizure of a company in Sicily owned by American corporations.

Australia and New Zealand brought a case to the ICJ against France in 1973 over radioactive fallout from French nuclear tests in the Pacific. The World Court ordered France to stop further testing until the court reached a final decision. When France announced it was stopping its nuclear tests permanently after 1974, the court stopped deliberating the case.

The International Court of Justice also issues what are called advisory opinions (opinions about cases and situations that do not have the force of law) when the General Assembly and the Security Council request it to do so. The World Court issued four advisory opinions having to do with Namibia, three of them requested by the General Assembly. The 1971 advisory opinion on the issue requested by the Security Council declared that South Africa's continuing presence in Namibia was illegal and that South Africa should immediately end its occupation.

A 1962 advisory opinion over the issue of the refusal of certain states to contribute to the expense of peacekeeping operations in the Middle East and the Congo declared that such expenses were to be borne by all UN member states in accordance with the charter. A 1988 advisory opinion declared that the United States was obligated to submit to arbitration its dispute with the United Nations about its order to close the New York office of the Palestine Liberation Organization (PLO) observer mission.

In spite of the impressive variety of its case load, the International Court of Justice has been used sparingly. In its 50 years of existence the World Court has only handled about 60 cases, and less than half of those have resulted in a judgment. The rest of the cases were dismissed either because the court lacked the jurisdiction (authority) to try the case, because the group applying for a case was not a proper member of the UN, or because one of the nations involved requested the case be dropped.

Part of the reason the ICJ has not been utilized more is limited access. Only countries—rather than individuals or organizations—are allowed to be a party to a dispute before the World Court, and only the General Assembly, the Security Council, or other authorized UN bodies or specialized agencies are permitted to request an advisory opinion. Furthermore, World Court proceedings are expensive and slow. Parties have to wait at least two years from the time they submit their case to the time they receive a judgment. For this reason most parties prefer to settle their disputes by quiet negotiations.

Nonetheless, the World Court has advanced the cause of international law. By successfully settling a number of important cases, it has strengthened the goal of ending

*The General Assembly and the Security Council can request the Court to issue advisory opinions, which do not have the force of law. This advisory opinion declared that South Africa's occupation of Namibia was illegal.*

conflict by law rather than by force. ICJ decisions, widely cited, have contributed to the development of law and law courts worldwide. While it cannot be said that the World Court has ushered in a new era of international law, it has taken an important step in that direction.

In his 1992 report on ways to strengthen the United Nations, *An Agenda for Peace,* Secretary-General Boutros Boutros-Ghali recommended more use of the World Court. "The docket [schedule] of the International Court of Justice has grown fuller but it remains an under-used resource for the peaceful [judgment] of disputes," he wrote. "Greater reliance on the Court would be an important contribution to United Nations peacemaking."

He recommended that all UN member states accept the general jurisdiction of the court before the end of the UN Decade of International Law, in the year 2000, and that they use the special chambers court when submission of a dispute to the full court is not practical. He also recommended that UN bodies turn to the court more frequently for advisory opinions and that the trust fund established to assist countries unable to afford the cost involved in bringing a dispute to the court be supported more fully.

## The International Law Commission
The General Assembly established the International Law Commission (ILC) in 1947 to develop and write international law. The commission, which meets annually in Geneva, consists of 34 members elected to five-year terms by the General Assembly. They serve the UN as legal experts rather than as representatives of their governments.

The commission offers the first versions of articles on subjects of international

# WAR CRIMES IN THE FORMER YUGOSLAVIA

In 1992 eleven-year-old Lenida Konjic was the only one in her family left after Serb militiamen raped and shot her mother and took her father and brothers to the mass execution of all the males in the village. Lenida somehow managed to make her way to the Bosnian city of Bosanski Novi and later was lucky to reach a refugee camp in a United Nations convoy. "At night we were so scared we couldn't sleep," she said about her time in Bosanski Novi. "We would just wait to be slaughtered."

Topcagic Muharem, 18, the only Muslim survivor in the village of Koritnik, said he will never forget the day Serbs herded more than 50 Muslim men, women, and children into a basement, tossed in hand grenades, then joked that the screams of the dying sounded "just like a mosque."

In response to the growing number of reported war crimes, the Security Council in October 1992 created a Commission of Experts to investigate and collect evidence, and in February 1993 it passed a resolution that established a War Crimes Tribunal for atrocities committed in the former Yugoslavia, with the Commission of Experts as its evidence-gathering wing.

The War Crimes Tribunal has 11 judges from around the world, chosen by the General Assembly. The court has adopted rules of evidence and as of mid-1994 was ready to receive proposed indictments at its seat in The Hague.

One problem with the proposed tribunal is that it still lacks a chief prosecutor, although the court regards the deputy, Graham Blewitt of Australia, as empowered to act in the absence of a chief. Another drawback has been that as long as peace negotiations are possible to bring the war to an end, there has been little interest in offending the parties by charging them with war crimes.

Nonetheless, evidence is being collected by both governments and nongovernmental organizations (NGOs). The human rights group Helsinki Watch has a list of Serbian officials it would like to see prosecuted.

The Commission of Experts already has reports of beatings, torture, starvation, and murder at more than 200 camps and detention centers, any one of which could provide evidence for many convictions. One of the best pieces of evidence is a mass grave outside Vukovar (one of the more than 100 mass graves that have been reported) that is reportedly full of the corpses of about 200 Croatians dragged out of a hospital and massacred by Serbs. There are also detailed reports about the murderous Serbian campaign of "ethnic cleansing" in the Prijedor area of northern Bosnia in 1992.

*The 11 judges of the International Tribunal on War Crimes in the former Yugoslavia meet for the first time in November 1993.*

law, either chosen by the commission or referred to it by the General Assembly or the Economic and Social Council. Most of these first versions of articles, such as the four articles that make up the Law of the Sea adopted in Geneva in 1958, serve as the basis for conventions and treaties that are later adopted by the assembly or by international conferences.

The International Law Commission produced a series of conventions about diplomatic immunity (the agreement between nations that diplomats serving in foreign countries cannot be arrested and tried for violations of the host countries' laws). They were the Vienna Convention on Diplomatic Relations (1961), the Vienna Convention on Consular Relations (1963), the Convention on Special Missions (1969), and the Convention on the Prevention and Punishment of Crimes against Internationally Protected Persons, including Diplomatic Agents (1973).

In the early 1990s the International Law Commission adopted the Code of Crimes against the Peace and Security of Mankind, which had been on the commission's schedule since 1947. The Code of Crimes against the Peace and Security of Mankind identifies as crimes the following: aggression; threat of aggression; intervention; colonial and other forms of foreign domination; international terrorism; the recruitment, financing, training, or use of mercenaries; illicit drug traffic; genocide;

apartheid; systematic or mass human rights violations; exceptionally serious war crimes; and willful and severe damage to the environment. The International Law Commission also discussed the idea of establishing an international criminal court that would be authorized to try crimes under the code.

In the early 1990s the ILC worked on issues having to do with state responsibility, the status of the diplomatic courier and the diplomatic bag not accompanied by diplomatic courier (the way countries often send messages to their diplomats overseas), international liability (who is at fault and must pay money) for injuries suffered from acts not prohibited by international law, and relations between states and international organizations.

In 1993, at the request of the General Assembly, the International Law Commission drafted and presented to the Assembly a 67-article preliminary draft statute for a new court with jurisdiction over violations of international treaties and law.

The new court would have jurisdiction over such matters as genocide, apartheid, prisoners of war, protection of civilians in time of war, hostage taking, and other issues addressed by international treaties. The court would also have jurisdiction over national laws when the states party to the case agree. The creation of such a court would be a giant step forward for international law, for the world, and for the United Nations in the 21st century.

CHAPTER 11

# Specialized Agencies

*Children at a day care center in Tanzania operated by a French non-governmental organization. Over half of the children at the center are AIDS orphans.*

With a quick smile and flashing eyes, Wingston Zulu of Zambia stood on the threshold of adulthood. It was 1990 and the promise of a scholarship to study abroad opened wide the door to an exciting new adventure.

"We were supposed to go to the Soviet Union in about five days time," he told a World Health Organization (WHO) team in Lasaka, "so they asked us to go for a quick medical check-up."

That routine examination brought devastating news. Wingston learned that he was HIV positive. That meant that he had contracted the human immunodeficiency virus that leads to the crippling acquired immune deficiency syndrome called AIDS. Transmitted primarily through sexual intercourse, HIV breaks down the body's defenses, eventually causing a series of AIDS-related illnesses.

"I couldn't believe it," said 26-year-old Wingston, remembering the day his group received their medical test results. "There were seven of us who went and five of us were found to be HIV positive."

Unfortunately, there is little hope for Wingston and the one in four other Zambian adults who are currently HIV positive. There is no cure for AIDS, and it is highly unlikely that an effective vaccine will be ready by the end of the century.

## The World Health Organization

The World Health Organization is but one of the 17 specialized agencies and two independent intergovernmental agencies which are related to the United Nations by special agreements. These 19 agencies are separate organizations that work with the United Nations and with each other under the supervision of the UN Economic and Social Council. Some of the most important of these organizations are discussed below.

At the 46th World Health Assembly held in Geneva in May 1993, the World Health Organization discussed the health of humankind around the globe. The assembly, which governs the World Health Organization, meets annually to direct the agency's work and make decisions about its policy, programs, and budget.

The focus of discussions at the 1993 assembly was WHO's campaign against deadly diseases—not only AIDS but also tuberculosis, malaria, poliomyelitis, leprosy, onchocerciasis (river blindness), tetanus, diphtheria, and the varied lung infections and diarrheal diseases that are the leading killers of infants and young children.

Dr. Hiroshi Nakajima, reelected by the assembly for a second five-year term as World Health Organization director-general, described the moral mission of his agency as "the building of universal peace through health for all." In 1977 the World Health Organization had declared the goal of the agency to be nothing less than "Health for All by the Year 2000."

While there has been progress in several areas—for example, in the WHO campaign to immunize 90 percent of all the world's children against the major communicable childhood diseases by the year 2000—deadly illnesses like AIDS and tuberculosis (TB) are spreading rapidly.

The spread of AIDS continues to be a global crisis. The World Health Organiza-

tion reported that in 1993 about 2 million more people had been infected with HIV, the virus that causes AIDS, most of them in Africa. Michael Merson, director-general of the WHO Global Program on AIDS, reported that nearly 70 percent of the world's 15 million people infected with HIV are in Africa. In some African cities, as many as one third of all people aged 15 to 49 are infected. Hardest hit are young people, since 60 per cent of new infections in Africa are among 15- to 24-year-olds.

The World Health Organization Global Program on AIDS, a major international campaign to control and prevent the deadly disease, has been in place since 1987. Since the AIDS crisis touches so many aspects of the health and development of nations in Africa and elsewhere, WHO works closely with the UN Development Programme, UNESCO, the UN Population Fund, and other UN and nongovernmental agencies.

On April 26—shortly before the 1993 World Health Assembly met—the World

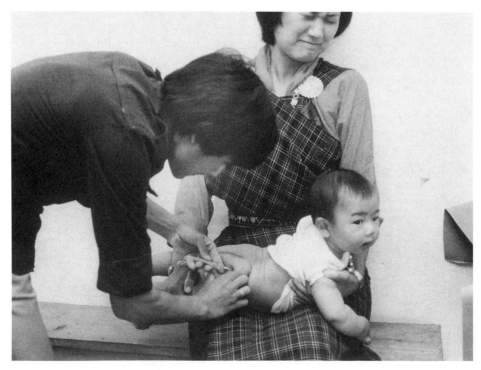

*A mother winces as her child receives a vaccination in Bhutan. The World Health Organization is waging a campaign to immunize the world's children against the major childhood diseases.*

# FIGHTING AIDS
# IN MADAGASCAR

A UN worker drives a jeep through the red-light district of Madagascar's capital distributing condoms and educational material. It is part of a campaign supported by the World Health Organization (WHO) to combat the spread of AIDS on this island nation off the eastern coast of Africa.

"At first we only distributed condoms to prostitutes," said one worker. "Now we also distribute them to their clients. Our goal is to limit sexually transmitted diseases, including the AIDS virus."

The campaign is aimed at people like Eva, who is the only bread-winner in her family, since the father of her three-year-old daughter went to prison for stealing. Eva also has to support her younger sister. Eva is a waitress, but because her salary is not enough to live on, she is also a prostitute. After her regular work, she goes to a disco to look for customers.

Prostitution is a growth industry in Madagascar because of wide-spread poverty. Although AIDS has not yet affected the island to the degree that it has countries on the African mainland, the risk of an epidemic is great.

To prevent the spread of sexually transmitted diseases, the government's Population Ministry, with the help of UN agencies, has embarked on a program that includes blood testing as well as education. UN agencies also help women set up small businesses that will provide them with alternative sources of income.

The AIDS crisis is spreading as more people are infected through heterosexual contacts. WHO predicts that by the year 2000 up to 18 million people will be infected worldwide. "If not controlled," warned former UN Secretary-General Javier Pérez de Cuéllar, "AIDS may ultimately prove to be the single greatest assault, beyond the deprivations of poverty, on the health and development of human beings."

Health Organization declared TB to be a worldwide emergency and warned that it would kill 30 million people over the next decade unless urgent measures were taken to combat it.

"Tuberculosis is humanity's greatest killer and it is out of control in many parts of the world," declared Dr. Arata Kochi, manager of the WHO Tuberculosis Program. "The disease, preventable and treatable, has been grossly neglected and no country is immune to it."

The World Health Organization is also renewing its campaign to control the spread of malaria and dengue, another mosquito-borne disease. Coordinated by the UN Spe-

*Liberians line up for a smallpox vaccination in 1963. Eventually, the fight against smallpox was won, with the only remaining samples of the virus preserved in laboratories in Russia and the United States.*

cial Program for Research and Training in Tropical Disease—a joint operation of the World Health Organization, the UN Development Programme, and the World Bank—the first human clinical trial of a promising new drug for the treatment of malaria recently began in the Netherlands.

The World Health Organization is almost as old as the UN itself. The idea for it originated at the United Nations Conference in San Francisco in 1945, and the organization officially came into existence on April 7, 1948 (April 7 is now observed as World Health Day).

Since its founding, the World Health Organization has promoted and coordinated research, disease prevention programs, and primary health care; conducted immunization campaigns; and provided countries with assistance to improve their health care. WHO works with other United Nations agencies, governments, and nongovernmental organizations to educate people about health issues—care of mothers and pregnant women, general health care, food, nutrition, safe water, sanitation, immunization against infectious diseases, treatment of common diseases and injuries, and the administration of drugs. The World Health Organization also helps countries build hospitals and medical and nursing schools.

## The Food and Agriculture Organization

The Food and Agriculture Organization (FAO) is the UN's largest specialized agency. Since it was founded in 1945 at a conference in Quebec, FAO has become the leading international organization for food and agriculture and the central UN agency for rural development. The goal of FAO is nothing less than the elimination of hunger throughout the world.

Member nations of FAO seek to raise the levels of nutrition and health standards of their people; improve the production, processing, marketing, and distribution of food; promote rural development; and help other countries solve their food shortages. FAO provides programs that improve soil and water management, increase crop and livestock production, encourage agricultural research, and make the transfer of farming technology to developing countries easier. The organization also promotes the conservation of forest and other natural resources; the prudent use of seed, fertilizers, and pesticides; the control of animal diseases; and the development of renewable sources of energy. FAO works closely with the International Fund for Agricultural Development, another UN specialized agency.

The Food and Agriculture Organization has been especially involved in dealing with food shortages in Africa. In North Africa the main threat to the food supply has been the screwworm fly, a parasitic insect that develops in sores and wounds or in the nostrils of warm-blooded animals. FAO and the International Fund for Agricultural Development invited representatives from donor countries and international organizations to pledging conferences on Screwworm Eradication in North Africa to raise money for projects designed to break the life cycle of the screwworm fly. Projects, jointly funded by FAO, the UN Development Programme, and the African Development Bank, operate out of the Rome-based Screwworm Emergency Center for North Africa, which was set up at the FAO headquarters in 1990.

FAO's Global Information and Early Warning System provides up-to-date information on food supplies around the world and identifies countries threatened by food shortages. FAO also has a Food Security Assistance Scheme that helps developing countries establish national food reserves. The Food and Agriculture Organization and the United Nations jointly sponsor the World Food Program, which collects food from member states and distributes it to areas beset by hunger and poverty.

The General Conference of FAO, composed of all its member states, meets every other year to assess the state of the world's food and agriculture, make policy, review programs, and approve the FAO budget. October 16—the day the Food and Agriculture Organization was founded—has been observed annually since 1979 as World Food Day.

## The World Bank

The purpose of the World Bank—the world's largest international lending body—is to channel the financial resources of developed countries to developing countries to raise their standard of living. As the largest single source of development aid for the developing world, the World Bank formerly financed the building of roads, railroads, and power stations, but now it concentrates more on projects that benefit poor people more directly.

A billion people around the world are now living on less than a dollar a day. To combat poverty the World Bank has adopted a two-part approach—encouragement of economic growth and improvement of social services. Today the World Bank helps poor people by getting them to participate in rural development and agriculture and education programs.

Environmental considerations are also an important factor in World Bank loans. Two years after its Environmental Department was established in 1987, the World Bank embarked on a policy of having scien-

*With the help of the Food and Agriculture Organization, anti-locust campaigns were launched throughout North Africa in the 1950s. Here, workers feed poison bait to locusts in Morocco.*

*Helped by two loans from the World Bank, South Africa was able to build this power station in the 1950s.*

tifically prepared environmental impact assessments made on intended projects. Because the World Bank has 1,800 projects worth several hundred billion dollars in about 100 countries around the world, it is helping make environmentally sustainable development a central focus in the plans of developing countries.

The World Bank consists of four agencies—the International Bank for Reconstruction and Development, the International Finance Corporation, the International Development Association, and the Multilateral Investment Guarantee Agency.

The World Bank's International Bank for Reconstruction and Development provides loans and technical assistance to countries for agriculture, rural development, and the construction of infrastructure—ports, power facilities, roads, and railways. The Bank for Reconstruction and Development came out of the same 1944 Bretton Woods Conference that produced the International Monetary Fund.

The charter of the Bank for Reconstruction and Development says that loans must be made only for productive purposes (for the kinds of projects already mentioned). Also, the loans must have a good chance of being repaid, and the bank must be sure that the funds are not available from other sources on reasonable terms.

The Bank for Reconstruction and Development is unique among intergovernmental organizations in that it relies primarily on private investors. Most of the money the bank lends comes from its own borrowing on world markets, recycled loans, and the sale of parts of its loans to other investors, most often commercial banks. It makes loans to member nations, their political subdivisions, or to private businesses operating in their territories.

The International Finance Corporation was established in 1956 to provide special help to the Bank of Reconstruction and Development's least developed member nations. The corporation supports private economic growth through the use of domestic and foreign capital (money) and lends money to private enterprises that contribute to development by attracting capital and experienced management and turning them into productive investments.

International Finance Corporation investments have been mostly in manufacturing, but they also have been in mining, energy, utilities, agriculture, and tourism. While the corporation is associated with the International Bank for Reconstruction and Development, its funds are separate. The corporation receives a wide range of services from the bank, and its membership is open to all International Bank of Reconstruction and Development members.

The International Development Association was established in 1960 to provide the same kind of development assistance as the International Bank of Reconstruction and Development, but on easier terms. The association provides interest-free loans (called "credits") to poor countries that the bank does not provide. Most association credits are for 50 years, with only a small fee charged for administrative costs.

To qualify for an International Development Association credit a country must be very poor and have a severe balance-of-payments problem (meaning that more money leaves the country than comes in). The applicant must also have a genuine commitment to development and have sufficient internal stability to benefit from a long-term credit.

The Multilateral Investment Guarantee Agency was established in 1988 to increase the flow of investment to developing countries by providing long-term political risk insurance. Investors are insured against such risks as the seizure of property by a government, transfer of money from one currency to another, civil unrest, and war.

They are also provided with advisory and consultative services.

## The International Labour Organization

The International Labour Organization (ILO), established in 1919 as an independent group under the League of Nations, became the UN's first specialized agency in 1946. Its purpose is to set international labor standards that will improve working conditions around the world. The ILO motto is "Poverty anywhere constitutes a danger to prosperity everywhere." Agency experts try to help member nations with vocational training, manpower planning,

*Pakistani farmers deliver sugarcane to a paper mill. The mill, built in the 1970s, was the first to use sugarcane residue as its principal raw material. The International Finance Corporation provided funds to build the plant.*

employment and management policies, occupational health and safety practices, social security, cooperatives, and small handicraft industries.

The ILO is unique among international intergovernmental organizations in that it allows workers and employers, as well as governments, to make agency decisions. At the annual meeting of the ILO's supreme body—the International Labour Conference—each member nation has four delegates: two represent the government, one represents employers, and one represents workers.

The International Labour Organization has adopted more than 300 international agreements and recommendations on wages, work hours, minimum ages for employment, workmen's compensation, social insurance, industrial safety, and human rights, but it cannot force governments to improve working conditions. The International Labour Organization promotes advanced study and training through the International Institute for Labor Studies in Geneva, which brings together experts from around the world, and the International Center

*This worker routinely handles metals that reach a temperature of 950° F. The International Labour Organization encourages member nations to maintain high standards for worker safety.*

# CHILDREN WHO WORK

*Children carry heavy loads at a brick factory in Bogotá, Colombia.*

The suffering that 19th-century factory owners used to inflict on European and North American children is now being felt by more than 100 million children around the world. Today's children pan gold in sweltering, malaria-ridden jungles in South America, risk physical deformity in rundown leather-tanning workshops in the Middle East, and face sharks and suffer ruptured eardrums on Asian deep-sea fishing operations.

Poor parents trapped in city slums and poverty-stricken rural areas often send their children to work because they have no other choice. There may be no schools, or they may cost too much, or the quality may be so low and the dropout rate so high that the parents see them as useless.

The problem of child labor has been a special concern of the International Labour Organization (ILO) since it was founded in 1919. *Combating Child Labour,* a book published by the ILO office in Geneva in 1988, details many aspects of the problem worldwide.

Even in places where there are laws against child labor, employers ignore the law, knowing it cannot be enforced by a handful of overworked inspectors unable to cope with thousands of illegal enterprises operating in the back alleys of a huge city. Moreover, most national labor laws have big loopholes. They often exempt family businesses and educational and training institutions, and many countries exempt agriculture and domestic service as well.

ILO studies show that the most effective work on behalf of children is being done by voluntary grass-roots groups. In the Philippines private groups set up mobile schools in tents near places where children work, and in Brazil they are trying to help the government cope with the millions of children who live and work in the streets.

Some children have organized themselves and have provided leadership to their communities. In 1976 a group of Peruvian teenagers launched Manthoc, a social action movement, in southern Lima to provide food, clothing, and medicine to poor people and to help care for small children and the elderly. Today, children continue to run the organization with help from Catholic Youth volunteers.

for Advanced Technical and Vocational Training in Turin, Italy, which trains directors of technical and vocational schools, union leaders, managers, instructors, and technicians, mostly from developing countries.

### The International Monetary Fund

The International Monetary Fund (IMF) originated at the same International Monetary and Financial Conference at Bretton Woods in 1944 that created the World Bank. Both agencies formally began work when the Articles of Agreement—known as the Bretton Woods Agreement—came into force in December 1945.

The IMF promotes international monetary cooperation, trade expansion, exchange stability (stability in the value of the various world currencies, for instance the dollar, pound, yen, and mark), a system of currency transactions between members, and the elimination of foreign exchange rules that hinder world trade. The three main duties the Bretton Woods Agreement gave to the IMF were to administer a code of conduct for currency exchange rates and payment transactions (how payments between countries are handled), to help members observe a code of conduct with respect to their trade imbalances (when goods imported do not equal goods exported), and to provide an organization where members can consult with each other about international money matters.

The IMF seeks to help nations with their balance-of-payments problems without having them resort to methods that might reduce national or international prosperity (such as seizing property or making other countries pay high fees to export goods into a country). By doing so, the IMF tries to make the international monetary system more stable and help the orderly growth of world trade. When the IMF lends to a member nation that is having trouble repaying its foreign loans, it asks that the nation show how it intends to solve its payments problems so it can repay the IMF within its normal repayment period of three to five years.

Developing countries like Tanzania and Jamaica have criticized the IMF for not understanding their needs. Because the fund was created before most developing countries achieved their independence, they claim that the fund is geared primarily toward solving the problems of developed countries.

Although most developed countries can accept and survive the strict conditions attached to IMF loans (usually involving cuts in public spending and currency devaluations), these same conditions can cause economic hardship as well as social unrest and political instability in developing countries. The economic policies of governments required to adhere to the terms of IMF loans have caused social unrest in Egypt, Zambia, and the Dominican Republic.

In 1987 Managing Director Michel Camdessus proposed a way to provide easy credit to 60 of the world's poorest countries, many of them in Africa. Since then, the fund has found new and more flexible ways to help developing countries by charging lower interest rates and extending the time they are allowed to take to repay their loans.

### The United Nations Educational, Scientific and Cultural Organization

The United Nations Educational, Scientific and Cultural Organization (UNESCO) came into existence in November 1946 to support international cooperation in the fields of education, science, culture, and communications and to increase respect for justice, the rule of law, human rights, and the basic freedoms proclaimed by the UN Charter and the Universal Declaration of Human Rights.

Convinced that ignorance of other people and their customs breeds suspicion, mistrust, and conflict and that the best way to prevent war is through education, UNESCO supports primary education programs designed to eliminate illiteracy and promote the values of freedom, tolerance, and justice.

In December 1993, UNESCO joined UNICEF and the UN Population Fund in sponsoring an education summit in New Delhi, attended by the heads of state of nine of the world's most populous countries—Bangladesh, Brazil, China, Egypt, India, Indonesia, Mexico, Nigeria, and Pakistan. These countries, which account for more than 70 percent of the world's illiterate adults and more than 50 percent of the world's children who are not in school, pledged to increase literacy rates and try to provide a primary education to all their citizens, especially women and girls.

UNESCO also trains teachers and administrators, finances school construction projects, and sponsors studies on racism, the environment, and the origins of war.

UNESCO's cultural programs focus on artistic creativity, the growth of cultures, and the preservation of art, books, monuments, and oral traditions. UNESCO also assists the media in developing countries by promoting cooperation between regional news organizations and conducting studies on the role of the media in economic development.

## Other Specialized Agencies

The International Civil Aviation Organization (ICAO) was created in 1947 to pro-

mote the safe and orderly growth of international aviation. ICAO sets international safety standards for aircraft, pilots, flight crews, air traffic controllers, ground crews, and security personnel at international airports. Its regulations govern international flights, customs, immigration, and procedures for public health officials. More than 165 nations belong to the International Civil Aviation Organization.

The International Fund for Agricultural Development (IFAD) seeks to end hunger and malnutrition in developing

*UNESCO provided the funds to build the Delhi Public Library in India. It now has a stock of more than 60,000 books, and it services more than 70,000 readers a month. Here, a young girl starts to read her book on the steps of the van that serves as a mobile lending library.*

# UNESCO IN INDONESIA

*The ancient Buddhist sanctuary of Borobudur in Java. UNESCO is assisting in the conservation and restoration of this magnificent temple.*

Jogjakarta, in central Java, Indonesia, is known for its beautiful Buddhist temples. Tourists flock there to admire the 9th-century shrine of Borobudur. But for Indonesians, Jogjakarta is more than a cultural attraction. It is also a learning center.

One of its educational institutions is the Multimedia Training Center (MMTC), which with support from UNESCO is training broadcast journalists to staff the country's expanding electronic media.

Indonesia—now the world's fifth-largest country in terms of population—is relying more and more on electronic media to unify the diverse peoples and cultures scattered across the 13,000 islands of the Indonesian archipelago. The state-owned television service has 10 broadcast stations that reach the far-flung population. The government estimates that 141 million people watch television every day.

The training at the Multimedia Training Center is rigorous. The day begins at four in the morning with a wake-up bell, followed by an obligatory military drill and exercise period. Besides completing a demanding academic schedule of classes, homework, and exams, students do fieldwork by visiting the local TV station and practicing on-camera interviews. They also travel to neighboring villages to attend village media awareness groups called *kelompencapirs*. There they gain firsthand information on how government officials monitor the reaction of villagers to government programming.

Victorine Limaswari, a scholarship student at MMTC, wants to become a television producer after she returns to her native island. "I would like to contribute my expertise to increase the quality of broadcasting in our local programming," she said.

With help from the UN, the Multimedia Training Center in Jogjakarta is training television and radio professionals to meet the needs of Indonesia's growing population.

countries by helping them increase their food production and improve nutrition. IFAD concentrates its efforts primarily on rural populations in Africa, Asia, and Latin America which suffer most from hunger and malnutrition. Since it was organized in 1977, IFAD has invested close to $3 billion in more than 300 projects in 100 developing countries.

The International Maritime Organization (IMO) promotes international cooperation on shipping matters by encouraging its member states and other maritime organizations to coordinate their activities and share technical and legal information. The IMO Convention, which was drafted at the 1948 UN Maritime Conference in Geneva and came into force in 1958, set up international regulations having to do with maritime safety, pollution, the training and certification of seafarers, and liability and compensation.

The International Telecommunication Union (ITU), founded in 1875 in Paris as the International Telegraph Union, became a UN specialized agency in 1947. It allocates radio-frequency spectrum and satellite positioning, produces guidelines, regulations, and studies, disseminates telecommunications information, and helps construct telecommunications facilities and equipment in developing countries. The ITU Plenipotentiary Conference meets every five years to set policy, while the Administrative Council, composed of 43 members elected by the Plenipotentiary Conference, meets annually to carry out that policy.

The United Nations Industrial Development Organization (UNIDO) was the first UN body ever converted into a specialized agency when 20 years after the General Assembly created it UNIDO went on to become a specialized agency in 1986. As the UN's central body for industrial development, UNIDO promotes industrialization in developing countries through investment, technical assistance, training programs, and the transfer of technology to and between developing countries.

The Universal Postal Union (UPU), which was established in 1875 by the Berne Treaty, became a UN specialized agency in 1948. UPU regulates international mail delivery and rates and provides technical assistance to postal systems in developing countries. The UPU central authority is the Universal Postal Congress, which meets every five years to review the Universal Postal Convention and its subsidiary agreements.

The World Intellectual Property Organization (WIPO) seeks to protect inventions, trademarks, copyrights, and other forms of industrial, literary, and artistic property by means of treaties, conventions, and agreements. Although it did not become a specialized UN agency until 1974, WIPO's origins go back to the Paris Convention for the Protection of Industrial Property (1883) and the Berne Convention for the Protection of Literary and Artistic

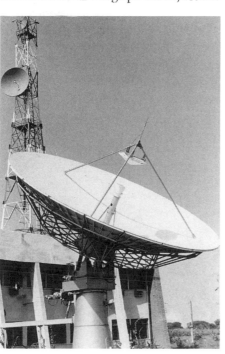

*To keep up with the rapid advances in the telecommunications industry, the government of India sought help from the International Telecommunication Union to construct this earth satellite station in New Delhi.*

*The World Meteoro-
logical Organization
is dedicated to the
international ex-
change of weather
information. This
satellite photograph
shows a storm
developing near
Hawaii.*

Works (1886). WIPO administers the International Union for the Protection of Industrial Property and the International Union for the Protection of Literary and Artistic Works, created by the Paris and Berne Conventions.

The World Meteorological Organization (WMO) is the successor to the International Meteorological Organization, which was established in 1873. Its main business is the international exchange of weather information. WMO's World Weather Watch coordinates all the information gathered from national weather service land stations and space satellites. WMO also tracks climate changes and the effects on the atmosphere of greenhouse gases, acid rain, and ozone layer depletion.

## The International Atomic Energy Agency

The International Atomic Energy Agency (IAEA)—one of the two independent intergovernmental agencies affiliated with the UN—promotes the peaceful use of nuclear energy around the world. However, it is in its capacity as an inspector of nuclear sites that the IAEA is best known. One of the agency's most important responsibilities is to inspect nuclear plants around the world to make sure countries are not using nuclear materials for military purposes in violation of the Non-Proliferation Treaty. IAEA encounters with uncooperative would-be nuclear powers like Iraq and North Korea have gotten considerable media coverage in recent years.

The IAEA began taking shape when an international conference at the UN headquarters in New York unanimously approved the creation of the IAEA in October 1956. The agency advises governments, especially those of developing countries, about nuclear energy programs, environmental issues, and nuclear safety standards. It also sponsors conferences, regional seminars, training courses, fellowships for advanced study, research grants, equipment loans, comprehensive safety regulations, and advice-giving missions on nuclear power planning and nuclear law.

The IAEA collects and distributes nuclear scientific and technological information through its International Nuclear Information System in Vienna. With the help of UNESCO, the IAEA operates three nuclear physics laboratories and the International Center for Theoretical Physics in Trieste, Italy. It also works with WHO to advance the use of radiation in medicine and biology.

*Experts from the
International Atomic
Energy Agency take
readings of highly
radioactive nuclear
fuel that was found
stored in under-
ground containers
near Baghdad in
1991.*

## The General Agreement on Tariffs and Trade

The General Agreement on Tariffs and Trade (GATT) is the other of the two independent intergovernmental organizations affiliated with the United Nations. GATT is a multilateral treaty (that is, a treaty between more than two nations) agreed to by more than 130 nations responsible for most of the world's trade. Established in 1948 and headquartered in Geneva, the staff of GATT serves as the principal international forum for discussing trade problems, setting rules for the conduct of world trade, reducing trade barriers, and settling trade disputes.

The latest round of GATT negotiations to lower tariffs and promote freer trade—called the Uruguay Round—began in Punta del Este, Uruguay, in 1986 and ended seven years later. On December 15, 1993, GATT director-general Peter Sutherland, who oversaw the last phase of the talks, banged the table with his gavel and declared, "I gavel the Uruguay Round as concluded."

Relieved that the United States and Europe had agreed to put aside their differences at the last minute, representatives from 117 GATT member nations in the brown-carpeted, granite-walled conference hall in Geneva leaped to their feet, applauded, cheered, and gave each other bear hugs.

The accord reduces tariffs by a third over six years and brings industries like accounting and farming into global trade agreements for the first time. As the first world trade accord since 1979, it is expected to boost international investment and business by opening markets to goods and services and encouraging countries to specialize in producing and exporting whatever they can make most efficiently. Brazil's representative, Luiz Felipe Palmeira Lampreia, called the accord, which covers more industries in more countries than any other trade agreement in history, "a major achievement."

Earlier GATT rounds had begun the process of reducing tariffs. The Kennedy Round (1964–1967) succeeded in getting the world's leading trading countries to cut their tariffs by more than $40 billion. The Tokyo Round (1973–1979), which dealt with international barriers to trade in industrial and agricultural products, resulted in a substantial 30 percent reduction of trade restrictions that affected world trade worth $300 billion.

Since 1968, GATT has operated the International Trade Center in Geneva jointly with the United Nations Conference on Trade and Development. The center provides developing countries with information and advice on export markets.

# Into the Future

An unprecedented summit meeting of the Security Council was held on January 31, 1992. For the first time in the 47-year history of the United Nations the leaders of the 15 countries represented on the council—the 5 permanent members (Britain, China, France, Russia, and the United States) as well as the 10 rotating members (Austria, Belgium, Cape Verde, Ecuador, Hungary, India, Japan, Morocco, Venezuela, and Zimbabwe)—sat at the horseshoe table in the Security Council chamber in New York to talk about the future of the UN.

"The international agenda is shifting from crisis management, in which the UN has for so long played a distinguished role, to crisis prevention," said British prime minister John Major. He opened the meeting in his capacity as leader of the country chairing the Security Council for the month of January. "The aim must be to equip the UN to lead in crisis prevention."

For five hours the leaders discussed what they expected from the UN and what their countries would offer in return. Several nations advocated a UN peacekeeping force capable of responding rapidly to a crisis. Russian president Boris Yeltsin called for "a special, quick-response mechanism to ensure peace and security." French president François Mitterrand promised to contribute a 1,000-member contingent to a UN rapid-use peacekeeping force. The leaders of the 10 nonpermanent member nations of the council also presented their ideas.

In their final statement, the heads of state who took part in the historic meeting pledged to strengthen the capacity of the UN in the areas of preventive diplomacy, peacemaking, and peacekeeping; acknowledged the importance of economic development and human rights for international peace and security; and encouraged member states to make a greater financial and political commitment to the United Nations.

The leaders asked the new secretary-general, Boutros Boutros-Ghali, to prepare by July 1, 1992, an "analysis and recommendations on ways of strengthening and making more efficient within the framework and provisions of the Charter the capacity of the United Nations for preventive diplomacy, for peacemaking and for peacekeeping." They wanted the secretary-general to tell the nations of the world what resources the UN needed to carry out its work.

The secretary-general responded to their request with a 48-page report called *An Agenda for Peace*. "In these past months," he wrote in the introduction, "a conviction has grown, among nations large and small, that an opportunity has been regained to achieve the great objectives of the

*This stamp, issued by the UN, shows the headquarters in New York City in front of the UN logo, with United Nations spelled out in the five original official languages of the organization.*

Charter—a United Nations capable of maintaining international peace and security, of securing justice and human rights and of promoting, in the words of the Charter, 'social progress and better standards of life in larger freedom.' This opportunity must not be squandered. The Organization must never again be crippled as it was in the era that has now passed."

His report urged member states "to enhance respect for human rights and fundamental freedoms, to promote sustainable economic and social development for wider prosperity, to [reduce] distress, and to curtail the existence and use of massively destructive weapons." In places where tensions may lead to conflict, he said the UN should employ preventive diplomacy in the form of fact-finding missions, confidence-building measures, early-warning alerts, demilitarized zones, and the deployment of UN civilians and possibly troops in a threatened country at the earliest possible stage to contain the conflict.

Because the Security Council could act much more decisively now that the cold war was over, the United Nations had regional security problems thrust at it as never before in its history. The problem was increased because most of the new UN missions demanded nation-building and peace-enforcement skills far beyond anything ever required by earlier peacekeeping assignments, for example, in Cyprus or in the Sinai. The conditions that were demanded by the UN for earlier peacekeeping operations—the consent of the opposing parties, clearly understood and accepted authority given to the UN, reliable local officials with whom to deal, and clear geographical lines—were not present in places like Bosnia, Somalia, and Cambodia. In each of these places at least one party to the conflict was determined to keep fighting, UN or no UN.

Traditional UN peacekeeping methods cannot work where there is no peace to keep, and economic and political sanctions available to the UN under its charter can do little to stop savage civil, ethnic, or religious conflicts that often result in the mass killing of ethnic minorities.

When diplomacy fails and punishment in the form of sanctions does not work, the Security Council must have sufficient military muscle to back up its decisions. This was the case when the UN responded with force to Iraq's aggression against Kuwait. Secretary-General Boutros Boutros-Ghali wrote in his report that the option of the Security Council "to take military action to maintain or restore international peace and security" after peaceful means have failed "is essential to the credibility of the United Nations as a guarantor of international security."

To give the UN this capacity, the secretary-general recommended that the Security Council negotiate agreements with member states to provide permanent standby forces to carry out council decisions. Secretary-General Boutros Boutros-Ghali also called for the use of UN peace-enforcement troops, composed of voluntary units from member states, to restore cease-fires that break down. Toward the end of his report the secretary-general recommended that the presidents and prime ministers of the nations on the Security Council meet every other year just before the fall meeting of the General Assembly and that the foreign ministers of these nations meet whenever necessary.

As the United Nations celebrates its 50th anniversary in 1995 and looks forward to its next 50 years, we would all do well to keep in mind the words with which the secretary-general concluded his report: "The United Nations was created with a great and courageous vision. Now is the time, for nations and peoples, and the men and women who serve it, to seize the moment for the sake of the future."

APPENDIX 1

# UNITED NATIONS MEMBER STATES

| MEMBER | DATE OF ADMISSION | MEMBER | DATE OF ADMISSION |
|---|---|---|---|
| Afghanistan | Nov. 19, 1946 | Cyprus | Sept. 20, 1960 |
| Albania | Dec. 14, 1955 | Czech Republic[3] | Jan. 19, 1993 |
| Algeria | Oct. 8, 1962 | Democratic People's | |
| Andorra | Jul. 28, 1993 | Republic of Korea | Sept. 17, 1991 |
| Angola | Dec. 1, 1976 | Denmark | Oct. 24, 1945 |
| Antigua and Barbuda | Nov. 11, 1981 | Djibouti | Sept. 20, 1977 |
| Argentina | Oct. 24, 1945 | Dominica | Dec. 18, 1978 |
| Armenia | Mar. 2, 1992 | Dominican Republic | Oct. 24, 1945 |
| Australia | Nov. 1, 1945 | Ecuador | Dec. 21, 1945 |
| Austria | Dec. 14, 1955 | Egypt | Oct. 24, 1945 |
| Azerbaijan | Mar. 2, 1992 | El Salvador | Oct. 24, 1945 |
| Bahamas | Sept. 18, 1973 | Equatorial Guinea | Nov. 12, 1968 |
| Bahrain | Sept. 21, 1971 | Eritrea | May 28, 1993 |
| Bangladesh | Sept. 17, 1974 | Estonia | Sept. 17, 1991 |
| Barbados | Dec. 9, 1966 | Ethiopia | Nov. 13, 1945 |
| Belarus[1] | Oct. 24, 1945 | Federated States of | |
| Belgium | Dec. 27, 1945 | Micronesia | Sept. 17, 1991 |
| Belize | Sept. 25, 1981 | Fiji | Oct. 13, 1970 |
| Benin | Sept. 20, 1960 | Finland | Dec. 14, 1955 |
| Bhutan | Sept. 21, 1971 | France | Oct. 24, 1945 |
| Bolivia | Nov. 14, 1945 | Gabon | Sept. 20, 1960 |
| Bosnia and Herzegovina | May 22, 1992 | Gambia | Sept. 21, 1965 |
| Botswana | Oct. 17, 1966 | Georgia | Jul. 31, 1992 |
| Brazil | Oct. 24, 1945 | Germany[4] | Sept. 18, 1973 |
| Brunei Darussalam | Sept. 21, 1984 | Ghana | Mar. 8, 1957 |
| Bulgaria | Dec. 14, 1955 | Greece | Oct. 25, 1945 |
| Burkina Faso | Sept. 20, 1960 | Grenada | Sept. 17, 1974 |
| Burundi | Sept. 18, 1962 | Guatemala | Nov. 21, 1945 |
| Cambodia | Dec. 14, 1955 | Guinea | Dec. 12, 1958 |
| Cameroon | Sept. 20, 1960 | Guinea-Bissau | Sept. 17, 1974 |
| Canada | Nov. 9, 1945 | Guyana | Sept. 20, 1966 |
| Cape Verde | Sept. 16, 1975 | Haiti | Oct. 24, 1945 |
| Central African Republic | Sept. 20, 1960 | Honduras | Dec. 17, 1945 |
| Chad | Sept. 20, 1960 | Hungary | Dec. 14, 1955 |
| Chile | Oct. 24, 1945 | Iceland | Nov. 19, 1946 |
| China[2] | Oct. 24, 1945 | India | Oct. 30, 1945 |
| Colombia | Nov. 5, 1945 | Indonesia | Sept. 28, 1950 |
| Comoros | Nov. 12, 1975 | Iran | Oct. 24, 1945 |
| Congo | Sept. 20, 1960 | Iraq | Dec. 21, 1945 |
| Costa Rica | Nov. 2, 1945 | Ireland | Dec. 14, 1955 |
| Cote d'Ivoire [Ivory Coast] | Sept. 20, 1960 | Israel | May 11, 1949 |
| Croatia | May 22, 1992 | Italy | Dec. 14, 1955 |
| Cuba | Oct. 24, 1945 | Jamaica | Sept. 18, 1962 |

| MEMBER | DATE OF ADMISSION | MEMBER | DATE OF ADMISSION |
|---|---|---|---|
| Japan | Dec. 18, 1956 | Papua New Guinea | Oct. 10, 1975 |
| Jordan | Dec. 14, 1955 | Paraguay | Oct. 24, 1945 |
| Kazakhstan | Mar. 2, 1992 | Peru | Oct. 31, 1945 |
| Kenya | Dec. 16, 1963 | Philippines | Oct. 24, 1945 |
| Kuwait | May 14, 1963 | Poland | Oct. 24, 1945 |
| Kyrgyzstan | Mar. 2, 1992 | Portugal | Dec. 14, 1955 |
| Lao People's Democratic | | Qatar | Sept. 21, 1971 |
| Republic | Dec. 14, 1955 | Republic of Korea | Sept. 17, 1991 |
| Latvia | Sept. 17, 1991 | Romania | Dec. 14, 1955 |
| Lebanon | Oct. 24, 1945 | Russian Federation[7] | Oct. 24, 1945 |
| Lesotho | Oct. 17, 1966 | Rwanda | Sept. 18, 1962 |
| Liberia | Nov. 2, 1945 | Saint Kitts and Nevis | Sept. 23, 1983 |
| Libya | Dec. 14, 1955 | Saint Lucia | Sept. 18, 1979 |
| Liechtenstein | Sept. 18, 1990 | Saint Vincent and the | |
| Lithuania | Sept. 17, 1991 | Grenadines | Sept. 16, 1980 |
| Luxembourg | Oct. 24, 1945 | Samoa | Dec. 15, 1976 |
| Macedonia, the former | | San Marino | Mar. 2, 1992 |
| Yugoslav Republic of[5] | Apr. 8, 1993 | Sao Tome and Principe | Sept. 16, 1975 |
| Madagascar | Sept. 20, 1960 | Saudi Arabia | Oct. 24, 1945 |
| Malawi | Dec. 1, 1964 | Senegal | Sept. 28, 1960 |
| Malaysia[6] | Sept. 17, 1957 | Seychelles | Sept. 21, 1976 |
| Maldives | Sept. 21, 1965 | Sierra Leone | Sept. 27, 1961 |
| Mali | Sept. 28, 1960 | Singapore | Sept. 21, 1965 |
| Malta | Dec. 1, 1964 | Slovak Republic[8] | Jan. 19, 1993 |
| Marshall Islands | Sept. 17, 1991 | Slovenia | May 22, 1992 |
| Mauritania | Oct. 27, 1961 | Solomon Islands | Sept. 19, 1978 |
| Mauritius | Apr. 24, 1968 | Somalia | Sept. 20, 1960 |
| Mexico | Nov. 7, 1945 | South Africa | Nov. 7, 1945 |
| Moldova | Mar. 2, 1992 | Spain | Dec. 14, 1955 |
| Monaco | May 28, 1993 | Sri Lanka | Dec. 14, 1955 |
| Mongolia | Oct. 27, 1961 | Sudan | Nov. 12, 1956 |
| Morocco | Nov. 12, 1956 | Suriname | Dec. 4, 1975 |
| Mozambique | Sept. 16, 1975 | Swaziland | Sept. 24, 1968 |
| Myanmar | Apr. 19, 1948 | Sweden | Nov. 19, 1946 |
| Namibia | Apr. 23, 1990 | Syria | Oct. 24, 1945 |
| Nepal | Dec. 14, 1955 | Tajikistan | Mar. 2, 1992 |
| Netherlands | Dec. 10, 1945 | Thailand | Dec. 16, 1946 |
| New Zealand | Oct. 24, 1945 | Togo | Sept. 20, 1960 |
| Nicaragua | Oct. 24, 1945 | Trinidad and Tobago | Sept. 18, 1962 |
| Niger | Sept. 20, 1960 | Tunisia | Nov. 12, 1956 |
| Nigeria | Oct. 7, 1960 | Turkey | Oct. 24, 1945 |
| Norway | Nov. 27, 1945 | Turkmenistan | Mar. 2, 1992 |
| Oman | Oct. 7, 1971 | Uganda | Oct. 25, 1962 |
| Pakistan | Sept. 30, 1947 | Ukraine | Oct. 24, 1945 |
| Panama | Nov. 13, 1945 | United Arab Emirates | Dec. 9, 1971 |

| MEMBER | DATE OF ADMISSION | MEMBER | DATE OF ADMISSION |
|---|---|---|---|
| United Kingdom | Oct. 24, 1945 | Venezuela | Nov. 15, 1945 |
| United Republic of | | Vietnam | Sept. 20, 1977 |
| Tanzania [9] | Dec. 14, 1961 | Yemen [10] | Sept. 30, 1947 |
| United States | Oct. 24, 1945 | Yugoslavia | Oct. 24, 1945 |
| Uruguay | Dec. 18, 1945 | Zaire | Sept. 20, 1960 |
| Uzbekistan | Mar. 2, 1992 | Zambia | Dec. 1, 1964 |
| Vanuatu | Sept. 15 1981 | Zimbabwe | Aug. 25, 1980 |

## NOTES

[1] On September 19, 1991, Byelorussia informed the United Nations that it had changed its name to Belarus.

[2] The Republic of China (Nationalist China) was an original member of the UN from October 24, 1945. After its defeat in the Chinese civil war in the late 1940s, it set up a government on the island of Taiwan. In 1971 the People's Republic of China (Communist China) took its place at the United Nations and replaced it as a permanent member of the Security Council.

[3] Czechoslovakia, which was an original member of the United Nations from October 24, 1945, divided into the Czech Republic and the Slovak Republic. Both of them were admitted to the UN on January 19, 1993.

[4] The Federal Republic of Germany (West Germany) and the German Democratic Republic (East Germany) were admitted to membership in the United Nations on September 18, 1973. In 1990 they united to form a single German state.

[5] This is a temporary name pending settlement of a dispute that arose over the use of its name.

[6] The Federation of Malaya, which joined the United Nations in 1957, changed its name to Malaysia on September 16, 1963.

[7] The Union of Soviet Socialist Republics (Soviet Union) was an original member of the United Nations from October 24, 1945. In the early 1990s its UN membership and seat on the Security Council was filled by the Russian Federation (Russia). The other former Soviet republics (Byelorussia and the Ukraine were already members) joined the UN as separate, independent states.

[8] See Note 3.

[9] Tanganyika, a member of the United Nations since December 14, 1961, and Zanzibar, a member since December 16, 1963, united to form the United Republic of Tanganyika and Zanzibar on April 26, 1964. Six months later the new country changed its name to the United Republic of Tanzania.

[10] Yemen was admitted to membership in the United Nations in 1947 and the People's Democratic Republic of Yemen (South Yemen) joined the UN in 1967. On May 22, 1990, the two countries merged.

# CHARTER OF THE UNITED NATIONS

## PREAMBLE

WE THE PEOPLES OF THE UNITED NATIONS DETERMINED

to save succeeding generations from the scourge of war, which twice in our lifetime has brought untold sorrow to mankind, and

to reaffirm faith in fundamental human rights, in the dignity and worth of the human person, in the equal rights of men and women and of nations large and small, and

to establish conditions under which justice and respect for the obligations arising from treaties and other sources of international law can be maintained, and

to promote social progress and better standards of life in larger freedom,

AND FOR THESE ENDS

to practice tolerance and live together in peace with one another as good neighbors, and

to unite our strength to maintain international peace and security, and

to ensure by the acceptance of principles and the institution of methods, that armed force shall not be used, save in the common interest, and

to employ international machinery for the promotion of the economic and social advancement of all peoples,

HAVE RESOLVED TO COMBINE OUR EFFORTS TO ACCOMPLISH THESE AIMS

Accordingly, our respective Governments, through representatives assembled in the city of San Francisco, who have exhibited their full powers found to be in good and due form, have agreed to the present Charter of the United Nations and do hereby establish an international organization to be known as the United Nations.

## CHAPTER I

### PURPOSES AND PRINCIPLES

*Article 1*
The Purposes of the United Nations are:

1. To maintain international peace and security, and to that end: to take effective collective measures for the prevention and removal of threats to the peace, and for the suppression of acts of aggression or other breaches of the peace, and to bring about by peaceful means, and in conformity with the principles of justice and international law, adjustment or settlement of international disputes or situations which might lead to a breach of the peace;

2. To develop friendly relations among nations based on respect for the principle of equal rights and self-determination of peoples, and to take other appropriate measures to strengthen universal peace;

3. To achieve international co-operation in solving problems of an economic, social, cultural or humanitarian character, and in promoting and encouraging respect for human rights and for fundamental freedoms for all without distinction as to race, sex, language or religion; and

4. To be a centre for harmonizing the actions of nations in the attainment of these common ends.

*Article 2*

The Organization and its Members, in pursuit of the Purposes stated in Article 1, shall act in accordance with the following Principles:

1. The Organization is based on the principle of the sovereign equality of all its Members.

2. All Members, in order to ensure to all of them the rights and benefits resulting from membership, shall fulfil in good faith the obligations assumed by them in accordance with the present Charter.

3. All Members shall settle their international disputes by peaceful means in such a manner that international peace and security, and justice, are not endangered.

4. All Members shall refrain in their international relations from the threat or use of force against the territorial integrity or political independence of any state, or in any other manner inconsistent with the Purposes of the United Nations.

5. All Members shall give the United Nations every assistance in any action it takes in accordance with the present Charter, and shall refrain from giving assistance to any state against which the United Nations is taking preventive or enforcement action.

6. The Organization shall ensure that states which are not Members of the United Nations act in accordance with these Principles so far as may be necessary for the maintenance of international peace and security.

7. Nothing contained in the present Charter shall authorize the United Nations to intervene in matters which are essentially within the domestic jurisdiction of any state or shall require the Members to submit such matters to settlement under the present Charter; but

this principle shall not prejudice the application of enforcement measures under Chapter VII.

## CHAPTER II

### MEMBERSHIP

*Article 3*

The original Members of the United Nations shall be the states which, having participated in the United Nations Conference on International Organization at San Francisco or having previously signed the Declaration by United Nations of 1 January 1942, sign the present Charter and ratify if in accordance with Article 110.

*Article 4*

1. Membership in the United Nations is open to all other peace-loving states which accept the obligations contained in the present Charter and, in the judgment of the Organization, are able and willing to carry out these obligations.

2. The admission of any such state to membership in the United Nations will be affected by a decision of the General Assembly upon the recommendation of the Security Council.

*Article 5*

A Member of the United Nations against which preventive or enforcement action has been taken by the Security Council may be suspended from the exercise of the rights and privileges of membership by the General Assembly upon the recommendation of the Security Council. The exercise of these rights and privileges may be restored by the Security Council.

*Article 6*

A member of the United Nations which has persistently violated the Principles contained in the present Charter may be expelled from the Organization by the General Assembly upon the recommendation of the Security Council.

# CHAPTER III

## ORGANS

*Article 7*

1. There are established as the principal organs of the United Nations: a General Assembly, a Security Council, an Economic and Social Council, a Trusteeship Council, an International Court of Justice and a Secretariat.

2. Such subsidiary organs as may be found necessary may be established in accordance with the present Charter.

*Article 8*

The United Nations shall place no restrictions on the eligibility of men and women to participate in any capacity and under conditions of equality in its principal and subsidiary organs.

# CHAPTER IV

## THE GENERAL ASSEMBLY

### Composition

*Article 9*

1. The General Assembly shall consist of all the Members of the United Nations.

2. Each member shall have not more than five representatives in the General Assembly.

### Functions and Powers

*Article 10*

The General Assembly may discuss any questions or any matters within the scope of the present Charter or relating to the powers and functions of any organs provided for in the present Charter, and, except as provided in Article 12, may make recommendations to the Members of the United Nations or to the Security Council or to both on any such questions or matters.

*Article 11*

1. The General Assembly may consider the general principles of co-operation in the maintenance of international peace and security, including the principles governing disarmaments and the regulation of armaments, and may make recommendations with regard to such principles to the Members or to the Security Council or to both.

2. The General Assembly may discuss any questions relating to the maintenance of international peace and security brought before it by any Member of the United Nations, or by the Security Council, or by a state which is not a Member of the United Nations in accordance with Article 35, paragraph 2, and except as provided in Article 12, may make recommendations with regard to any such questions to the state or states concerned or to the Security Council or to both. Any such question on which action is necessary shall be referred to the Security Council by the General Assembly either before or after discussion.

3. The General Assembly may call the attention of the Security Council to situations which are likely to endanger international peace and security.

4. The powers of the General Assembly set

forth in this Article shall not limit the scope of Article 10.

*Article 12*

1. While the Security Council is exercising in respect of any dispute or situation the functions assigned to it in the present Charter, the General Assembly shall not make any recommendation with regard to that dispute or situation unless the Security Council so requests.

2. The Secretary-General, with the consent of the Security Council, shall notify the General Assembly at each session of any matters relative to the maintenance of international peace and security which are being dealt with by the Security Council and shall similarly notify the General Assembly, or the Members of the United Nations if the General Assembly is not in session, immediately the Security Council ceases to deal with such matters.

*Article 13*

1. The General Assembly shall initiate studies and make recommendations for the purpose of:

   a: promoting international co-operation in the political field and encouraging the progressive development of international law and its codification;

   b: promoting international co-operation in the economic, social, cultural, educational and health fields, and assisting in the realization of human rights and fundamental freedoms for all without distinction as to race, sex, language or religion.

2. The further responsibilities, functions and powers of the General Assembly with respect to matters mentioned in paragraph 1 (b) above are set forth in Chapters IX and X.

*Article 14*

Subject to the provisions of Article 12, the General Assembly may recommend measures for the peaceful adjustment of any situation, regardless of origin, which it deems likely to impair the general welfare or friendly relations among nations, including situations resulting from a violation of the provisions of the present Charter setting forth the Purposes and Principles of the United Nations.

*Article 15*

1. The General Assembly shall receive and consider annual and special reports from the Security Council; these reports shall include an account of the measures that the Security Council has decided upon or taken to maintain international peace and security.

2. The General Assembly shall receive and consider reports from the other organs of the United Nations.

*Article 16*

The General Assembly shall perform such functions with respect to the international trusteeship system as are assigned to it under Chapters XII and XIII, including the approval of the trusteeship agreements for areas not designated as strategic.

*Article 17*

1. The General Assembly shall consider and approve the budget of the Organization.

2. The expenses of the Organization shall be borne by the Members as apportioned by the General Assembly.

3. The General Assembly shall consider and approve any financial and budgetary arrangements with specialized agencies referred to in Article 57 and shall examine the administrative budgets of such specialized

agencies with a view to making recommendations to the agencies concerned.

## Voting

*Article 18*

1. Each member of the General Assembly shall have one vote.

2. Decisions of the General Assembly on important questions shall be made by a two-thirds majority of the members present and voting. These questions shall include: recommendations with respect to the maintenance of international peace and security, the election of the non-permanent members of the Security Council, the election of the members of the Economic and Social Council, the election of members of the Trusteeship Council in accordance with paragraph 1 (c) of Article 86, the admission of new Members to the United Nations, the suspension of the rights and privileges of membership, the expulsion of Members, questions relating to the operation of the trusteeship system, and budgetary questions.

3. Decisions on other questions, including the determination of additional categories of questions to be decided by a two-thirds majority, shall be made by a majority of the members present and voting.

*Article 19*

A Member of the United Nations which is in arrears in the payment of its financial contributions to the Organization shall have no vote in the General Assembly if the amount of its arrears equals or exceeds the amount of the contributions due from it for the preceding two full years. The General Assembly may, nevertheless, permit such a Member to vote if it is satisfied that the failure to pay is due to conditions beyond the control of the Member.

## Procedure

*Article 20*

The General Assembly shall meet in regular annual sessions and in such special sessions as occasion may require. Special sessions shall be convoked by the Secretary-General at the request of the Security Council or of a majority of the Members of the United Nations.

*Article 21*

The General Assembly shall adopt its own rules of procedure. It shall elect its President for each session.

*Article 22*

The General Assembly may establish such subsidiary organs as it deems necessary for the performance of its functions.

# CHAPTER V

## THE SECURITY COUNCIL

## Composition

*Article 23*

1. The Security Council shall consist of fifteen Members of the United Nations. The Republic of China, France, the Union of Soviet Socialist Republics, the United Kingdom of Great Britain and Northern Ireland and the United States of America shall be permanent members of the Security Council. The General Assembly shall elect ten other Members of the United Nations to be non-permanent members of the Security Council, due regard being specially paid, in the first instance to the contribution of Members of the United Nations to the maintenance of international peace and security and to the other purposes of the Organization, and also to equitable geographical distribution.

2. The non-permanent members of the Security Council shall be elected for a term of two years. In the first election of the non-permanent members after the increase of the membership of the Security Council from eleven to fifteen, two of the four additional members shall be chosen for a term of one year. A retiring member shall not be eligible for immediate re-election.

3. Each member of the Security Council shall have one representative.

## Functions and Powers

*Article 24*

1. In order to ensure prompt and effective action by the United Nations, its Members confer on the Security Council primary responsibility for the maintenance of international peace and security, and agree that in carrying out its duties under this responsibility the Security Council acts on their behalf.

2. In discharging these duties the Security Council shall act in accordance with the Purposes and Principles of the United Nations. The specific powers granted to the Security Council for the discharge of these duties are laid down in Chapters VI, VII, VIII and XII.

3. The Security Council shall submit annual and, when necessary, special reports to the General Assembly for its consideration.

*Article 25*

The Members of the United Nations agree to accept and carry out the decisions of the Security Council in accordance with the present Charter.

*Article 26*

In order to promote the establishment and maintenance of international peace and security with the least diversion for armaments of the world human and economic resources, the Security Council shall be responsible for formulating, with the assistance of the Military Staff Committee referred to in Article 47, plans to be submitted to the Members of the United Nations for the establishment of a system for the regulation of armaments.

## Voting

*Article 27*

1. Each member of the Security Council shall have one vote.

2. Decisions of the Security Council on procedural matters shall be made by an affirmative vote of nine members.

3. Decisions of the Security Council on all other matters shall be made by an affirmative vote of nine members including the concurring votes of the permanent member; provided that, in decisions under Chapter VI, and under paragraph 3 of Article 52, a party to a dispute shall abstain from voting.

## Procedure

*Article 28*

1. The Security Council shall be so organized as to be able to function continuously. Each member of the Security Council shall for this purpose be represented at all times at the seat of the Organization.

2. The Security Council shall hold periodic meetings at which each of its members may, if it so desires, be represented by a member of the government or by some other specially designated representative.

3. The Security Council may hold meetings at such places other than the seat of the Organization as in its judgment will best facilitate its work.

*Article 29*

The Security Council may establish such subsidiary organs as it deems necessary for the performance of its functions.

*Article 30*

The Security Council shall adopt its own rules of procedure, including the method of selecting its President.

*Article 31*

Any Member of the United Nations which is not a member of the Security Council may participate, without vote, in the discussion of any question brought before the Security Council whenever the latter considers that the interests of that Member are specially affected.

*Article 32*

Any Member of the United Nations which is not a member of the Security Council or any state which is not a Member of the United Nations, if it is a party to a dispute under consideration by the Security Council, shall be invited to participate, without vote, in the discussion relating to the dispute. The Security Council shall lay down such conditions as it deems just for the participation of a state which is not a Member of the United Nations.

## CHAPTER VI

### PACIFIC SETTLEMENT OF DISPUTES

*Article 33*

1. The parties to any dispute, the continuance of which is likely to endanger the maintenance of international peace and security, shall, first of all, seek a solution by negotiation, enquiry, mediation, conciliation, arbi-tration, judicial settlement, resort to regional agencies or arrangements, or other peaceful means of their own choice.

2. The Security Council shall, when it deems necessary, call upon the parties to settle their dispute by such means.

*Article 34*

The Security Council may investigate any dispute, or any situation which might lead to international friction or give rise to a dispute, in order to determine whether the continuance of the dispute or situation is likely to endanger the maintenance of international peace and security.

*Article 35*

1. Any Member of the United Nations may bring any dispute, or any situation of the nature referred to in Article 34, to the attention of the Security Council or of the General Assembly.

2. A state which is not a Member of the United Nations may bring to the attention of the Security Council or of the General Assembly any dispute to which it is a party if it accepts in advance, for the purposes of the dispute, the obligations of pacific settlement provided in the present Charter.

3. The proceedings of the General Assembly in respect of matters brought to its attention under this Article will be subject to the provisions of Articles 11 and 12.

*Article 36*

1. The Security Council may, at any stage of a dispute of the nature referred to in Article 33 or of a situation of like nature, recommend appropriate procedures or methods of adjustment.

2. The Security Council should take into consideration any procedures for the settle-

ment of the dispute which have already been adopted by the parties.

3. In making recommendations under this Article the Security Council should also take into consideration that legal disputes should as a general rule be referred by the parties to the International Court of Justice in accordance with the provisions of the Statute of the Court.

*Article 37*

1. Should the parties to a dispute of the nature referred to in Article 33 fail to settle it by means indicated in the Article, they shall refer it to the Security Council.

2. If the Security Council deems that the continuance of the dispute is in fact likely to endanger the maintenance of international peace and security, it shall decide whether to take action under Article 36 or to recommend such terms of settlement as it may consider appropriate.

*Article 38*

Without prejudice to the provisions of Articles 33 to 37, the Security Council may, if all the parties to any dispute so request, make recommendations to the parties with a view to a pacific settlement of the dispute.

# CHAPTER VII

## ACTION WITH RESPECT TO THREATS TO THE PEACE, BREACHES OF THE PEACE, AND ACTS OF AGGRESSION

*Article 39*

The Security Council shall determine the existence of any threat to the peace, breach of the peace, or act of aggression and shall make recommendations, or decide what measures shall be taken in accordance with Articles 41 and 42, to maintain or restore international peace and security.

*Article 40*

In order to prevent an aggravation of the situation, the Security Council may, before making the recommendations or deciding upon the measures provided for in Article 39, call upon the parties concerned to comply with such provisional measures as it deems necessary or desirable. Such provisional measures shall be without prejudice to the rights, claims or position of the parties concerned. The Security Council shall duly take account of failure to comply with such provisional measures.

*Article 41*

The Security Council may decide what measures not involving the use of armed force are to be employed to give effect to its decisions, and it may call upon the Members of the United Nations to apply such measures. These may include complete or partial interruption of economic relations and of rail, sea, air, postal, telegraphic, radio and other means of communication, and the severance of diplomatic relations.

*Article 42*

Should the Security Council consider that measures provided for in Article 41 would be inadequate or have proved to be inadequate, it may take such action by air, sea or land forces as may be necessary to maintain or restore international peace and security. Such action may include demonstrations, blockade, and other operations by air, sea, or land forces of Members of the United Nations.

*Article 43*

1. All Members of the United Nations, in order to contribute to the maintenance of

international peace and security, undertake to make available to the Security Council, on its call and in accordance with a special agreement or agreements, armed forces, assistance and facilities, including rights of passage, necessary for the purpose of maintaining international peace and security.

2. Such agreement or agreements shall govern the numbers and types of forces, their degree of readiness and general location, and the nature of the facilities and assistance to be provided.

3. The agreement or agreements shall be negotiated as soon as possible on the initiative of the Security Council. They shall be concluded between the Security Council and Members or between the Security Council and groups of Members and shall be subject to ratification by the signatory states in accordance with their respective constitutional processes.

### Article 44

When the Security Council has decided to use force it shall, before calling upon a Member not represented on it to provide armed forces in fulfillment of the obligations assumed under Article 43, invite that Member, if that Member so desires, to participate in the decisions of the Security Council concerning the employment of contingents of that Member's armed forces.

### Article 45

In order to enable the United Nations to take urgent military measures, Members shall hold immediately available national air-force contingents for combined international enforcement action. The strength and degree of readiness of these contingents and plans for their combined action shall be determined, within the limits laid down in the special agreement or agreements referred to

in Article 43, by the Security Council with the assistance of the Military Staff Committee.

### Article 46

Plans for the application of armed force shall be made by the Security Council with the assistance of the Military Staff Committee.

### Article 47

1. There shall be established a Military Staff Committee to advise and assist the Security Council on all questions relating to the Security Council's military requirements for the maintenance of international peace and security, the employment and command of forces placed at its disposal, the regulation of armaments, and possible disarmament.

2. The Military Staff Committee shall consist of the Chiefs of Staff of the permanent members of the Security Council or their representatives. Any Member of the United Nations not permanently represented on the Committee shall be invited by the Committee to be associated with it when the efficient discharge of the Committee's responsibilities requires the participation of that Member in its work.

3. The Military Staff Committee shall be responsible under the Security Council for the strategic direction of any armed forces placed at the disposal of the Security Council. Questions relating to the command of such forces shall be worked out subsequently.

4. The Military Staff Committee, with the authorization of the Security Council and after consultation with appropriate regional agencies, may establish regional sub-committees.

*Article 48*

1. The action required to carry out the decisions of the Security Council for the maintenance of international peace and security shall be taken by all the Members of the United Nations or by some of them, as the Security Council may determine.

2. Such decisions shall be carried out by the Members of the United Nations directly and through their action in the appropriate international agencies of which they are members.

*Article 49*

The Members of the United Nations shall join in affording mutual assistance in carrying out the measures decided upon by the Security Council.

*Article 50*

If preventive or enforcement measures against any state are taken by the Security Council, any other state, whether a Member of the United Nations or not, which finds itself confronted with special economic problems arising from the carrying out of those measures shall have the right to consult the Security Council with regard to a solution of those problems.

*Article 51*

Nothing in the present Charter shall impair the inherent right of individual or collective self-defence if an armed attack occurs against a Member of the United Nations, until the Security Council has taken measures necessary to maintain international peace and security. Measures taken by Members in the exercise of this right of self-defence shall be immediately reported to the Security Council and shall not in any way affect the authority and responsibility of the Security Council under the present Charter to take at any time such action as it deems necessary in order to maintain or restore international peace and security.

# CHAPTER VIII

## REGIONAL ARRANGEMENTS

*Article 52*

1. Nothing in the present Charter precludes the existence of regional arrangements or agencies for dealing with such matters relating to the maintenance of international peace and security as are appropriate for regional action, provided that such arrangements or agencies and their activities are consistent with the Purposes and Principles of the United Nations.

2. The Members of the United Nations entering into such arrangements or constituting such agencies shall make every effort to achieve pacific settlement of local disputes through such regional agencies before referring them to the Security Council.

3. The Security Council shall encourage the development of pacific settlement of local disputes through such regional arrangements or by such regional agencies either on the initiative of the states concerned or by reference from the Security Council.

4. This Article in no way impairs the application of Articles 34 and 35.

*Article 53*

1. The Security Council shall, where appropriate, utilize such regional arrangements or agencies for enforcement action under its authority. But no enforcement action shall be taken under regional arrangements without the authorization of the Security Council, with the exception of measures against any enemy state, as defined in paragraph 2

of this Article, provided for pursuant to Article 107 or in regional arrangements directed against renewal of aggressive policy on the part of any such state, until such time as the Organization may, on request of the Governments concerned, be charged with the responsibility for preventing further aggression by such a state.

2. The term enemy state as used in paragraph 1 of this Article applies to any state which during the Second World War has been an enemy of any signatory of the present Charter.

*Article 54*

The Security Council shall at all times be kept fully informed of activities undertaken or in contemplation under regional arrangements or by regional agencies for the maintenance of international peace and security.

# CHAPTER IX

## INTERNATIONAL ECONOMIC AND SOCIAL CO-OPERATION

*Article 55*

With a view to the creation of conditions of stability and well-being which are necessary for peaceful and friendly relations among nations based on respect for the principle of equal rights and self-determination of peoples, the United Nations shall promote:
   a. higher standards of living, full employment, and conditions of economic and social progress and development;
   b. solutions of international economic, social, health, and related problems; and international cultural and educational co-operation; and

   c. universal respect for, and observance of, human rights and fundamental freedoms for all without distinction as to race, sex, language, or religion.

*Article 56*

All Members pledge themselves to take joint and separate action in co-operation with the Organization for the achievement of the purposes set forth in Article 55.

*Article 57*

1. The various specialized agencies, established by intergovernmental agreement and having wide international responsibilities, as defined in their basic instruments, in economic, social, cultural, educational, health, and related fields, shall be brought into relationship with the United Nations in accordance with the provisions of Article 63.

2. Such agencies thus brought into relationship with the United Nations are hereinafter referred to as specialized agencies.

*Article 58*

The Organization shall make recommendations for the co-ordination of the policies and activities of the specialized agencies.

*Article 59*

The Organization shall, where appropriate, initiate negotiations among the states concerned for the creation of any new specialized agencies required for the accomplishment of the purposes set forth in Article 55.

*Article 60*

Responsibility for the discharge of the functions of the Organization set forth in this Chapter shall be vested in the General Assembly and, under the authority of the General Assembly, in the Economic and Social Council, which shall have for this purpose the powers set forth in Chapter X.

# CHAPTER X

## THE ECONOMIC AND SOCIAL COUNCIL

### Composition

*Article 61*

1. The Economic and Social Council shall consist of fifty-four Members of the United Nations elected by the General Assembly.

2. Subject to the provisions of paragraph 3, eighteen members of the Economic and Social Council shall be elected each year for a term of three years. A retiring member shall be eligible for immediate re-election.

3. At the first election after the increase in the membership of the Economic and Social Council from twenty-seven to fifty-four members, in addition to the members elected in place of the nine members whose term of office expires at the end of that year, twenty-seven additional members shall be elected. Of these twenty-seven additional members, the term of office of nine members so elected shall expire at the end of one year, and of nine other members at the end of two years, in accordance with arrangements made by the General Assembly.

4. Each member of the Economic and Social Council shall have one representative.

### Functions and Powers

*Article 62*

1. The Economic and Social Council may make or initiate studies and reports with respect to international economic, social, cultural, educational, health, and related matters and may make recommendations with respect to any such matters to the General Assembly, to the Members of the United Nations, and to the specialized agencies concerned.

2. It may make recommendations for the purpose of promoting respect for, and observance of, human rights and fundamental freedoms for all.

3. It may prepare draft conventions for submission to the General Assembly, with respect to matters falling within its competence.

4. It may call, in accordance with the rules prescribed by the United Nations, international conferences on matters falling within its competence.

*Article 63*

1. The Economic and Social Council may enter into agreements with any of the agencies referred to in Article 57, defining the terms on which the agency concerned shall be brought into relationship with the United Nations. Such agreements shall be subject to approval by the General Assembly.

2. It may co-ordinate the activities of the specialized agencies through consultation with and recommendations to such agencies and through recommendations to the General Assembly and to the Members of the United Nations.

*Article 64*

1. The Economic and Social Council may take appropriate steps to obtain regular reports from the specialized agencies. It may make arrangements with the Members of the United Nations and with the specialized agencies to obtain reports on the steps taken to give effect to its own recommendations and to recommendations on matters falling within its competence made by the General Assembly.

2. It may communicate its observations on these reports to the General Assembly.

*Article 65*

The Economic and Social Council may furnish information to the Security Council and shall assist the Security Council upon its request.

*Article 66*

1. The Economic and Social Council shall perform functions as fall within its competence in connexion with the carrying out of the recommendations of the General Assembly.

2. It may, with the approval of the General Assembly, perform services at the request of Members of the United Nations and at the request of specialized agencies.

3. It shall perform such other functions as are specified elsewhere in the present Charter or as may be assigned to it by the General Assembly.

## Voting

*Article 67*

1. Each member of the Economic and Social Council shall have one vote.

2. Decisions of the Economic and Social Council shall be made by a majority of the members present and voting.

## Procedure

*Article 68*

The Economic and Social Council shall set up commissions in economic and social fields and for the promotion of human rights, and such other commissions as may be required for the performance of its functions.

*Article 69*

The Economic and Social Council shall invite any Member of the United Nations to participate, without vote, in its deliberations on any matter of particular concern to that Member.

*Article 70*

The Economic and Social Council may make arrangements for representatives of the specialized agencies to participate, without vote, in its deliberations and in those of the commissions established by it, and for its representatives to participate in the deliberations of the specialized agencies.

*Article 71*

The Economic and Social Council may make suitable arrangements for consultation with non-governmental organizations which are concerned with matters within its competence. Such arrangements may be made with international organizations and, where appropriate, with national organizations after consultation with the Member of the United Nations concerned.

*Article 72*

1. The Economic and Social Council shall adopt its own rules of procedure, including the method of selecting its President.

2. The Economic and Social Council shall meet as required in accordance with its rules, which shall include provision for the convening of meetings on the request of a majority of its members.

# CHAPTER XI

## DECLARATION REGARDING NON-SELF-GOVERNING TERRITORIES

*Article 73*

Members of the United Nations which have or assume responsibilities for the administration of territories whose peoples have not yet attained a full measure of self-government recognize the principle that the interests of the inhabitants of these territories are paramount, and accept as a sacred trust the obligation to promote to the utmost, within the system of international peace and security established by the present Charter, the well-being of the inhabitants of these territories and, to this end:

a. to ensure, with due respect for the culture of the peoples concerned, their political, economic, social, and educational advancement, their just treatment, and their protection against abuses;

b. to develop self-government, to take due account of the political aspirations of the peoples, and to assist them in the progressive development of their free political institutions, according to the particular circumstances of each territory and its peoples and their varying stages of advancement;

c. to further international peace and security;

d. to promote constructive measures of development, to encourage research, and to co-operate with one another and, when and where appropriate, with specialized international bodies with a view to the practical achievement of the social, economic, and scientific purposes set forth in this Article; and

e. to transmit regularly to the Secretary-General for information purposes, subject to such limitation as security and constitutional considerations may require, statistical and other information of a technical nature relating to economic, social, and educational conditions in the territories for which they are respectively responsible other than those territories to which Chapters XII and XIII apply.

*Article 74*

Members of the United Nations also agree that their policy in respect of the territories to which this Chapter applies, no less than in respect of their metropolitan areas, must be based on the general principle of good-neighbourliness, due account being taken of the interests and well-being of the rest of the world, in social, economic, and commercial matters.

# CHAPTER XII

## INTERNATIONAL TRUSTEESHIP SYSTEM

*Article 75*

The United Nations shall establish under its authority an international trusteeship system for the administration and supervision of such territories as may be placed thereunder by subsequent individual agreements. These territories are hereinafter referred to as trust territories.

*Article 76*

The basic objectives of the trusteeship system, in accordance with the Purposes of the United Nations laid down in Article 1 of the present Charter, shall be:

a. to further international peace and security;

b. to promote the political, economic, social, and educational advancement of the inhabitants of the trust territories, and their progressive development towards self-government or independence as may be appropriate to the particular circumstances of each territory and its people and the freely expressed wishes of the peoples concerned, and as may be provided by the terms of each trusteeship agreement;

c. to encourage respect for human rights and for fundamental freedoms for all without distinction as to race, sex, language, or religion, and to encourage recognition of the interdependence of the peoples of the world; and

d. to ensure equal treatment in social, economic, and commercial matters for all Members of the United Nations and their nationals, and also equal treatment for the latter in the administration of justice, without prejudice to the attainment of the foregoing objectives and subject to the provisions of Article 80.

*Article 77*

1. The trusteeship system shall apply to such territories in the following categories as may be placed thereunder by means of trusteeship agreements:

a. territories now held under mandate;

b. territories which may be detached from enemy states as a result of the Second World War; and

c. territories voluntarily placed under the system by states responsible for their administration.

2. It will be a matter for subsequent agreement as to which territories in the foregoing categories will be brought under the trusteeship system and upon what terms.

*Article 78*

The trusteeship system shall not apply to territories which have become Members of the United Nations, relationship among which shall be based on respect for the principle of sovereign equality.

*Article 79*

The terms of trusteeship for each territory to be placed under the trusteeship system, in-

cluding any alteration or amendment, shall be agreed upon by the states directly concerned, including the mandatory power in the case of territories held under mandate by a member of the United Nations, and shall be approved as provided for in Articles 83 and 85.

*Article 80*

1. Except as may be agreed upon in individual trusteeship agreements, made under Articles 77, 79 and 81, placing each territory under the trusteeship system, and until such agreements have been concluded, nothing in this Chapter shall be construed in or of itself to alter in any manner the rights whatsoever of any states or any peoples or the terms of existing international instruments to which Members of the United Nations may respectively be parties.

2. Paragraph 1 of this Article shall not be interpreted as giving grounds for delay or postponement of the negotiation and conclusion of agreements for placing mandated and other territories under the trusteeship system as provided for in Article 77.

*Article 81*

The Trusteeship agreements shall in each case include the terms under which the trust territory will be administered and designate the authority which will exercise the administration of the trust territory. Such authority, hereinafter called the administering authority, may be one or more states or the Organization itself.

*Article 82*

There may be designated, in any trusteeship agreement, a strategic area or areas which may include part or all of the trust territory to which the agreement applies, without prejudice to any special agreement or agreements made under Article 43.

*Article 83*

1. All functions of the United Nations relating to strategic areas, including the approval of the terms of the trusteeship agreements and of their alteration or amendment, shall be exercised by the Security Council.

2. The basic Objectives set forth in Article 76 shall be applicable to the people of each strategic area.

3. The Security Council shall, subject to the provisions of the trusteeship agreements and without prejudice to security considerations, avail itself of the assistance of the Trusteeship Council to perform those functions of the United Nations under the trusteeship system relating to political, economic, social, and educational matters in the strategic areas.

*Article 84*

It shall be the duty of the administering authority to ensure that the trust territory shall play its part in the maintenance of international peace and security. To this end the administering authority may make use of volunteer forces, facilities, and assistance from the trust territory in carrying out the obligations toward the Security Council undertaken in this regard by the administering authority, as well as for local defence and the maintenance of law and order within the trust territory.

*Article 85*

1. The functions of the United Nations with regard to the trusteeship agreements for all areas not designated as strategic, including the approval of the terms of the trusteeship agreements and of their alteration or amendment, shall be exercised by the General Assembly.

2. The Trusteeship Council, operating under the authority of the General Assembly,

shall assist the General Assembly in carrying out these functions.

# CHAPTER XIII

## THE TRUSTEESHIP COUNCIL

### Composition

*Article 86*

1. The Trusteeship Council shall consist of the following Members of the United Nations:

   a. those Members administering trust territories;
   b. such of those Members mentioned by name in Article 23 as are not administering trust territories; and
   c. as many other Members elected for three-year terms by the General Assembly as may be necessary to ensure that the total number of members of the Trusteeship Council is equally divided between those members of the United Nations which administer trust territories and those which do not.

2. Each member of the Trusteeship Council shall designate one specially qualified person to represent it therein.

### Functions and Powers

*Article 87*

The General Assembly and, under its authority, the Trusteeship Council, in carrying out their functions, may:

   a. consider reports submitted by the administering authority;
   b. accept petitions and examine them in consultation with the administering authority;

c. provide for periodic visits to the respective trust territories at times agreed upon with the administering authority; and;

d. take these and other actions in conformity with the terms of the trusteeship agreements.

### Article 88

The Trusteeship Council shall formulate a questionnaire on the political, economic, social, and educational advancement of the inhabitants of each trust territory, and the administering authority for each trust territory within the competence of the General Assembly shall make an annual report to the General Assembly upon the basis of such questionnaire.

## Voting

### Article 89

1. Each member of the Trusteeship Council shall have one vote.

2. Decisions of the Trusteeship Council shall be made by a majority of the members present and voting.

## Procedure

### Article 90

1. The Trusteeship Council shall adopt its own rules of procedure, including the method of selecting its President.

2. The Trusteeship Council shall meet as required in accordance with its rules, which shall include provision for the convening of meetings of the request of a majority of its members.

### Article 91

The Trusteeship Council shall, when appropriate, avail itself of the assistance of the Economic and Social Council and of the specialized agencies in regard to matters with which they are respectively concerned.

## CHAPTER XIV

## THE INTERNATIONAL COURT OF JUSTICE

### Article 92

The International Court of Justice shall be the principal judicial organ of the United Nations. It shall function in accordance with the annexed Statute of the Permanent Court of International Justice and forms an integral part of the present Charter.

### Article 93

1. All Members of the United Nations are *ipso facto* parties to the Statute of the International Court of Justice.

2. A state which is not a Member of the United Nations may become a party to the Statute of the International Court of Justice on conditions to be determined in each case by the General Assembly upon the recommendation of the Security Council.

### Article 94

1. Each Member of the United Nations undertakes to comply with the decisions of the International Court of Justice in any case to which it is a party.

2. If any party to a case fails to perform the obligations incumbent upon it under a judgment rendered by the Court, the other party may have recourse to the Security Council, which may, if it deems necessary, make recommendations or decide upon measures to be taken to give effect to the judgment.

*Article 95*

Nothing in the present Charter shall prevent Members of the United Nations from entrusting the solution of their differences to other tribunals by virtue of agreements already in existence or which may be concluded in the future.

*Article 96*

1. The General Assembly or the Security Council may request the International Court of Justice to give an advisory opinion on any legal question.

2. Other organs of the United Nations and specialized agencies, which may at any time be so authorized by the General Assembly, may also request advisory opinions of the Court on legal questions arising within the scope of their activities.

# CHAPTER XV

## THE SECRETARIAT

*Article 97*

The Secretariat shall comprise a Secretary-General and such staff as the Organization may require. The Secretary-General shall be appointed by the General Assembly upon the recommendation of the Security Council. He shall be the chief administrative officer of the Organization.

*Article 98*

The Secretary-General shall act in that capacity in all meetings of the General Assembly, of the Security Council, of the Economic and Social Council, and of the Trusteeship Council, and shall perform such other functions as are entrusted to him by these organs. The Secretary-General shall make an annual report to the General Assembly on the work of the Organization.

*Article 99*

The Secretary-General may bring to the attention of the Security Council any matter which in his opinion may threaten the maintenance of international peace and security.

*Article 100*

1. In the performance of their duties the Secretary-General and the staff shall not seek or receive instructions from any government or from any other authority external to the Organization. They shall refrain from any action which might reflect on their position as international officials responsible only to the Organization.

2. Each Member of the United Nations undertakes to respect the exclusively international character of the responsibilities of the Secretary-General and the staff and not to seek to influence them in the discharge of their responsibilities.

*Article 101*

1. The staff shall be appointed by the Secretary-General under regulations established by the General Assembly.

2. Appropriate staffs shall be permanently assigned to the Economic and Social Council, the Trusteeship Council, and, as required, to other organs of the United Nations. These staffs shall form a part of the Secretariat.

3. The paramount consideration in the employment of the staff and in the determination of the conditions of service shall be the necessity of securing the highest standards of efficiency, competence, and integrity. Due regard shall be paid to the importance of recruiting the staff on as wide a geographical basis as possible.

# CHAPTER XVI

## MISCELLANEOUS PROVISIONS

*Article 102*

1. Every treaty and every international agreement entered into by any Member of the United Nations after the present Charter comes into force shall as soon as possible be registered with the Secretariat and published by it.

2. No party to any such treaty or international agreement which has not been registered in accordance with the provision of paragraph 1 of this Article may invoke that treaty or agreement before any organ of the United Nations.

*Article 103*

In the event of a conflict between the obligations of the Members of the United Nations under the present Charter and their obligations under any other international agreement, their obligations under the present Charter shall prevail.

*Article 104*

The Organization shall enjoy in the territory of each of its Members such legal capacity as may be necessary for the exercise of its functions and the fulfilment of its purposes.

*Article 105*

1. The Organization shall enjoy in the territory of each of its Members such privileges and immunities as are necessary for the fulfilment of its purposes.

2. Representatives of the Members of the United Nations and officials of the Organization shall similarly enjoy such privileges and immunities as are necessary for the independent exercise of their functions in connexion with the Organization.

3. The General Assembly may make recommendations with a view to determining the details of the application of paragraphs 1 and 2 of this Article or may propose conventions to the Members of the United Nations for this purpose.

# CHAPTER XVII

## TRANSITIONAL SECURITY ARRANGEMENTS

*Article 106*

Pending the coming into force of such special agreements referred to in Article 43 as in the opinion of the Security Council enable it to begin the exercise of its responsibilities under Article 42, the parties to the Four-Nation Declaration, signed at Moscow, 30 October 1943, and France, shall, in accordance with the provisions of paragraph 5 of that Declaration, consult with one another and as occasion requires with other Members of the United Nations with a view to such joint action on behalf of the Organization as may be necessary for the purpose of maintaining international peace and security.

*Article 107*

Nothing in the present Charter shall invalidate or preclude action, in relation to any state which during the Second World War has been an enemy of any signatory to the present Charter, taken or authorized as a result of that war by the Governments having responsibility for such action.

# CHAPTER XVIII

## AMENDMENTS

*Article 108*

Amendments to the present Charter shall come into force for all Members of the

United Nations when they have been adopted by a vote of two thirds of the members of the General Assembly and ratified in accordance with their respective constitutional processes by two thirds of the Members of the United Nations including all the permanent members of the Security Council.

*Article 109*

1. A General Conference of the Members of the United Nations for the purpose of reviewing the present Charter may be held at a date and place to be fixed by a two-thirds vote of the members of the General Assembly and by a vote of any nine members of the Security Council. Each Member of the United Nations shall have one vote in the conference.

2. Any alteration of the present Charter recommended by a two-thirds vote of the conference shall take effect when ratified in accordance with their respective constitutional processes by two thirds of the Members of the United Nations including all the permanent members of the Security Council.

3. If such a conference has not been held before the tenth annual session of the General Assembly following the coming into force of the present Charter, the proposal to call such a conference shall be placed on the agenda of that session of the General Assembly, and the conference shall be held if so decided by a majority vote of the members of the General Assembly and by a vote of any seven members of the Security Council.

# CHAPTER XIX

## RATIFICATION AND SIGNATURE

*Article 110*

1. The present Charter shall be ratified by the signatory states in accordance with their respective constitutional processes.

2. The ratifications shall be deposited with the Government of the United States of America, which shall notify all the signatory states of each deposit as well as the Secretary-General of the Organization when he has been appointed.

3. The present Charter shall come into force upon the deposit of ratifications by the Republic of China, France, the Union of Soviet Socialist Republics, the United Kingdom of Great Britain and Northern Ireland and the United States of America, and by a majority of the other signatory states. A protocol of the ratifications deposited shall thereupon be drawn up by the Government of the United States of America which shall communicate copies thereof to all the signatory states.

4. The states signatory to the present Charter which ratify it after it has come into force will become original Members of the United Nations on the date of the deposit of their respective ratifications.

*Article 111*

The present Charter, of which the Chinese, French, Russian, English, and Spanish texts are equally authentic, shall remain deposited in the archives of the Government of the United States of America. Duly certified copies thereof shall be transmitted by that Government to the Governments of the other signatory states.

IN FAITH WHEREOF the representatives of the Governments of the United Nations have signed the present Charter.

DONE at the city of San Francisco the twenty-sixth day of June, one thousand nine hundred and forty-five.

# UNIVERSAL DECLARATION OF HUMAN RIGHTS

## PREAMBLE

Whereas recognition of the inherent dignity and of the equal and inalienable rights of all members of the human family is the foundation of freedom, justice and peace in the world,

Whereas disregard and contempt for human rights have resulted in barbarous acts which have outraged the conscience of mankind, and the advent of a world in which human beings shall enjoy freedom of speech and belief and freedom from fear and want has been proclaimed as the highest aspiration of the common people,

Whereas it is essential, if man is not to be compelled to have recourse, as a last resort, to rebellion against tyranny and oppression, that human rights should be protected by the rule of law,

Whereas it is essential to promote the development of friendly relations between nations,

Whereas the peoples of the United Nations have in the Charter reaffirmed their faith in fundamental human rights, in the dignity and worth of the human person and in the equal rights of men and women and have determined to promote social progress and better standards of life in larger freedom,

Whereas Member States have pledged themselves to achieve, in co-operation with the United Nations, the promotion of universal respect for and observance of human rights and fundamental freedoms,

Whereas a common understanding of these rights and freedoms is of the greatest importance for the full realization of this pledge,

Now, therefore,

THE GENERAL ASSEMBLY

proclaims

THIS UNIVERSAL DECLARATION OF HUMAN RIGHTS

as a common standard of achievement for all peoples and all nations, to the end that every individual and every organ of society, keeping this Declaration constantly in mind, shall strive by teaching and education to promote respect for these rights and freedoms and by progressive measures, national and international, to secure their universal and effective recognition and observance, both among the peoples of Member States themselves and among the peoples of territories under their jurisdiction.

### Article 1

All human beings are born free and equal in dignity and rights. They are endowed with reason and conscience and should act towards one another in a spirit of brotherhood.

### Article 2

Everyone is entitled to all the rights and freedoms set forth in this Declaration, without distinction of any kind, such as race, colour, sex, language, religion, political or other opinion, national or social origin, property, birth or other status. Furthermore, no distinction shall be made on the basis of the political, jurisdictional, or international status of the country or territory to which a person belongs, whether it be independent, trust, non-self-governing or under any other limitation of sovereignty.

*Article 3*

Everyone has the right to life, liberty, and security of person.

*Article 4*

No one shall be held in slavery or servitude; slavery and the slave trade shall be prohibited in all their forms.

*Article 5*

No one shall be subjected to torture or to cruel, inhuman or degrading treatment or punishment.

*Article 6*

Everyone has the right to recognition everywhere as a person before the law.

*Article 7*

All are equal before the law and are entitled without any discrimination to equal protection of the law. All are entitled to equal protection against any discrimination in violation of this Declaration and against any incitement to such discrimination.

*Article 8*

Everyone has the right to an effective remedy by the competent national tribunals for acts violating the fundamental rights granted him by the constitution or by law.

*Article 9*

No one shall be subjected to arbitrary arrest, detention or exile.

*Article 10*

Everyone is entitled in full equality to a fair and public hearing by an independent and impartial tribunal, in the determination of his rights and obligations and of any criminal charge against him.

*Article 11*

1. Everyone charged with a penal offence has the right to be presumed innocent until proved guilty according to law in a public trial at which he has had all the guarantees necessary for his defence.

2. No one shall be held guilty of any penal offence on account of any act or omission which did not constitute a penal offence, under national or international law, at the time when it was committed. Nor shall a heavier penalty be imposed than the one that was applicable at the time the penal offence was committed.

*Article 12*

No one shall be subjected to arbitrary interference with his privacy, family, home or correspondence, nor to attacks upon his honour and reputation. Everyone has the right to protection of the law against such interference or attacks.

*Article 13*

1. Everyone has the right to freedom of movement and residence within the borders of each State.

2. Everyone has the right to leave any country, including his own, and to return to his country.

*Article 14*

1. Everyone has the right to seek and to enjoy in other countries asylum from persecution.

2. This right may not be invoked in the case of prosecutions genuinely arising from non-political crimes or from acts contrary to the purposes and principles of the United Nations.

*Article 15*

1. Everyone has the right to a nationality.

2. No one shall be arbitrarily deprived of his nationality nor denied the right to change his nationality.

*Article 16*

1. Men and women of full age, without any limitation due to race, nationality or religion, have the right to marry and to found a family. They are entitled to equal rights as to marriage, during marriage and at its dissolution.

2. Marriage shall be entered into only with the free and full consent of the intending spouses.

3. The family is the natural and fundamental group unit of society and is entitled to protection by society and the State.

*Article 17*

1. Everyone has the right to own property alone as well as in association with others.

2. No one shall be arbitrarily deprived of his property.

*Article 18*

Everyone has the right to freedom of thought, conscience and religion; this right includes freedom to change his religion or belief, and freedom, either alone or in community with others and in public or private, to manifest his religion or belief in teaching, practice, worship and observance.

*Article 19*

Everyone has the right to freedom of opinion and expression; this right includes freedom to hold opinions without interference and to seek, receive and impart information and ideas through any media and regardless of frontiers.

*Article 20*

1. Everyone has the right to freedom of peaceful assembly and association.

2. No one may be compelled to belong to an association.

*Article 21*

1. Everyone has the right to take part in the government of his country, directly or through freely chosen representatives.

2. Everyone has the right of equal access to public service in his country.

3. The will of the people shall be the basis of the authority of government; this will shall be expressed in periodic and genuine elections which shall be by universal and equal suffrage and shall be held by secret vote or by equivalent free voting procedures.

*Article 22*

Everyone, as a member of society, has the right to social security and is entitled to realization, through national effort and international co-operation and in accordance with the organization and resources of each State, of the economic, social and cultural rights indispensable for his dignity and the free development of his personality.

*Article 23*

1. Everyone has the right to work, to free choice of employment, to just and favourable conditions of work and to protection against unemployment.

2. Everyone, without any discrimination, has the right to equal pay for equal work.

3. Everyone who works has the right to just and favourable remuneration ensuring for himself and his family an existence worthy of human dignity, and supplemented, if necessary, by other means of social protection.

4. Everyone has the right to form and to join trade unions for the protection of his interests.

*Article 24*
Everyone has the right to rest and leisure, including reasonable limitation of working hours and periodic holidays with pay.

*Article 25*
1. Everyone has the right to a standard of living adequate for the health and well-being of himself and of his family, including food, clothing, housing and medical care and necessary social services, and the right to security in the event of unemployment, sickness, disability, widowhood, old age or other lack of livelihood in circumstances beyond his control.

2. Motherhood and childhood are entitled to special care and assistance. All children, whether born in or out of wedlock, shall enjoy the same social protection.

*Article 26*
1. Everyone has the right to education. Education shall be free, at least in the elementary and fundamental stages. Elementary education shall be compulsory. Technical and professional education shall be made generally available and higher education shall be equally accessible to all on the basis of merit.

2. Education shall be directed to the full development of the human personality and to the strengthening of respect for human rights and fundamental freedoms. It shall promote understanding, tolerance and friendship among all nations, racial or religious groups, and shall further the activities of the United Nations for the maintenance of peace.

3. Parents have a prior right to choose the kind of education that shall be given to their children.

*Article 27*
1. Everyone has the right freely to participate in the cultural life of the community, to enjoy the arts and to share in scientific advancement and its benefits.

2. Everyone has the right to the protection of the moral and material interests resulting from any scientific, literary or artistic production of which he is the author.

*Article 28*
Everyone is entitled to a social and international order in which the rights and freedoms set forth in this Declaration can be fully realized.

*Article 29*
1. Everyone has duties to the community in which alone the free and full development of his personality is possible.

2. In the exercise of his rights and freedoms, everyone shall be subject only to such limitations as are determined by law solely for the purpose of securing due recognition and respect for the rights and freedoms of others and of meeting the just requirements of morality, public order and the general welfare in a democratic society.

3. These rights and freedoms may in no case be exercised contrary to the purposes and principles of the United Nations.

*Article 30*
Nothing in this Declaration may be interpreted as implying for any State, group or person any right to engage in any activity or to perform any act aimed at the destruction of any of the rights and freedoms set forth herein.

APPENDIX 4

# *ACRONYMS OF MAJOR UN ORGANIZATIONS AND AGENCIES*

| | | | |
|---|---|---|---|
| **ECOSOC** | Economic and Social Council | **UNCTAD** | UN Conference on Trade and Development |
| **FAO** | Food and Agriculture Organization | **UNDP** | UN Development Programme |
| **GATT** | General Agreement on Tariffs and Trade | **UNDRO** | Office of the UN Disaster Relief Coordinator |
| **Habitat** | UN Center for Human Settlements | **UNEP** | UN Environment Programme |
| **IAEA** | International Atomic Energy Agency | **UNESCO** | UN Educational, Scientific and Cultural Organization |
| **IBRD** | International Bank for Reconstruction and Development | **UNFPA** | UN Population Fund |
| | | **UNHCR** | Office of the UN High Commissioner for Refugees |
| **ICAO** | International Civil Aviation Organization | **UNICEF** | UN Children's Fund |
| **ICJ** | International Court of Justice | **UNIDO** | UN Industrial Development Organization |
| **IDA** | International Development Association | **UNIFEM** | UN Development Fund for Women |
| **IFAD** | International Fund for Agricultural Development | **UNITAR** | UN Institute for Training and Research |
| **IFC** | International Finance Corporation | **UNRWA** | UN Relief and Works Agency for Palestine Refugees in the Near East |
| **ILO** | International Labour Organization | **UNU** | United Nations University |
| **IMF** | International Monetary Fund | **UPU** | Universal Postal Union |
| | | **WFC** | World Food Council |
| **IMO** | International Maritime Organization | **WFP** | World Food Program |
| | | **WHO** | World Health Organization |
| **INSTRAW** | UN International Research and Training Institute for the Advancement of Women | **WIPO** | World Intellectual Property Organization |
| **ITU** | International Telecommunication Union | **WMO** | World Meteorological Organization |

APPENDIX 5

# ADDRESSES OF MAJOR UN ORGANIZATIONS

## UN HEADQUARTERS

United Nations
United Nations Plaza
New York, NY 10017, U.S.A.

United Nations
Palais des Nations
CH-1211 Geneva 10, Switzerland

United Nations
Vienna International Centre
P.O. Box 500
A-1400 Vienna, Austria

## UN SPECIALIZED AGENCIES

**Food and Agriculture Organization**
Via delle Terme di Caracalla
00100 Rome, Italy

**General Agreement on Tariffs and Trade Center**
Centre William Rappard
154 Rue de Lausanne
CH-1211 Geneva 21, Switzerland

**International Atomic Energy Agency**
Vienna International Center
Wagramerstrasse 5, P.O. Box 100
A-1400 Vienna, Austria

**International Civil Aviation Organization**
1000 Sherbrooke Street West, Suite 327
Montreal, Quebec H3A 2R2, Canada

**International Fund for Agricultural Development**
Via del Serafico 107
00142 Rome, Italy

**International Labour Organization**
4, Route des Morillons
CH-1211 Geneva 22, Switzerland

*UN headquarters in New York City. The tall building on the right is the Secretariat. The General Assembly is on the left.*

**International Maritime Organization**
4 Albert Embankment
London SE1 7SR, United Kingdom

**International Monetary Fund**
700 19th Street, N.W.
Washington, D.C. 20431, U.S.A.

**International Tele-communication Union**
Place des Nations
CH-1211 Geneva 20, Switzerland

**UNESCO**
7, Place de Fontenoy
75700 Paris, France

**United Nations Industrial Development Organization**
Wagramerstrasse 5
Vienna XXII, Austria

**Universal Postal Union**
Weltpoststrasse 4
Berne, Switzerland

**World Intellectual Property Organization**
34, Chemin des Colombettes
CH-1211 Geneva 20, Switzerland

**World Bank**
1818 H Street, N.W.
Washington, D.C. 20433, U.S.A.

**World Health Organization**
20, Avenue Appia
CH-1211 Geneva 27, Switzerland

**World Meteorological Organization**
41, Avenue Giuseppe-Motta
CH-1211 Geneva 20, Switzerland

# FURTHER READING

## GENERAL HISTORIES OF THE UN

Dudley, George A. *A Workshop for Peace: Designing the United Nations Headquarters*. Cambridge: The Architectural History Foundation/MIT Press, 1994.

Evans, Gareth. *Cooperating for Peace: The Global Agenda for the 1990s and Beyond*. Concord, Mass.: Paul and Company Publishers Consortium, 1993.

Goodrich, Leland. *The United Nations in a Changing World*. New York: Columbia University Press, 1974.

Greenfield, Stanley, ed. *Who's Who in the United Nations and Related Agencies*. 2nd ed. Detroit: Omnigraphics, 1992.

Hilderbrand, Robert. *Dumbarton Oaks: The Origins of the United Nations and the Search for Postwar Security*. Chapel Hill: University of North Carolina Press, 1990.

Knock, Thomas. *To End All Wars: Woodrow Wilson and the Quest for a New World Order*. New York: Oxford University Press, 1992.

Luard, Evan. *A History of the United Nations*. New York: St. Martin's, 1982.

Muller, Joachim. *The Reform of the United Nations*. New York: Oceana, 1992.

Osmanszyk, Edmund. *The Encyclopedia of the United Nations and International Agreements*. 2nd ed. London: Taylor & Francis, 1990.

Riggs, Robert, and Jack Plano. *The United Nations: International Organization and World Politics*. 2nd ed. Belmont, Calif.: Wadsworth, 1994.

Rikhye, Indar, and Kjell Skjelsback, eds. *The United Nations and Peacekeeping: Results, Limitations, and Prospects— The Lessons of 40 Years of Experience*. New York: St. Martin's, 1991.

Roberts, Adam, and Benedict Kingsbury, eds. *United Nations, Divided World: The UN's Role in International Relations*. 2nd ed. New York: Oxford University Press, 1993.

Tessitore, John, and Susan Woolfson, eds. *A Global Agenda: Issues Before the General Assembly of the United Nations*. Lanham, Md.: University Press of America. Published annually.

Urquhart, Brian. *A Life in Peace and War*. New York: Harper & Row, 1987.

Yoder, Amos. *The Evolution of the United Nations System*. 2nd ed. Washington, D.C.: Taylor & Francis, 1993.

Zacher, Mark. *Dag Hammarskjöld's United Nations*. New York: Columbia University Press, 1970.

## BIOGRAPHIES AND AUTOBIOGRAPHIES

Hammarskjöld, Dag. *Markings*. New York: Knopf, 1964.

Hareven, Tamara. *Eleanor Roosevelt: An American Conscience*. Chicago: Quadrangle Books, 1968.

Lash, Joseph. *Eleanor: The Years Alone*. New York: Norton, 1972.

Lie, Trygve. *In the Cause of Peace: Seven Years with the United Nations*. New York: Macmillan, 1954.

MacKenzie, Lewis. *Peacekeeper: The Road to Sarajevo*. Vancouver: Douglas & McIntyre, 1993.

Nassif, Ramses. *U Thant in New York, 1961–1971: A Portrait of the Third UN Secretary General*. London: C. Hurst, 1988.

Patterson, Charles. *Marian Anderson*. New York: Franklin Watts, 1988.

Thant, U. *View from the UN*. New York: Doubleday, 1978.

Urquhart, Brian. *Hammarskjöld*. New York: Knopf, 1972.

———. *Ralph Bunche: An American Life*. New York: Norton, 1993.

## UN PUBLICATIONS

Department of Public Information. *Basic Facts about the United Nations*. New York: United Nations, 1992.

Department of Public Information. *Everyone's United Nations*. 11th ed. New York: United Nations, 1994.

Department of Public Information. *Yearbook of the United Nations*. New York: United Nations. Published annually.

**For a complete listing of UN publications, contact:**

United Nations Publications
2 United Nations Plaza
Room DC2-853
New York, NY 10017
Telephone: 800-253-9646
    or 212-963-8302

# INDEX

# ACKNOWLEDGMENTS

I would like to express my gratitude to the following people at the UN for their assistance: Joyce Rosenblum, United Nations photo librarian, Jean Ando, reference librarian, United Nations Children's Fund (UNICEF); Aliye Pekin Celik, United Nations Center for Human Settlements (Habitat); Heather Courtney, public information assistant, United Nations High Commissioner for Refugees (UNHCR); William Lee, United Nations Relief and Works Agency for Palestine Refugees in the Near East (UNRWA); Dulcie de Montagnac and Gabor Szilyagi, United Nations Environment Programme (UNEP); Steve Roswick, *Secretariat News;* Zohreh Tabatabai, Fiftieth Anniversary Secretariat; United Nations Department of Public Information; and "World Chronicle," the UN television program.

My editors at Oxford—Nancy Toff, Tara Deal, and Paul McCarthy—deserve much of the credit for this book. Their dedication, patience, and hard work helped shape and improve the project on its long journey to completion.

My thanks also to John Tessitore, director of communications, United Nations Association of the United States of America (UNA-USA), for reading an early draft of the manuscript and making helpful suggestions.